THE COLLAPSE OF THE WAR SYSTEM

ISBN: 978-1-905451-53-1

A CIP catalogue for this book is available from the National Library.

This book was published by Saor-Ollscoil Press in cooperation with Choice Publishing, Ireland
Tel: ++353 (0)41 9841551 Email: info@choicepublishing.ie
www.choicepublishing.ie
www.saor-ollscoil.ie Email: info@saor-ollscoil.ie

To Anthony Muggeant

THE COLLAPSE OF THE WAR SYSTEM

DEVELOPMENTS IN THE PHILOSOPHY OF PEACE IN THE TWENTIETH CENTURY

Best Wishes

John Jacob English

Saor-Ollscoil Press
in association with Choice Publishing
2007

14/01/2008

About the Author

John Jacob English PhD is Director of Saor-Ollscoil na hÉireann (The Free University of Ireland) and teaches the Study of Peace course at the college.
He is convenor of the Peace Theories Commission of the International Peace Research Association (IPRA).
He organises the Visions of Peace Project. This project was established as a result of the Visions of Peace conference 2000 which was organised by Saor-Ollscoil as part of UNESCO's Decade for the Culture of Peace Programme.
The author was awarded the *Visionary of Peace Award 2007* by the Education for Peace Foundation (Ireland)

Contact the author at:
www.visionsofpeace.ie
info@visionsofpeace.ie

About Saor-Ollscoil Na hÉireann

Saor-Ollscoil na hÉireann (The Free University of Ireland) is a small independent university college established in Dublin, Ireland in 1986.
Saor-Ollscoil was established as a University of Civil Society with the motto 'Beholden to None'.
The college offers Degrees in the Liberal Arts to mature students who have a love of learning for its own sake and a wish to develop their capacity for logical reasoning and clear thinking. Saor-Ollscoil has an open and flexible system to suit the needs of mature students.
The college offers post graduate degrees by research in relevant areas.

Saor-Ollscoil na hÉireann
55 Prussia Street
Dublin 7
Ireland
www.saor-ollscoil.ie

"Before the Cathedral comes
the vision of the Cathedral."

Anon.

Acknowledgements

I would like to thank all the people who have contributed to the existence of Saor-Ollscoil Na hÉireann; in particular, Kevin O Byrne and Mairéad Ní Chíosóig for their dedication to the concept of education in its truest sense and Dr. Bernard O Connor for his long-term commitment to the Saor-Ollscoil. Particular acknowledgements to Dr. John de Courcy Ireland and Col. Ned Doyle for their inspiration on the questions of peace. Thanks too Brendan Duddy SJ and Sheikh Dr. Shaheed Satardien and a special thanks to Seán Sourke and John Cullen for their deliberations over the years.

Thanks to the Students at Saor-Ollscoil who, in their maturity, create an exciting and challenging educational environment.

Lastly to Marian Naughton and our two families who put up with us and to Tansy the office cat whose job was to flick everything from the table onto the floor and work it into some hidden corner.

Go raibh mile maith agaimh go léir.

JJE

Table of Contents

To The Reader...

There is one thing stronger than all the armies in the world and that is an idea whose time has come.
Victor Hugo

MOVING BEYOND THE PROPAGANDA AND THE ILLUSIONS

Peace should never be seen as some conflict-free utopia. Even the simplest understanding of peace will show that peace is not the absence of conflict but the ability of coping with conflict by peaceful means. Peace will not reduce our security, or our creativity, or our capacity for change. It will actually have the opposite effect. It is violence and the culture of violence that is destroying our security and our capacity for real progressive cultural evolution. The good news is that there is nothing in the nature of Man (Homo Sapiens - the intelligent animal) that enslaves us to violence or aggression. There is nothing in the nature of our social systems that condemns our cultures to perpetual violence. In fact all the information, knowledge and wisdom that is required for us as individuals and for our societies to live in peace are well know and freely available. We should not be waiting for some magical breakthrough in the near future in our understanding of ourselves and our societies that would suddenly create a peaceful world.

It is not necessary for every new generation to try and create or recreate the wheel. The creation of the framework for peace is not now beyond our human imagination or capacity. All the fundamental principles associated with the reduction and elimination of violence and violent aggression in individuals are well known. All the basic information that would prevent group conflicts from degenerating into large-scale violence are also well known. This knowledge has been available for a long time, and it may well be as Mahatma Gandhi said: '*Puratana* and *Sanatana* – Old and Eternal'. The question we might ask is why there seems to be an almost total failure in the application of the awareness of this knowledge and information, particularly by those people who could make a difference in our world?

It is correct and realistic to recognise that at the beginning of the Twenty First Century there are those cultures that cling to and legitimise the use of violence for a whole range of ideological and pathological reasons. These legitimisations range from the self-interest of the power elites in all areas of human society, in politics through economics to religion. But these legitimisations reflect more about the nature of power than the nature of violence. In any explanation for or against the use of violence the differences between what can be termed: 'functional violence' and 'demented violence' is of critical importance. The more traditional attempts to try and understand and explain the use of violence are functional in nature - in that the logical explanation for the use of violence seems to be the most realistic. When violence is used without logic or function then it is generally seen as demented violence - however defined. It will be easy enough to point out that: 'functional violence' can be or can become: 'demented violence' without losing its functionality and vice versa. A particular genocidal policy or procedure may or may not be functional in nature but at the coalface of the implementation its functionality is not the most important consideration.

In any analysis of the role of violence in society it is important to go beyond the more traditional framework of victim and aggressor. The 'who' part of the question should never become the central issue. The analysis should never be based on what the X's did to the Y's. From a purely analytical point of view it is not important whether the X's did it the Y's or the Y's did it to the X's; whether as in Jonathan Swift's: *Gulliver's Travels* the Big-Endians did it to the Little-Endians or the Little-Endians did it to the Big-Endians. The vital issue is the development of the awareness that what was done regardless of the victim-aggressor dichotomy was totally unacceptable and criminal in the very worse sense. We must accept that no amount of justification can reduce the responsibility on those who inflict violence either directly or indirectly on others. It cannot be logically argued that the use of aircraft to kill civilians is legitimate in one conflict and criminal in another. The propaganda that supports this type of hypocrisy must have some limits in reality.

The slow dawning of the realisation that we actually have the knowledge that is required to create peace will of course require a paradigm shift in our cultural evolution. But paradigm shifts do happen and the tipping point for the paradigm for peace is much closer than may seem at first glance. Leo Tolstoy predicted that war and violence and the absurdities associated with them would be abolished within one hundred years of the clear statement of the problem. It seems that it will take a little more than the one hundred years. But for very fundamental reasons the ideology of violence will not survive another hundred years. Because if we do not make that paradigm shift into a culture of peace there will be no culture in which a culture of violence will survive even in the short term. This was the central message given by the then Secretary General of the United Nations Boutros Boutros Ghali in his: *Agenda for Peace* (1992) in the light of his knowledge of just how close on a number of occasions our civilization came to creating nuclear omnicide. Very few species have ever got a second chance at survival and the collapse of the Cold War may have created the possibility of a second chance. The concept of preparing for and waging wars to end wars is just one of the *Alice in Wonderland* pieces of propaganda that underpins the ideology of violence. If war brought about peace and violence brought about non-violence we would be living in a very peaceful culture. If war and violence solved problems then most of our problems would be solved. The culture of war and violence has to be built on a whole tissues of lies or as Tolstoy calls them a series of: 'childish absurdities'. But the rejection of these absurdities may be nearer than we think.

There may or may not be a: 'Turning Point' when people wake up some morning and say we reject violence in all its forms because we see the damage it has done to our culture, to our creativity, to our vision and to our future possibilities. The process of demystifying violence has been far more gradual. The process has involved de-romanticising, de-rationalising, de-legitimising, and de- culturising the concepts of violence. For much of the twentieth century there had been a naive belief that science, however defined, could rise above the traditional passions of mankind. That science would be the foundation upon which we could build a new enlightenment – a new civilization. But there were always the doubters. Einstein in the: *Manifesto to Europeans* (1915) asked how could scientists do in the name of the state what once had been done in the name of religion? It may well be that in relation to the actuality of war and violence, reason and science have not and will not contribute to the paradigm shift that is required, but that reason and science have a negative influence on our cultural paradigm.

We might ask how relevant is any peace theory to conflicts that are deeply routed in historical or cultural grievances or to the use of violence that may have its source deep in the reptilian part of the human brain? It is easy to say that peace theories might be fine in the abstract, but in the real world of violent conflict, in the unbelievable cruelty associated with economic and social exploitation, then we might be justified in dismissing theory. Or to say that theories are fine in theory but in the world of real-politic, only force or power matters. To paraphrase the quotation of the Romans: 'In times of War, the Law is Silenced', we can now state: 'In times of Violence, the Theories are Silenced'.

The collapse of the ideology of war will of course not automatically bring about the collapse of the ideology of violence, but it surely follows that a culture of peace cannot be built on a culture of violence. The ideology of war is one of the central foundations of the ideology of violence and just as the horse comes before the cart the collapse of the ideology of war will be a major step in the collapse of the ideology of violence.

27th August 2007
JJE

1

THE NATURE OF THE DEBATE

Quarry the rock with razors or moor the vessel with a thread of silk,
then you may hope such delicate instruments as human knowledge
and human reason to contend against those giants,
the passion and the pride of Men

Cardinal John Henry Newman (1801-1890)

The goal one should have in front of one in the education of a person is to form in them the heart, the judgement, the mind, in that order..., if, (the person) had allowed his heart to be corrupted, science in his hands will be like weapons in the hands of a madman

A conclusion of peace nullifies all existing reasons for a future war,
even if these are not yet known to the contracting parties,
and no matter how acutely and carefully they may be pieced together out of old documents

Immanuel Kant (1724-1804)

A definition of insanity in relation to war and the use of violence:
To keep doing the same things and expect different results.

SETTING THE FRAMEWORK

The twentieth century has seen a significant evolution in the debate on the nature of war and peace and on the nature of violence and non-violence. Some of the greatest scientists and philosophers of that century have contributed to the evolution of this debate. Yet the questions, "why war?"[1] and more significantly, "why peace?" and the implications of these questions are still problematic for many people. In any analysis of the forces that have dominated the twentieth century the ideology of violence may well seem, at first glance, to predominate over the philosophy of peace. The history of that century has seen some of the most destructive wars and conflicts ever recorded. The ideologies of violence on which these wars and conflicts were constructed have not gone away. The fundamental forces, which have created such enormous levels of violence, are even more dangerous today than ever before.

But the possibility of human society transcending collective violence has become less of a Utopian dream and more of a practical necessity dictated by developments in science and technology, if not in ethics and morality. The practicality of individuals resolving conflict without the resort to violence and the possibilities of societies resolving conflict without the resort to war have begun to be critically and scientifically examined.[2] The practical application of the knowledge arising from this examination may not yet have resulted in any significant achievements in reducing levels of violence, but those who advocate the functional nature of war and the utilitarian nature of violence are now on the defensive.

This book sets out to show that the foundations for a philosophy of peace have been clearly laid and that the ideological basis of war and the utilitarian basis of violence have been critically undermined. No other century has seen such an onslaught on

---

[1] Albert Einstein and Sigmund Freud, *Why War?* (London: 1934).
[2] Raimo Vayrynen, ed., *The Quest For Peace* (International Social Science Council, London: Sage, 1987).

the philosophical and ideological basis of war and violence. This onslaught from so many different sides has eroded the very foundations on which war and violence have traditionally been rationalized, justified and normalized. The ancient institution of war, without losing its inherent fascination, has become substantially discredited. Many of the romantic myths about war and violence have been challenged and undermined. For decades the ideologies of the twentieth century had preached that successive wars, revolutions and the use of violence would be followed by social, political and economic bliss. The twentieth century has shown more than any other century that the utopian belief in the power of violence is false.

"Before the Cathedral comes the vision of the Cathedral," in this sense a philosophy of peace has been constructed in the twentieth century, which will have enormous positive influence on the twenty first century. The changes that have taken place in the critical analysis of the utility of war and violence, of aggression and conflict, will have far-reaching and fundamental effects on the future evolution of the science of human understanding. The peace philosophies of Leo Tolstoy, Bertrand Russell, Mahatma Gandhi and Albert Einstein are used as the outline of the evolution of the philosophy of peace. These individuals and their ideas are chosen partly on an arbitrary basis, but also because they are central to the evolution of the debate. The ideas put forward or adopted by them are central to the understanding of any philosophy of peace. These individuals and their ideas reflect almost the entire fabric of the contemporary and historical arguments and debate.

PEACE BY DICTIONARY DEFINITION

Because of the ambiguity associated with the word *peace* and related concepts and ideas it is important to clarify some of the basic definitions. Many different meanings and many different ideas have become associated with the concept of peace. There has always been some confusion about the meaning given at different times and in different cultures to the concept, value and function of peace.

In order to analyse some of the concepts associated with the idea of peace in recent times, it is helpful to look closely at some of the modern dictionary definitions associated with the word. A selection of ideas associated with the meaning of the word *peace* from a number of authoritative English dictionaries (Oxford, Collins), reveals at least five distinct meanings: see Table 1:1

Table 1:1
PEACE IS: BY DICTIONARY DEFINITION

1. The state existing (between nations) during the absence of war.
2. A state of harmony between people or groups.
3. Law and order within a state.
4. The absence of mental anxiety.
5. A state of stillness or silence.

These five definitions of peace are selected because they cover most of the important modern meanings associated with the concept of peace. Some of these words and related concepts have various other assumptions associated with and built into their meaning. These assumptions are sometimes invisible because they are almost taken for granted within the language we use. Classical and historical definitions of peace have changed considerably from culture to culture and over time in the same culture. The meaning of *Shalom (Peace)* is certainly different from the meaning of *Pax (Peace).* Again the cultural significance of *Ahimsa (Non-injury)* will be quite different from the meanings of *Agape (Brotherly Love)* or *Irene (Peace).*

St. Augustine's classical definition of peace as "The Tranquility of Order" is still very attractive but quite different from the definition by Hugo Grotius of peace as "The short interval between two conflicts." Any number of definitions of peace can be found in historical studies, while contemporary definitions seem to be more all-inclusive. The definition of peace produced at the end of the Yamoussoukro (UNESCO) Conference is a good example, peace is seen as "The dominant moral force of modern civilisation...it necessitates the establishment of a new international order that is more just and better adapted to human progress".[3] In the papal encyclical *Pacem in Terris (Peace on Earth)* Pope John XXIII outlined the possible construction of peace as requiring: "Truth as its foundation, Justice as its Rule, Love as its driving force, Liberty as its atmosphere."[4] While it may seem impossible to get any logical consensus from such a wide range of definitions, the definitions themselves reflect a very comprehensive set of attempts to produce an agreed and coherent understanding of what, for many, is a confused and complexing concept.

THE CONCEPTUALISATION OF THE DEFINITIONS

Dictionary definitions are valuable to a limited extent but cannot help to explain some of the misunderstandings which arise when some of these words are used to describe historical experience or to explain contemporary events. The meaning of the word *war* would seem to be quite clear. A general non-legal understanding of war, as a violent conflict between two groups, is accepted by most people. But the clarity of such a definition can be very deceptive. For example Clausewitz observed that war is: "only part of political intercourse, therefore by no means an independent thing in itself."[5] Two important points follow from this interpretation of war. Firstly, because war is not an independent variable:

> An understanding of war cannot be based solely on a definition of war, which can only isolate the set of wars from the set of non-wars. Rather, it is necessary to appreciate conceptually how war fits into a broader context…

And secondly,

> Because war is a political phenomenon, a theory of war

[3] UNESCO, Yamoussoukro Conference Final Report, (1989), 20.
[4] John XXIII, *Pacem in Terris* (New York: America Press, 1989).
[5] Anatol Rapoport, introduction to *On War* by Carl von Clausewitz ed. Anatol Rapoport (London: Penguin, 1968), 402.

> should be subsumed under a more general theory of politics. Thus, a conceptualisation of war requires that we first understand what is meant by politics.[6]

It is not very helpful to explain one concept by introducing another one. If we attempt to explain the idea of war by looking at the meaning of politics, then in order to explain politics we may have to look at the meaning of morality and ethics and so on. We do not even have to accept the idea that war is a political phenomenon.

In one sense any definition of peace would have to include an identification of concepts associated with non-peace: see Table 1:2

Table 1:2

SOME CONCEPTS ASSOCIATED WITH NON-PEACE.

1. War.	4. Conflict.
2. Violence.	5. Insecurity.
3. Aggression.	6. Injustice.

Identifying and defining the components of non-peace may be as equally valid as identifying and defining the components of peace. There is a definite positive or negative relationship between any two opposing concepts such as violence and non-violence or security and insecurity. Dieter Senghaas in "The Quest for Peace"[7] says:

> Transcending collective violence and peace are, to some extent, synonymous concepts. Peace, however has to be defined more broadly as a political "modus vivendi", characterised both by the absence of direct violence and by an increasing degree of political liberty and social justice. Both in modern and modernizing societies such a broad definition is essential since according to all historical and present experience the absence of direct violence cannot be maintained without sustained efforts in

[6] T. Clifton Morgan, "The Concept of War." *Peace and Change.* Vol. XV. No. 4, (October 1990), 413-441.

[7] Dieter Senghaas in *The Quest for Peace* ed. by Raimo Vayrynen, International Social Science Council, (London: Sage, 1987)

> the realisation of liberty and justice. If such political efforts are lacking, or remain insufficient, the use of direct violence is likely to re-emerge. Only when political and social orders are considered as fairly legitimate, do people, in general, abstain from the resort to open violence[8].

The cultural enterprise for peace has deep roots in the various religious, artistic and philosophical traditions. Theodore F. Lentz in his *Towards a Science of Peace*[9] outlines a very pessimistic picture of the possibilities of a culture of peace: "Unless the science of peace enables us to find the road to survival there will be no culture in which to carry on a science of culture."[10] Many attempts have been made to outline and limit the legitimate field of peace studies. But it is very problematic to try and prioritise the biological approach to peace over the theological approach; or the economic understanding of peace in preference to the psychological understanding. The philosophy of peace must take the morphological approach to the subject even allowing for the risks that are inherent in this approach for any subject: see Table 1:3

Table 1:3
THE MORPHOLOGY OF PEACE

1. Theology of Peace.	5. The Politics of Peace.
2. Biology of Peace.	6. The Economics of Peace.
3. Psychology of Peace.	7. The Ideology of Peace.
4. Sociology of Peace.	8. The Science of Peace.

John Macquarrie in: *The Concept of Peace* [11] identifies the complexity of the problems that arise in trying to arrive at a workable concept. Macquarrie believes that Christian theology offers one of the most comprehensive and rich concepts of

---

[8] Ibid., 3.
[9] Theodore F. Lentz, *Towards A Science Of Peace* (London: Halcyon Press, 1955).
[10] Ibid., 4.
[11] John Macquarrie, *The Concept of Peace* (London: SCM Press, 1973).

peace. He makes an important distinction between the techniques and concepts of peace:

> One must not for a moment underrate the importance of the techniques of peace, the objective knowledge of one kind or another which is essential to the realisation of peace and which is scattered throughout many groups of specialists. But while acknowledging this, one must also be clear that another kind of knowledge is needed too, and needed just as urgently. This I have called 'an intellectual grasp of what peace essentially is.' It is the concept of peace. This is something of a different order from the technical knowledge we have been considering.[12]

PEACE STUDIES AND THE IDEA OF A UNIVERSITY

The idea of identifying and tracing the philosophy of peace as it evolved in the twentieth century arose from a number of different influences. One of the most important of these was my own experience in preparing and teaching a course in peace studies for undergraduate students, starting tentatively in 1986 and working through into the 1990s. During the nineteen eighties the academic debate on the nature and constitution of peace studies was still in a state of flux. In the summer of 1989 The Annals of the American Academy of Political and Social Science, produced an in-depth study of *Peace Studies: Past and Future.*[13] The conceptual boundaries of peace studies were outlined in this and other studies in some detail.[14] Some general agreement on the nature of peace studies would seem to have been arrived at. The study of peace would involve a number of areas of substantive focus and these were clearly outlined in the special volume of the Annals: see Table 1:4

---

[12] Ibid., 11.

[13] George A. Lopez et al, ed. "Peace Studies Past and Future" *The Annals of the American Academy of Political and Social Science*, Vol. 504. (London: Sage, July 1989).

[14] Peadar Cremin ed. *Education for Peace*, (Dublin: Education Studies Association of Ireland 1993).

Table 1:4
SUBSTANTIVE AREAS OF PEACE STUDIES

1. The analysis of the causes and consequences of violent conflict.

2. The study of theories and techniques of managing, reducing, and resolving conflict.

3. The examination of those norms, values, rules, and institutions that are necessary for constructing peace.

Within these broad concepts George A. Lopez identified nine distinct areas of legitimate inquiry which can be said to constitute the sub-fields of peace studies.[15] These various developments in peace studies were carried out against the background of a bitter academic debate which questioned the very nature and value of peace studies. In one of a number of critical studies carried out during the nineteen eighties Baroness Cox states:

> Peace studies is not a genuine educational discipline, and therefore cannot be taught as one.[16]

More importantly the authors of: *Peace Studies: A Critical Survey* go on to state that:

> Enormous issues of principle are raised by any inquiry into the academic and intellectual standing of a university discipline.[17]

This is precisely where the debate on peace studies was at its most challenging and most vulnerable. The debate on the role of peace studies within the academic structures of the modern university system raised some fundamental questions about the

---

[15] Lopez, et al., 11.
[16] Caroline Cox and R. Scruton, "Peace Studies: A Critical Survey" (London: Alliance of Publishers for the Institute for European Defence and Strategic Studies. Occasional Paper No. 7 1984), 7.
[17] Ibid., 10.

nature and the role of the university itself within the modern world. Peace studies by its very nature challenges the more traditional and conservative concepts of the university in society. The debate about the function of the university is as old as the concept of the university itself. It has attracted some of the greatest minds. Cardinal John Henry Newman in an outstanding series of lectures given in 1852 and published as *The Idea of the University* [18] set the framework for much of the modern debate. Newman took up the debate on the role of education almost where Aristotle and Plato had left off:

> I am asked what is the end of University Education, and of the Liberal or Philosophical Knowledge which I conceive it to impart: I answer, that what I have already said had been sufficient to show that it has a very tangible, real, and sufficient end, though the end cannot be divided from the knowledge itself. Knowledge is capable of being its own end.[19]

He had already given his outline of the positive aspects of liberal education as the following:

> A habit of mind is formed which lasts through life, of which the attributes are, freedom, equitableness, calmness, moderation, and wisdom; or what in a former Discourse I have ventured to call a philosophical habit.[20]

Within the modern university system the struggle to establish peace studies as a legitimate academic subject reflected much of the debate on the role of the university in society. The research, development, and construction of weapons of mass destruction of nuclear, chemical, and biological basis was only made possible by the active participation of universities at every level. Many universities are so involved in the culture of the defence industries that they are very restrained in their ability to analyse

---

[18] John Henry Newman, *The Idea of the University* ed. Frank M. Turner. (New Haven: Yale University Press, 1966).
[19] Ibid., 78.
[20] Ibid., 77.

critically the military-industrial complexes and the vast vested interests that are associated with their world-views.

During the Cold War the continent of Europe became saturated with weapons of mass extermination. The opposition to this madness was left in general to small groups of peace activists. The universities wanted all of the privileges but were prepared to take none of the moral responsibilities. Jean-Jacques Rousseau gave a very clear warning of the dangers that may arise when education takes this direction when he said:

> The goal one should have in front of one in the education of a person is to form in them the heart, the judgement, the mind, in that order ..., if, (the person) had allowed his heart to be corrupted, science in his hands will be like weapons in the hands of a madman.[21]

It would be hard to find a more clear or direct warning in relation to the nuclear madness of the 20th century. Peace studies, in essence, set out to undermine the ideology of violence and the mythologies of force that have become central aspects of our modern culture.

Should the university attempt to make a contribution to a more free and more peaceful society? Cardinal Newman saw this contribution as imperative to the role of the university in any society. In the more recent debate Noam Chomsky, that bane of western political systems expressed similar opinions:

> The university will be able to make its contribution to a free society only to the extent that it overcomes the temptation to conform unthinkingly to the existing patterns of power and privilege.[22]

The questions that arise when considering the role of the university in establishing a just society raise a number of

---

[21] John Hope Mason, *The Indispensable Rousseau.* (London: Quartet, 1979), 20.
[22] Noam Chomsky, *Deterring Democracy*. London: Vintage, 1992.

important questions and are seen as problematic from an academic point of view. Within the field of peace studies the role of the university has been clearly stated:

> The task of a university in an economically unjust and environmentally self-destructive world is an ethical one: to analyse the causes of this world situation and to try to find 'a rational, ethical (and Christian) solution' to its problems of falsehood, injustice, want and oppression.[23]

THE STUDY OF PEACE VERSUS THE STUDY OF WAR

The long and hard-won quest for legitimacy within the university system had a major influence upon the evolution of the concept of peace studies. One of the more important effects of this debate was that the subjects of war and violence were seen as much more legitimate than the subjects of peace and non-violence. Kenneth Boulding, one of the founding fathers of peace research, argued that:

> It makes sense to have a discipline centred around conflict, because conflict is a virtually universal phenomenon in all social and even some biological systems. The patterns of conflict - the ways in which conflicts originate, develop, and are resolved - may demonstrate some similarity in different situations and at different levels of social interaction.[24]

The study of conflict is, of course, central to the study of peace just as the study of disease is central to the study of health. The problem arises when the study of conflict dominates peace studies to the exclusion of the study of peace. Conflict studies is not peace studies. The philosophical foundation on which peace studies should be built has a different foundation to conflict and

---

[23] Rodolfo Cardenal, "*The Role of the University in Establishing a Just Society*" Irish School of Ecumenics paper in *Irish Times* (15th July 1994), 6.
[24] Peter Van Den Dungen, "Peace Research and the Search For Peace" *International Journal of World Peace*, Vol. XI. No. 3, (Jul.-Sept. 1985), 36.

related studies. In the introduction to *A Reader In Peace Studies* the editors state the following:

> It is up to the individual reader to decide which, if any, of the approaches represented here are most likely to achieve a more peaceful and just world.[25]

Initially this statement may be seen as an objective caution to the student entering on a subjective field of study and as such it is a legitimate statement of caution. But it is also a coded language for a much more important statement. It, in effect, implies that peace studies is an area of studies that has no moral or philosophical foundation. Peace studies without a firm philosophical foundation, without a philosophy of peace, is a "studies" set adrift with no foundation on which to build.
Professor O'Connell, Nigel Young and others working at the School of Peace Studies in Bradford, produced a number of studies on the problems and possibilities of peace studies.[26] In relation to the teaching of peace studies at university level O'Connell outlined three distinct possibilities. Firstly, peace studies could be taught as a degree subject in its own right. Secondly, peace studies could be taught as a minor component within a degree course. Thirdly, peace studies could be taught as a value or focus within existing subjects. While accepting that there has to be limitations on the extension of peace studies into so many different areas, O'Connell outlines a very broad approach to the field of peace studies. Within this broad approach the central concepts of peace, freedom and justice can only be understood and developed within the academic framework of philosophy and theology. Without a sound framework in these areas, the study of peace in international relations or ethnic conflict, etc. will be very restricted and problematic.

---

[25] Paul Smoker, Ruth Davies and Barbara Munske, ed. *A Reader in Peace Studies* (Oxford: Pergamon, 1990), xii.

[26] James O'Connell, "Approaches to the Study of Peace", Conference Paper: Education for Peace, University of Limerick, (1991).

THE UNESCO PRINCIPLE

The peace research agenda as set out by the International Peace Research Association (IPRA) identified fifteen major areas of peace research ranging from Aggression and Attitude Formation to Politics and Sexism.[27] There was plenty of information and research on specific topics within the peace research agenda; in conflict resolution, in aggression, in arms races, in the causes of war and many other areas. It would seem that a better understanding of many of these areas of study is vital to the development of peace studies. In order properly to debate and critically analyse the question of nuclear deterrence it was necessary for students to know the difference between an SS20 and a Cruise missile.

For a number of years the peace studies course at the Saor-Ollscoil na hEireann, in line with many other peace studies courses, was shaped both by the Cold War and its political fall-out on the peace research agenda.[28] But the fact that students could complete a peace studies course in so many universities and still not even be aware of the views of Leo Tolstoy, Albert Einstein or Bertrand Russell on peace, was a major weakness in the course structures. Many peace studies courses, in order to justify themselves in the broader academic debate on the role of peace studies, seemed to have given up the study of general principles and concentrated on specific details of arms and insecurity, of conflict and its dynamics. In the *World Encyclopaedia of Peace* published in 1986 the concept of a philosophy of peace is not even considered important enough to receive its own entry. In this encyclopaedia, written by some of the leading peace educators and researchers, it is almost impossible to find any evidence that there exists an enormous amount of critical philosophy on peace and related concepts.

The United Nations Educational, Scientific and Cultural Organisation was founded in 1946. The main purpose of the

---

[27] IPRA.

[28] Conference Papers on the Teaching of Peace and Conflict Studies at British Universities, University of Bradford, (1989).

organisation, according to its constitution, was to support the principles of the United Nations: "to save succeeding generations from the scourge of war"[29]. The preamble to the UNESCO constitution states quite clearly that:

> Since wars begin in the minds of men, it is in the minds of men that the defences of peace must be constructed.[30]

This belief has been reaffirmed by UNESCO on numerous occasions since then. In a publication of "What Is UNESCO?" in 1992 it was restated as the main driving principle of the organisation. In this study the examination of the evolution of the philosophy of peace in the twentieth century will show that the basis of this UNESCO principle is false. All the evidence would seem to show that wars begin both in the hearts and minds of men and women, and it is in the hearts and minds of men and women that the defences of peace must be constructed. This is not just a semantic difference of interpretation but reflects a fundamentally different understanding.

In 1993 UNESCO produced an: "action programme to promote a culture of peace"[31]. This programme was intended to promote and consolidate the study and research of various aspects of what is meant by a culture of peace. By implication any understanding of a culture of peace would have to contribute to the comprehension of a culture of violence. In a paper on the culture of peace Michael Wessells attempts to contrast the two cultural paradigms. What he terms cultures of violence are outlined within the following framework:

> Cultures of violence are supported by a psychological infrastructure of individual beliefs and social norms and values that emphasise violence as a means of achieving power, protection, wealth, prestige, and self and group

---

[29] United Nations, *The Charter of the United Nations*, (26th June 1945), 1.
[30] United Nations, *The Constitution of the United Nations Educational, Scientific and Cultural Organisation.*
[31] UNESCO. Executive Board Document (27 C/ 126) (1993).

esteem, and social dominance.[32]

One example of a culture of violence he gives from North American cities. In the "combat zones" of inner cities many children are socialised into systems of discrimination, hatred and violence. He believes that in many cases the components of the culture of violence can be transmitted across generations.
A culture of peace can be defined in an equally broad narrative. It is recognised that conflict is an essential feature of all social systems. It is believed by many psychologists and sociologists that conflict has very beneficial effects on interpersonal relationships and social change. But within this framework:

> A culture of peace should be viewed not as a conflict-free Utopia but as a culture in which individuals, groups and nations have productive, co-operative relations with one another and manage their inevitable conflicts constructively.[33]

THE STUDY OF WAR AND PEACE

During the last fifty to sixty years the study of the causes of war and violence has made considerable progress. Both Sorokin in his: *Social and Cultural Dynamics* published in 1937[34] and Wright in his: *A Study of War* published in 1941[35] laid the foundations for the modern study of the phenomena of war and violence. The main contributions of both Sorokin and Wright were that they established a scientifically based multi-disciplinary approach to the study of war. Within this approach a variety of perspectives could contribute to the study of war and violence as complex social phenomena. The work of Lewis Fry

---

[32] Michael G. Wessells. "The Role of Peace Education in a Culture of Peace." *Peace Environment and Education*. Vol. IV. No. 18, (1994), 39.
[33] Ibid., 41.
[34] Pitirin Sorokin, *Social and Cultural Dynamics* (New York: American Books, 1937.
[35] Quincy Wright, *A Study of War* 2 vols. (Chicago: University of Chicago Press, 1965).

Richardson[36] also helped to lay the foundation for the modern study of the causes of war and violence. In the *Statistics of Deadly Quarrels* Richardson states:

> Wars and indeed all deadly quarrels, arise from measurable conditions surrounding, and measurable relations between, nations, groups and individuals.[37]

The approach taken by Sorokin, Wright and Richardson - the statistical and historical analysis of the institution of war and violence in all their forms - has provided a wealth of information for studying the social phenomena of war and violence:

> In the conversion of war from a subject of speculation and propaganda to one of scientific analysis, all three of these pioneers, as well as others, have played key roles.[38]

These studies opened up a whole range of questions about the function of war and violence in human society. They gave a more scientific approach and rational basis to questions that had been debated for generations.
Questions about the functionally of war in human society by implication led to questions about the functionally of peace. Quincy Wright in particular opened up a whole new approach to the study of peace in the development of his approach to the study of war. In volume II of: *A Study of War*, Wright opens the section with a discussion on the scientific method and how it might be used in the study of war:

> The analysis of war attempted in this section is not intended for aesthetic realisation or for moral guidance but for scientific understanding.[39]

---

[36] Lewis Fry Richardson, *Arms and Insecurity* ed. N. Rashevsky and E. Trucco, (London: Stevens, 1960); *The Statistics of Deadly Quarrels* ed. Quincy Wright, (London: Stevens, 1960).
[37] Richardson, *Statistics.*
[38] Joel David Singer, "From 'A Study of War' to Peace Research: Some Criteria and Strategies" *Journal of Conflict Resolution.* Vol. XIV. No. 4, (1970), 527.
[39] Wright, Vol. II. 681.

The more formal approach to the study of peace and the development of peace research began during the 1950s. The pioneering work of Johan Galtung[40] at the Peace Research Institute in Oslo (PRIO) laid the foundation for the development of peace research. With the establishment in 1964 of the International Peace Research Association (IPRA), peace research began to develop its own paradigm.[41] In the scientific community there has been a general trend towards conceptualising both war and peace as very complex social phenomena.

These phenomena range across the whole spectrum of human understanding from differences in international politics to differences in individual psychology. Apart from the work being done within the peace research community, numerous scholars from widely different academic fields have contributed to the investigation and analysis of the study of peace. Gaston Bouthoul,[42] wrote over thirty books and hundreds of articles and developed the science of *polemology*. Konrad Lorenz developed a theory of aggression[43] which opened the way for much debate during the 1960s. The list of those who have contributed to the study of peace in the twentieth century is almost endless but much of the basic logic of these contributions can be summed up in the words of Julian Huxley:

> Science is organised and tested knowledge; and in that knowledge lies the potential control of phenomena. In regard to war, science can have two functions, the one promoting and the other impeding war. It can amass knowledge about the methods of prosecuting war so as to make war more efficient; or it can amass knowledge

---

[40] Nils P. Gelditsch, *Johan Galtung: A Bibliography of his Writings 1951-1980* (Oslo: PRIO, 1980).

[41] Johan Galtung, *Towards a Definition of Peace Research* (Paris: UNESCO, 1979).

[42] Gaston Bouthoul, *War* (New York: Walker, 1970). Most publications in French.

[43] Konrad Lorenz, *On Aggression* (London: Methuen, 1966).

> about the nature, causes and activities of war with a view to checking or preventing it.[44]

In general terms the more recent approaches to the study of war and peace can be divided along a number of distinct lines. Two kinds of theoretical perspectives and two distinct methodological approaches can be identified:

> At the theoretical level, war, as well as conflict and co-operation, can be conceived on the one hand as resulting mostly from national decision-making processes within governments...On the other hand a large body of literature views the causes of international political actions, and wars in particular, as broad socio-political forces and movements that are beyond the control of any particular rulers.[45]

Singer and Small in their: *The Wages of War*[46] and Francis Beer in his *Peace Against War*[47] cover a vast survey of theories and statistical findings which reflect most of the more recent methodical approaches to the study of war and peace.

THE PHILOSOPHY OF WAR

Anatol Rapoport in his introduction to Clausewitz's *On War*[48] identifies three distinct philosophies of war. He believes that the philosophy of war as outlined by Clausewitz has had a profound influence on the military and political history of Europe throughout the nineteenth century and up to the present day. Rapoport identifies the three philosophies of war as the political, the eschatological and the cataclysmic. The political philosophy of war is the one most associated with the work of Clausewitz. The key concepts of this approach to war can be

---

[44] Julian Huxley, *Essays of a Humanist* (London: Chatto and Windus, 1964).
[45] Urs Luterbacheer, "Last Words about War". *Journal of Conflict Resolution*, Vol. XXVII. No. 1, (1984)165-182.
[46] Joel David Singer and Melvin Small. *The Wages of War 1816-1915* (New York: Wiley, 1972).
[47] Francis Beer, *Peace Against War*. (an Francisco: Freeman 1981).
[48] Clausewitz, 13-15.

identified with three words. War, in theory, is a *rational instrument of national policy.* Each of these words has a very clear and precise definition. The decision to wage war ought to be rational, war should be waged only for a specific purpose and its objectives should advance the interests of the whole group or nation that is asked to wage it.

The cataclysmic philosophy of war is the complete opposite of the political philosophy. War is seen as a disaster that afflicts humanity. No one in particular can be held responsible for it and no one can in reality gain from it, in particular those politicians and generals who are convinced that they are in control. Under this approach war is related to certain dynamic properties of the international system. Wars are seen to occur when the system breaks down. The eschatological philosophy of war is used by Rapoport to cover the varieties of war not included by the two main categories. The main theme in the eschatological approach is the unfolding of some grand divine or religious design, a final war that will usher in a new era of God's kingdom on earth or of economic and social prosperity. According to Rapoport one of these three philosophies will tend to dominate the understanding of war at any particular time, although elements of all three can also be found simultaneously.

The question, "Why war?" has been debated by philosophers and theologians as well as military strategists down through the ages. *The Art of War* by Sun Tzu[49] believed to have been composed during the fourth century B. C., is one of the early classics in the analysis of war in all its forms and functions. Liddell Hart, states that *The Art of War* has "never been surpassed in comprehensiveness and depth of understanding."[50] Liddell Hart believed that Carl von Clausewitz's classic: *On War*[51] which had such an important effect on European military thought, was not as balanced as Sun Tzu's analysis. Developments in the philosophy of war are of course very much

---

[49] Sun Tzu. *The Art of War* translated and introduced by Samuel B. Griffith. (London: Oxford University Press, 1971).
[50] Ibid., v.
[51] Clausewitz.

related to the developments in other areas of science and rational understanding. W.B.Gallie in his study *Understanding War:* states that:

> The scientific revolution of the sixteenth and seventeenth centuries...the Cartesian cult of rationality, efficiency and economy in all walks of life, all played their parts in wearing down the centuries-old assumption that war was one of the great unthinkables and therefore one of the great constants of human life.[52]

Clausewitz's *On War* published posthumously between 1832-35 set the framework for much of the later debate on the philosophy of war. Clausewitz set out his arguments on the logic of war in his first chapter. He believed that: "War is an act of force which theoretically can have no limits." Clausewitz states that: "to introduce into the philosophy of war itself a principle of moderation would be an absurdity."[53] In one sense Clausewitz did not invent something that was not already in existence. The militarisation of political thought which Clausewitz describes has had a long tradition in European society. J. F. C. Fuller in his study *The Decisive Battles of the Western World* states:

> It was gunpowder (that) shattered the mediaeval order physically and morally. War as a trial of moral values by battle, in which the Church refereed for God, gradually gave way to a new certainty: that war is a means towards a political end in which the deciding factor is power. As war was secularised, peace followed suit, idealism gave way to realism...[54]

There were other much more utilitarian objections to war. The basis for Bentham's *Plan for a Universal and Perpetual Peace*[55]

---

[52] W. B. Gallie, *Understanding War* (London: Routledge, 1991), 38.
[53] Clausewitz, 102.
[54] J. K. C. Fuller, *The Decisive Battles of the Western World* ed. John Terrine. (London: Granada, 1970). 322.
[55] Jeremy Bentham, *A Plan for a Universal and Perpetual Peace* (London: Grotious Society, 1927).

was that wars were no longer rational or economical. War, according to Bentham, no longer paid either the victor or the vanquished. For nineteenth century utilitarians such as Richard Cobden and John Bright, profit and peace went hand in hand. The central principle underlying the utilitarian world-view was the belief that only the traditional ruling classes wanted war. They, and a small elite of business interests in arms manufacturing, were the only people who would gain from war. "The people," if only they were allowed to speak for themselves, would opt for peace. Free trade and peace went hand in hand and were in the best interests of all the people of England. Cobden only slowly accepted that when "the people" did speak, they could well be fanatic in their support of war:

> Cobden could only explain this phenomenon by suggesting that somehow the entire English people had been infected with aristocratic vices.[56]

In their analysis of war Cobden and Wright fell under similar misconceptions as later researchers. They based their analysis on the belief that the motives for going to war were rational, economic and practical. They totally underestimated the importance of irrational and psychological motivations in the support and the pursuit of war. There is a world of a difference between the various theories of war and the actual realities of war. One of the great attractions of Clausewitz's analysis of war is his attempt to marry the reality with the theory. He has no doubt about the importance of theoretical principles in shaping reality. In simple terms it should be possible to trace effects to causes and to identify what Clausewitz called primary elements. Clausewitz starts his study with what seems to be a very simple question, "What is War?" It is the clarity of his answers to these simple questions that has made his contribution to the philosophy of war so significant.

THE PHILOSOPHY OF PEACE

---

[56] Howard, 45.

R.G. Collingwood in his *The Idea of History*[57] identifies some of the problems that arise in any attempt to outline the idea of a "philosophy of something." He believes that the name "philosophy of history" was invented in the eighteenth century by Voltaire, who meant it to be no more than critical or scientific history. Collingwood outlines his own ideas in his preliminary discussions:

> When we speak of the "philosophy of something" (e.g. of art, of religion, of history) we mean to designate a body of thoughts which arise in us when we think about that thing. These thoughts must be philosophical; that is, they must be universal and necessary…no thoughts can claim to be the philosophy of a subject unless they arise universally and necessarily in the mind of everyone who thinks about that subject.[58]

In relation to the possibilities of a philosophy of peace, Collingwood's analysis of the structure of human nature is quite significant. In criticising the earlier approaches to the science of human nature he rejects the fallacious concept that the human mind and human nature are constant and can be understood in the same way as the science of nature:

> If, on the other hand, that which we understand better is our own understanding, an improvement in that science is an improvement not only in its subject but its object also. By coming to think more truly about the human understanding we are coming to improve our own understanding. Hence the historical development of the science of human nature entails an historical development in human nature itself. [59]

---

[57] R.G. Collingwood, *The Idea of History* (Oxford: Oxford University Press, 1993).
[58] Ibid., 335.
[59] Ibid., 84.

The debate on the nature of intelligence and the evolution of knowledge may be significant but it is not a central part of the structure of the philosophy of peace.
A more practical approach might be gained by asking a number of simple but pertinent questions in relation to the structure of the philosophy of peace. A philosophy of peace should produce a general theory of peace. This general theory of peace would help explain and clarify the following questions:

1. Peace is?
2. Peace will be established by?
3. Peace can be maintained by?

The philosophy of peace should help to analyse and clarify the concepts that are associated with these explanations. In this sense the study of peace is more problematic than the study of war. A number of other approaches can be taken which would help expand the understanding of the framework of the philosophy of peace. The concept of peace could be and has been analysed at three distinct levels: the level of international relations, the level of the social structure and at the level of the individual. A second set of questions would arise from this approach:

1. What international conditions would create an environment which would establish as a *fait accompli (an accomplished fact)* the resolution of conflict by peaceful means?

2. What social and economic conditions would create a cultural system where violence would be rejected as a means of supporting, or changing that system.

3. What personal factors and conditions would help individuals reject the use of violence under all circumstances?

A philosophy of peace constructed around any of these questions would have to be based firmly on the traditional knowledge, understanding and wisdom that is to be found within the great religious traditions of mankind. It would also have to build on the scientific knowledge of human understanding that has made such significant progress in the twentieth century. The four individuals whose beliefs and ideas are identified in this study reflect this duality of approach. The basis of a philosophy of peace would have to reject the narrow ideologies of socialism and capitalism and the materialistic and militaristic world-view that they have manufactured.

2

THE EUROPEAN CULTURE OF VIOLENCE

For the masses, the real Christ is Alexander, Caesar, Charlemagne, Napoleon.
Pierre-Joseph Proudhon (1809-1865)

Violence and war (had) become the leading instruments of civilisation
because they dedicate men to non-material ends
Georges Sorel (1847-1922)

At the level of individuals, violence is a cleansing force.
It frees the native from his inferiority complex and restores his self-respect
Franz Fanon (1925-1961)

WAR AND HUMAN PROGRESS

In a masterly work: *War and Human Progress: An Essay on the Rise of Industrial Civilisation.*[1] Professor John Nef debated a number of important questions concerning the culture of violence and industrial civilisation. In a review of the book published at the time, Professor Hugh Trevor-Roper[2] sets this work above and beyond the more traditional debate on the theory of war and capitalism. Nef identifies a clear relationship between what he sees as "The revolution in the art of war" and "The birth of modern science and industrialism." But he goes far beyond the historical relationship between war and industrial development. Industrial and technological developments have always had a direct influence on the nature of war and the structural basis of violence. War and scientific progress have evolved an almost symbiotic relationship. The relationship between war and violence and the cultural aspects of civilisations have not been as clearly identified. Nef starts his study by looking at the relationship between what he calls "the new warfare" and the "Genesis of industrialism" from the late fifteenth century. One of the central aspects of this debate centres around the material restraints on the conduct of war. In this context it can be seen that industrial development and scientific progress have removed many of the traditional restraining factors in relation to the structure of war and the nature of violence.

There had always been a belief or a hope in European society that the introduction of more and more destructive technologies of violence might somehow lead to the restriction of their use. In 1139 Pope Innocent II placed under an interdict the use of the crossbow: "The Church held it to be a barbarous instrument, unfit for Christian warfare."[3] Its condemnation was confirmed

[1] John U. Nef *War and Human Progress: An Essay on the Rise of Industrial Civilisation* (New York: Norton, 1968).
[2] Hugh Trevor Roper, review of Nef, *War and Human Progress*, in *Sunday Times*, 1951.
[3] Nef, 135.

on a number of subsequent occasions. The Church was attempting to put some restraint on the violence that seemed to be so inherent in human nature. The mediaeval Church was acting very much like the modern state. It believed that if the Church was in a position to sanctify some violence and outlaw other types of violence, then it could reduce and possibly control the amounts of violence that arise out of natural grievances and disputes. In a similar way the modern state has taken on the monopoly of the legitimate use of violence. The legitimisation of state violence and the modern state's monopoly of that legitimisation is the cornerstone of a world-view and an ideology which would be far different if that cornerstone was to be seriously questioned or undermined.

Nef identifies what he considers to be a fundamental change in the attitudes of European society to war and to war fighting. He gives as a practical example of this the Surrender at Breda (1634-1635); the conditions of the surrender reflected all the best in the culture of Christian humanism. This compares with the type of actions still being undertaken by authorities in the sixteenth century against perceived enemies. One such example is the sentence passed upon St. Edmund Champion in 1681:

> Ye shall be drawn…upon hurdles to the place of execution, and there be hanged and let down alive, and your privy parts cut off, and your entrails taken out and burned in your sight; then your heads to be cut off and your bodies divided into four parts, to be disposed of at her Majesty's pleasure.[4]

At roughly the same as the surrender at Breda, Hugo Grotius (1583-1645) was writing his *De jure belli et pacis (On the Laws of War and Peace).* In effect the Church had lost whatever moral authority it had to restrict fighting and the carnage that arose from such fighting. In many cases the Christian Church itself was the source of the conflict. The attempts to restrict the damage done and suffering inflicted by war would have to

[4] Michael Mc Mahon. Saints. London. MQ Publications. 2006 p.327

evolve outside or alongside the traditional Christian restraints. A law of nations based on rational thought was, according to Grotius, the essential foundation for any prospect of universal peace. Nef examines what he terms the "Restraints of European Culture on Violence." During the seventeenth and eighteenth centuries there was, according to Nef, a growing distaste for the use of violence based on a number of different factors:

> It consisted in the improvement of manners, customs, and laws, and in the perfection of thought and of art of many kinds, from letters to music and architecture.[5]

This growing distaste for the use of violence can also be traced to the developing influence of rational thought upon political discourse and an increasing belief that the development of commerce, the peaceful exchange of goods, was beneficial to all. The growth of religious toleration, slowly but surely, was to have a major impact as a restraining factor on the use of unrestrained violence. More importantly there was the development of the belief that the interest of great states can be served better by peace than by war: "Kings themselves were deeply affected by the pacifistic positions held by theologians, philosophers, and men of letters."[6]

In the age before nationalism became the dominant ideology and in the period after the end of the major wars of religion, wars came to be seen in an older and more cynical light as the sport of Kings. Before and to a certain extent after the First World War, the thesis that the introduction of more frightful instruments of death might impose limits on war or perhaps even led to the abandonment of war became even more popular.

TOYNBEE'S HISTORICAL ANALYSIS

In his monumental work, *A Study of History* Arnold J. Toynbee[7] puts forward a number of theories in relation to the rise and fall

---

[5] Nef. 250.

[6] Ibid., 258.

[7] Arnold J. Toynbee, *A Study of History* abridged in two vols., by D. C. Somervell. (Oxford: Oxford University Press, 1974).

of civilisations. The threads of these theories are to be found throughout his massive study of history. Toynbee outlined a thesis on the relationship between militarism and civilisation which he developed in his latter works. *In A Study of History,* he identifies 26 civilisations based on distinct cultural structures and patterns. Of these 26 civilisations, Toynbee claimed 16 were now dead and buried. Of the remaining ten survivors, two were almost finished, the Nomads and the Polynesian. Of the last eight civilisations, according to Toynbee, seven out of the eight were under threat of either annihilation or assimilation by the eighth; that is by western "industrial" civilisation[8]. This grand picture put forward by Toynbee has suffered more than its fair share of criticism. But Toynbee's *Study of History* introduced many concepts that are still very useful today. Toynbee describes and identifies what he calls an "Universal State," which, like the Roman Empire, sees a dominant state becoming a dominant cultural empire.

In his latter works *Civilisation on Trial* (1948) and *War and Civilisation* (1950), Toynbee identifies some of the forces which have dominated the growth and decline of civilisations. Toynbee identified what he termed "The Suicidalness of Militarism" and he classified war and militarism as the most potent cause of the breakdown of society. He rejects the idea that each civilisation has a natural cycle with a beginning, a middle and an end stage, which works itself out over time. He goes on to say:

> The dead civilisations are not dead by fate, or "in the course of nature," and therefore our living civilisation is not doomed inexorably in advance to "join the majority" of its species. Though sixteen civilisations may have perished already to our knowledge, and nine others may be now at the point of death, we - the twenty-sixth are not compelled to submit the riddle of our fate to the blind arbitrament of statistics.[9]

---

[8] Ibid., Vol. I. 244.

[9] Ibid., Vol. I 254.

Toynbee's theories on the death of civilisations are based on the complex analysis of social, environmental, religious and many other historical forces. In one sense his view is very pessimistic; most of the civilisations he studies have broken down or gone into disintegration.

In 1975, the last year of his life, Toynbee wrote: "The two congenital social maladies of civilisations have been war and social injustice." He believed quite strongly that industrial civilisation has so far wrestled unsuccessfully with this disease. In his final analysis, Toynbee went back to his original belief in his theory that the growth of war and violence was the major cause of the breakdown of societies and the death of civilisations.[10]

Lewis Mumford in his magnum opus *The City in History*[11] outlined a slightly different thesis in the developmental relationship between war and violence and the evolution of civilisation.

> Too easily have historians imputed war chiefly to man's savage past, and have looked upon war as an incursion of so called primitive nomads, the "have-nots," against normally "peaceful" centres of industry and trade. Nothing could be further from the historic truth. War and domination, rather than peace and co-operation, were ingrained in the original structure of the ancient city.[12]

In page after page of *The City in History* Mumford puts forward his ideas on the parasitic relationship between the rise of the city and the institutionalisation of violence:

> Under the aegis of the city, violence thus became normalised, and spread far beyond the centres where

[10] Ibid., Vol. II. 392.
[11] Lewis Mumford, *The City in History* (London: Pelican, 1961).
[12] Ibid., 57.

> the great collective manhunts and sacrificial orgies were first instituted.[13]

Whatever the origins of the city, Mumford believed that urban power and its contribution to the capacity of war-fighting quickly became the most important force in determining the structure and institutions of the city.

> If civilised society has not yet outgrown war, as it outgrew less respectable manifestations of primitive magic, like child sacrifice and cannibalism, it is partly because the city itself in its structure and institutions continued to give war both a durable concrete form and a magical pretext for existence. Beneath all war's technical improvements lay an irrational belief, still deeply embedded in the collective unconscious: only by wholesale human sacrifice can the community be saved.[14]

PROUDHON'S ANALYSIS OF WAR AND PEACE

Pierre-Joseph Proudhon (1809-1865) was one of the most radical writers on social reform in the middle part of the nineteenth century and is important for his influence on later thinkers such as Marx. He is best known for his economic theories in relation to property and society, his most famous statement that "property is theft" reflects the paradoxical nature of much of his thinking. He seemed to deliberately go out of his way to make contradictory statements on every major issue, but he "shared his century's confidence that reason and science would bring about social progress and expand human freedom."[15] Proudhon attempted in his own way to discover the laws which he believed governed society and he made his mark in the early study of sociology. The publication of *The*

---

[13] Ibid., 56.
[14] Ibid., 58.
[15] Peter Marshall, *Demanding the Impossible* (London: Fontana Press, 1973), 235.

Philosophy of Misery[16] brought a direct response from Marx in his *The Misery of Philosophy*[17]. Proudhon's ideas on the questions of war and society can be found throughout most of his writings but in particular in his publication of *War and Peace* in 1861. One of the keys to understanding Proudhon's ideas on war and peace is his belief that at some stage in human development war will give way to peace. He believed that this development might take place towards the end of the nineteenth century. Tolstoy stated that Proudhon's *War and Peace* was to have a profound influence upon his thinking. Proudhon did not reject war in the same comprehensive manner as Tolstoy. Proudhon stated:

> War is divine, that is to say it is primordial, essential to life and to the production of men and society. It is deeply seated in human consciousness and its idea embraces all human relationships.[18]

Proudhon attempted to identify the causes of war in a number of areas of human relationships. "On other occasions he gives an economic explanation and argues that its primary cause is poverty. He also depicts war in its logical terms as: "the abstract formulation of the dialectic"[19]. In *War and Peace* Proudhon outlined or restated a thesis that was to become only too familiar in the twentieth century. He regarded war as a constructive force which had contributed much to humanity and to the dignity of Man. In this world-view, wars conferred upon the common man a kind of dignity that ordinary industrial life was failing to provide. Proudhon wrote: "For the masses, the real Christ is Alexander, Caesar, Charlemagne, Napoleon."[20]

Much of what Proudhon thought and wrote was both inconsistent and paradoxical. In his attempt at producing a

---

[16] Pierre-Joseph Proudhon, *The Philosophy of Misery*.London. Kessinger.2004
[17] Karl Marx. *The Poverty of Philosophy*. London. Prometheus.1995
[18] Stewart Edwards ed., *Selected Writings of Pierre-Joseph Proudhon* trans. Elizabeth Fraser. (London: Macmillan, 1969), 23.
[19] Marshall, 251.
[20] Nef, 405.

philosophy of human nature based on his own analysis of political ethics and human behaviour, he produced his own unique approach to some of the more controversial issues in relation to human progress. At one level Proudhon believed that human beings were naturally aggressive, selfish and domineering. He rejected any religious interpretation that might reduce these tendencies in human culture. At the same time that he was identifying the destructive passions of human nature, he believed that man was capable of rational control and that this rational control was the key to human progress. Proudhon believed that the Christian doctrine on war had never really become a dominant force in European civilisation. The idea that war by its very nature was evil, and peace by its nature virtuous, had lost much of its meaning and value. For Proudhon, the view of war as an ennobling spiritual experience seemed to become more relevant with the continuing decline in any spiritual consensus of the emerging industrial civilisation.

GEORGES SOREL: REFLECTIONS ON VIOLENCE

This theme was taken up by Georges Sorel (1847-1922) in his *Reflections on Violence* in which he identified and criticised the age-old association of violence with barbarism. He rejected the idea that gentleness is the mark of civilisation, and that acts of collective and individual violence alike should be regarded as barbarous. For Sorel:

> Violence and war (had) become the leading instruments of civilisation because they dedicate men to non-material ends.[21]

The complexities of Sorel's thought have been outlined and debated in a number of studies.[22] Sorel was a radical in the classical sense of radicalism. He disliked and distrusted liberalism, conservatism and, in the end, socialism and Marxism.

---

[21] Ibid., 407.

[22] Robert Nisbet, *The Social Philosophers: Community and Conflict in Western Thought* (London: Heinemann, 1974).

In one of his most famous works: *Reflections on Violence*[23] Sorel attacked the "liberal" concepts and ideas which were critical of the use of violence. But he also criticised the socialists and revolutionaries who saw violence as a tool of the revolution. Sorel was not advocating violence for its own sake. His position on violence was much more subtle than that; he believed that the greatest danger to any society was not violence, but materialism and decadence, and that these dangers were greatest in societies where violence was pasteurised behind legal frameworks.

In one of his other major works: *The Illusions of Progress*[24] Sorel attacked the concept of progress in much the same way as he had attacked the concept of violence. Peace has always been considered the greatest of blessings and the essential condition of all material progress, and it is for this reason that industrial societies have so often been contrasted favourably with military ones.[25] Sorel's world-view was set firmly in the tradition of those who questioned the benefits of industrialisation. In this framework: "Reason and science had not emancipated man; they had enslaved and debased him."[26] For Sorel, social, political or any fundamental cultural change was never gradual, uniform or easy. Sorel believed that in historical terms violence was the key to many of the great social developments. He emphasised in many of writings the creative role of violence, he believed that "Proletarian violence" was the only means of transforming society. Proletarian violence not only makes the future revolution certain, but it seems also to be the only means by which the European nations - at present stupefied by humanitarianism - can recover their former energy.[27]
What Sorel was attempting to do was to reconfirm beyond doubt the legitimacy and authenticity of violence as a means to an end. Violence was not only to be seen as a means to an end but also as the only way of achieving fundamental social change in

---

[23] Georges Sorel, *Reflections on Violence* trans. T. E. Hulme.(London: George Unwin and Allen, 1917).
[24] Georges Sorel, *The Illusions of Progress* trans. John Stanley and Charlotte Stanley. (Berkeley and Los Angeles: University of California Press, 1969).
[25] Sorel, *Reflections*, 205.
[26] Sorel, *Illusions,* xi.
[27] Ibid., 92.

society. Nisbet believes that the concept of the *heroic age* and the role of the *hero* were key factors in Sorel's manifesto for violence:

> Those willing to engage in violence, irrespective of its consequences, are manifestly more heroic, more trustworthy, more dedicated than those who profess commitment to goals but shrink from the means necessary to achieve them; so argues Sorel in his ethics of violence.[28]

Many of Sorel's ideas were seen even by his revolutionary contemporaries as being very radical. His ideas nevertheless represent and reflect a very important contribution in the historical analysis of the components in the culture of violence in European society. Similar ideas were expressed at a much later stage by Frantz Fanon (1925-1961) in: *The Wretched of the Earth*[29] and to a lesser extent: *On Violence* by Hannah Arendt.[30] For Fanon, violence was seen as a cleansing force that was an essential factor in the contribution to the search for freedom and the liberation of oppressed people:

> At the level of individuals, violence is a cleansing force. It frees the native from his inferiority complex and restores his self-respect.[31]

Fanon's analysis was dominated by his ideas on the problems and the relationships between the coloniser and the colonised. But in his theories "concerning violence" he attempted to cover the whole gambit of human relationships:

> Illuminated by violence, the consciousness of the people rebels against any pacification. From now on the demagogues, the opportunists and the magicians have a

---

[28] Nisbet, 303.
[29] Frantz Fanon, *The Wretched of the Earth* trans. Constance Farrington. (London: Pelican, 1983).
[30] Hannah Arendt, *On Violence* (London: Harvest, 1969).
[31] Fanon, 74.

difficult task.[32]

Fanon's ideas and his language make no concessions whatever to the possibility of peaceful social change or to the contribution that a less radical approach might make. *The Wretched of the Earth* became a clarion call taken up by revolutionary groups all over the world. Hannah Arendt, in her influential books, *The Origins of Totalitarianism* and *On Revolution*, takes a less radical line on the use of violence and the possible logical justifications that can be made around its defence. The critical debate for Arendt centred around revolution rather than war. Because of the technical developments in the means of destruction Arendt believed that wars on a world scale could not be justified on any rational grounds. The main thrust of her arguments centres around the relationship between war and revolution and the rational justifications that are given to support their respective uses:

> It is important to remember that the idea of freedom was introduced into the debate of the war question after it had become quite obvious that we had reached a state of technical development where the means of destruction were such as to exclude their rational use.[33]

Her analysis of the justification and glorification of violence centred, as she believed, around the concept of revolution, has made a critical contribution to the development of the debate. Wars and revolutions have, she believed, thus far:

> Determined the physiognomy of the twentieth century. And as distinguished from the nineteenth century ideologies - such as nationalism and internationalism, capitalism and imperialism, socialism and communism, which, though still invoked by many as justifying causes, have lost contact with the major realities of our world - war and revolution still constitute its two central political

---

[32] Ibid.
[33] Arendt, 14.

issues.[34]

The professional revolutionaries of the twentieth century were, she believed, the fools of history. Fools, not in a personal sense, but in their beliefs in the various theories of historical necessity. She outlined her own views on the rational justifications for revolutions in a very clear and unambiguous manner:

> And we also know to our sorrow that freedom has been better preserved in countries where no revolution ever broke out, no matter how outrageous the circumstances of the powers that be, and that there exist more civil liberties even in countries where the revolution was defeated than in those where revolutions have been victorious.[35]

THE DARWINIAN LEGACY: THE BIOLOGY OF PEACE AND WAR

Darwin's direct influence on the ideology of war or on the philosophy of peace is not that significant. However the influence of The *Origin of Species* cannot be underestimated; because, as the philosopher John Dewey said:

> In laying hands upon the sacred ark of absolute permanency. (*The Origin of Species)* introduced a mode of thinking that in the end was bound to transform the logic of knowledge, and hence the treatment of morals, politics and religion[36]

For many people Darwin gave a scientific rationality to Hobbes theory of human society as "the war of all against all." For this reason alone it would be a mistake to underestimate the Darwinian contribution to the debate on the culture of violence. Darwin opened a "Pandora's box" in relation to biological speculations about the role of violence and aggression in species

---

[34] Ibid., 11.
[35] Ibid., 115.
[36] John Dewey, "The Influence of Darwin on Philosophy" in *Darwin* ed. P. Appleman. (New York: Norton, 1970), 393.

evolution. The debate broadened out into almost all areas of social discourse. The debate on the biology of evolution had a profound effect on the study of human behaviour and human moral values.

The various doctrines of "biological militarism" and "conflict sociology" that became popular towards the end of the nineteenth century had their origins in different interpretations of Darwin's theory of evolution. The debate concerning the "biology of war" reached a peak in the years leading up to the start of the First World War. *The Origin of Species* was the "Bible" on which various schools of interpretation developed. The "War biologists," basing their theories on the perceived biologically aggressive nature of the human species, saw war as an adaptive response to long-term evolutionary pressures. But paradox abounded at the same time, and using the same "Bible," other biologists saw war as a biological disaster for the human species. Both sides distorted for their own purposes the challenging questions raised by Darwin. In a much earlier work, Malthus in *An Essay on the Principle of Population*[37] had identified both "positive" and "negative" checks on population growth. Malthus had listed the positive checks on population as famine, epidemics, poverty and war; and arising out of these he identified "a struggle for existence". Darwin himself would have been aware of Malthus's work and was probably influenced by these ideas.

In his book *Darwinism, War and History*, Paul Cook[38] outlines the development of various ideas associated with what he identifies as "peace biology" or "scientific pacifism." He compares these arguments with the various theories of war and aggression that developed around the concepts of the "survival of the fittest." Both Herbert Spencer and T. H. Huxley are identified as key figures in the unfolding of the debate. With

---

[37] Thomas Malthus, *An Essay on the Principles of Population as it Affects the Future Improvement of Society* (1798) ed. Geoffrey Gilbert. (Oxford: Oxford University Press, 1993).
[38] Paul Cook, *Darwinism: War and History*. (Cambridge: Cambridge University Press, 1994).

developments during the nineteenth century in science and economic progress it seemed to many that war and militarism were an outmoded phase of history. But the terrible losses and the dramatic social upheavals caused by the First World War raised a number of questions concerning the "Liberal Peace Myth." The essential element of this myth as built up during the nineteenth century was: "Faith in enlightened science and culture, human malleability and a better future."[39] Some of the central questions in the debate on man as the "fighting ape" may now seem dated. But many of the major elements in the historical debate are to be found in the work of E. O. Wilson and in the modern development of sociobiology.[40] The debate on the "violent nature" of the human species has taken a number of different turns. The question of whether the human species can construct a biologically independent culture is still moot.

MARXIST-LENINIST THEORY OF WAR AND PEACE

In his book *Just and Unjust Wars* Michael Walzer identifies some of the problems which arise in any attempt to outline Marx's doctrine on war and peace. There are, as Walzer pointed out, some major difference between Marx's theory of war and the position he adopted when confronted with the actualities of war, in particular the Franco-Prussian war of 1870:

> But Marx was not only a philosopher and a letter-writer; he was also a political leader and the spokesman of a mass movement. In these latter roles, his world-historical view of the significance of war was less important than the particular judgments he was called upon to make.[41]

Marx and Engels had both dismissed pacifism as a form of bourgeois ideology. While they supported the contemporary struggle against the war preparations of the capitalist countries, they saw no real meaning in this type of pacifist protest. For

---

[39] Ibid., 153.

[40] Edward O. Wilson, *Sociology: The New Synthesis..* (Cambridge, Mass.: 1975).

[41] Michael Walzer, *Just and Unjust Wars* (New York: Basic Books, 1992), 66.

them the problem of war was centrally a problem of capitalism. The main thrust of the Marxist analysis of peace is within the context of war as a social phenomenon. Within this tradition, peace was seen as a positive by-product of the establishment of socialism and communism. Real or eternal peace in the political sense can only be achieved by the worldwide establishment of socialism. But Marx was under no illusion about the limited role that the military could play in international stability:

> If limits are to be fixed by military interests, there will be no end to claims, because every military line is necessarily faulty, and may be improved by annexing some outlying territory; and moreover, they can never be fixed finally and fairly because they always must be imposed by the conqueror upon the conquered and consequently carry within them the seeds of fresh wars.[42]

Marx and Engels never underestimated the nature of war in society. Engels identified war as one of his main areas of study and he was called "the general" given his detailed knowledge and understanding of both the science and the art of war. The defeat of the revolutions of 1848 brought about decisive changes in the perception of war of both Marx and Engels. Engels saw in war a great experiment where theory and practice could be brought together and his writings reflect an attempt to produce what has been described as a dialectic of war. Marx saw war as one of: "humanity's eternal problems."[43] The simple theoretical solution of this problem was, for Marx, the destruction of private property and the establishment of a society based on communist principles and integrity. In his *The Civil War in France* Marx identified a society: "whose rule would be peace, because its natural ruler would be everywhere the same - Labour."[44]

Before the First World War very high hopes had been raised that the solidarity of the working classes, as manifested in the

---

[42] Ibid., 121.

[43] David McLellan, *The Thoughts of Karl Marx* (London: Macmillan, 1995), 242.

[44] Karl Marx and Friedrich Engels, *The Selected Works* (Moscow: Progress, 1973) 490.

various organisations and meetings of the Communist International, would contribute significantly to reducing the possibilities of major war in Europe. The International had been founded:

> To encourage working men of different countries to support each other's struggles, by vindicating the simple laws of morals and justice in foreign affairs.[45]

The various congresses of the First International made statement after statement rejecting war as a form of "Bourgeois conspiracy" against the working class. The third congress put forward a very clear view on how wars could be prevented:

> Nothing can put an end to war except social reorganisation...the peoples can henceforward lessen the frequency of war by opposing those who make war or declare war...The congress urges the workers to cease work should war break out in their respective countries.[46]

Bitter experience was to show that International solidarity at any level was not able to withstand the forces of nationalistic jingoism that were unleashed in Europe in 1914.

LENIN'S JUST WAR THEORY

In *Socialism and War*[47] Lenin clearly identified the types of war, both civil and international, that socialists could consider as both necessary and legitimate. He describes how the socialist attitude to war was fundamentally different from both the bourgeois pacifists and the anarchists. The major difference, according to Lenin, was that socialists understood the inevitable connection between war and class struggle: "We understand that wars

---

[45] McLellan, 94.

[46] Istvan Kende, "The History of Peace: Concepts and Organisations from the Late Middle Ages to the 1870s" *Journal of Peace Research*. Vol. XXVI. No. 3, (1989), 244.

[47] V. I. Lenin, *Socialism and War* Collected Works. Vol. XXI. (1915), (London: Progress Publishers, 1960-80), 299-304.

cannot be abolished unless classes are abolished and socialism is created."[48] Lenin originally dismisses as irrelevant the traditional just war concepts:

> Imagine a slave-holder who owns 100 slaves warring against another who owns 200 slaves, for a more "just" redistribution of slaves.[49]

But then Lenin's analysis of war goes on to create what in effect is his own Marxist theory of the just war. According to this theory, international and civil wars can be beneficial to the development of mankind by helping to destroy reactionary institutions. The French revolution and the French revolutionary wars were seen by Lenin as a prime example. Even if these wars contained an element of plunder and the conquest of foreign territory by the French, this did not take from their progressive nature. They led to the undermining and overthrow of the forces of absolutism and feudalism. Lenin identified the wars that he believed as fully legitimate, progressive and necessary:

> Wars waged by the oppressed class against the oppressor class, by slaves against slaveholders, by serfs against land-owners, and wage-workers against the bourgeois.[50]

The Marxist-Leninist theology of peace underwent some important changes with the establishment of the Soviet Union and the formulation by Lenin of the doctrine of peaceful co-existence: "which was to become the core of the Marxist-Leninist theory of peace."[51] But among many communists there was the general belief that the revolutions to bring about communism could only be carried out by armed violence. The capitalist system would not die peacefully. Lenin's period of

---

[48] Bernard Semmel, ed., *Marxism and the Science of War* (London: Oxford University Press, 1981), 164.
[49] Ibid., 166.
[50] Ibid., 164.
[51] Julian Lider, "Marxist-Leninist Concepts of Peace and Peaceful Co-existence" in *World Encyclopaedia of Peace* Vol. I. ed. Linus Pauling et al. (Oxford: Pergamon, 1986), 588.

peaceful co-existence was to be used as a period of economic recovery and military build up of the Soviet Union for the wars with the capitalist states which were inevitable. The thesis that a socialist revolution is the precondition for a stable peace remained the underlying basis of Marxist Leninist ideology of war.

A number of important developments in the communist ideology of war and peace were brought about with the various pressures building up in the international system. The rise of fascism in Europe and the experience of the Second World War did not fit into the traditional interpretations. *The Manifesto for Peace*, signed in Moscow in 1957, shows how much some of the ideas had changed:

> We declare that we are fully aware of our responsibility for the destiny of mankind; world war is not unavoidable, war can be prevented, peace can be secured and consolidated.[52]

This manifesto can be seen within a framework of Soviet propaganda but it also reflects important changes and genuine attempts by the communist ideologists to come to terms with the possibility of a lasting peace, short of total victory, for the communist ideology.

THE IDEOLOGY OF TOTALITARIANISM

Developments in the understanding of the ideology and culture of totalitarianism in its various modern forms in the twentieth century have had a profound influence on the philosophy of peace. The debate on the theory of totalitarianism has taken many twists and turns, dictated in part, by the ideological necessities of the Cold War system. Martin Kitchen[53] in his study of the structures of totalitarianism identifies six distinct characteristics that are basic features in all forms of totalitarian

---

[52] Ibid., 582.
[53] Martin Kitchen, *Fascism* (London: Macmillan, 1976).

dictatorships. Totalitarian ideologies reached their peak in the Soviet Union under Lenin and Stalin, and in Germany under the Nazi party. Other countries such as China under Mao Tse Tung, adapted totalitarian ideologies to suit their own circumstances. One of the central common denominators in the various totalitarian experiences was their understanding and conception of the ideology of violence. In trying to describe and explain the rise of fascism in Europe, there has been identified a set of easily discernible common characteristics in the variety of forms which it took in different countries:

> A political ideology of militant nationalism, proclaiming the state as paramount, the idolisation of a particular leader or political leadership, a mechanism of totalitarian social control including the apparatus and techniques of mass manipulation, and the central control of economy and culture[54]

The ideology of fascism reached its nemesis in the rise of Nazism in Europe. The historical roots of fascism have traditionally been traced back to the philosophical ideals of Machiavelli, Hegel, Nietzsche, Sorel and many others. Nietzsche's philosophical radicalism and acute criticism of bourgeois values laid part of the foundation on which various fascist ideologies were based. Many different interpretations of the historical phenomenon of fascism have been given. It has been seen as a reactionary movement against both liberalism and socialism. Many Marxists held the view that fascism was the: "final phase of bourgeois society." Organski believed that fascism was part of a process of transition from a pre-industrial to a post-industrial society.

In many ways the strength and appeal of fascism took both liberals and the more liberal socialists by surprise:

> A few nineteenth-century sages - a Burckhardt, a Nietzsche - had some inkling of the forces that might be unchained in mass industrialised societies, but nothing in

[54] Linus Pauling, et al., ed. *World Encyclopedia of Peace* Vol. I. (Oxford: Pergamon, 1986), 307.

> the thinking of Bentham and Mill, on the one hand, nor of Marx and Engels on the other, had prepared their followers for the emergence of movements which were both populist and authoritarian, which harnessed mass opinion to a militarist ethic, which were equally hostile to traditional class-structures and to democratic values, and which had no interest whatever in world peace.[55]

Whatever the explanations given to help define the phenomenon of fascism, the core of the fascist ideology was the belief in the legitimacy of the use of violence for political ends. Within this context the use of violence was glorified and rationalised and violence was seen as a cleansing force for the nation. This type of analysis is not peculiar to fascism. But fascism arose within an historical context when traditional certainties and moral standards had been destroyed or undermined. In the culture of fascism, restraints on the use of violence had no basis other than the political ambitions of power.

RATIONALISING THE IRRATIONAL

The question of violence, like the question of justice, can be seen as one of the core questions in any political philosophy, in that it raises some of what has been called the eternal questions common to all philosophy. In general, both the historical and contemporary attempts to explain violence in human society have been made along a number of distinct and sometimes exclusive paths. Many philosophers following the Platonic tradition see the use of violence both as rational and utilitarian. Within this tradition, violence is seen as rational in the Clausewizian sense as an instrument of political policy. It is seen as utilitarian in the Machiavellian sense, as the ends justifying the means. In general terms violence is seen as a central part of conflict and conflict itself is seen as a normal, and by some, as a positive part of human relationships and political structures. Sometimes the level of violence in a particular

---

[55] Michael Howard, *War and the Liberal Conscience* (Oxford: Oxford University Press, 1981), 100-101.

conflict spills over the level of any rational understanding or utilitarian justification. But this is not considered to invalidate any of the rational theories of justification.
There is a distinct historical tradition of the moral and ethical justifications and rationalisations of violence:

> Moral justifications of violence certainly seem to be a very general feature of ideologies of violence. The justifications then of violence are the higher ethical imperatives of justice, liberty, and historical necessity.[56]

But the opposite tradition also exists which identifies the use of violence as both irrational and anti-utilitarian, and morally unacceptable. The attempts to build a synthesis between these two opposing views can be identified as another legitimate historical tradition. Both the concepts of violence and aggression are such expansive concepts that numerous different approaches can be taken to their analysis and interpretation. It is hoped to trace some of the arguments that have been traditionally given to rationalise and justify the use of violence under certain political and social conditions. At the beginning of the twentieth century the ideology of political violence was supported by a number of core mythologies.

PHILOSOPHICAL VISIONS AND THE CULTURE OF VIOLENCE

Attempts at understanding the reality of war and the utilitarian nature of violence have traditionally been justified and rationalised around a number of distinct philosophical visions. These can be classified around a number of different headings. While each of these visions are related and interrelated to one another, there is a core in each vision which is separate and independent. At the same time it is possible to identify a number of traditional and conventional explanations and justifications for the culture of violence. see Table 4:1

[56] Leo Kuper, *The Pity of It All* (London: Duckworth, 1977), 116-117.

Table 4:1

PHILOSOPHICAL VISIONS OF WAR	TRADITIONAL JUSTIFICATIONS
1. The Historical Vision	1. The Rational Justification
2. The Religious or Spiritual Vision	2. The Utilitarian Justification
3. The Romantic Vision	3. The Romantic Explanation
4. The Machiavellian Vision	4. The Expediency Theory

Each of these approaches has the ability to a greater or lesser extent to create its own logical framework and to establish its own set of justifications and rational explanations within that logical framework.

1. The Historical Vision

The historical justification for the necessity of war and violence is one of the more important explanations in the cultural rationalisation of violence in the modern world. In this explanation it is believed that the highest political principles known to Man, such as Liberty, Equality and Fraternity, can only be achieved and maintained by the use of force. *Si vis pacem, para bellum,* "if you desire peace, prepare for war" is the concept most associated with this vision. The historical explanation of peace through security, or balance of power, or deterrence, is as important in the historical context for city-states as for great empires. The development of the modern nation-state has given a new lease of life to this explanation. The central part of this explanation is utilitarian by nature. The state, or the ruling elite, must in order to survive, take certain actions to defend and protect itself and to promote its own interests.

2. The Religious or Spiritual Vision

One of the most important religious contributions to the culture of violence is the theory of the "Just War". The Religious vision of war understands war and violence as a necessary evil which can be partly justified by the inherent weakness in human nature. In philosophical terms this tradition attempts to addresses the problem of evil in human society. It creates a framework of ethical justification which can side-step the moral issues of right and wrong. If war and violence are a result of the evil in the world or the evil in Man's nature than war and violence cannot be abolished in the imperfect human society. The best that religion can offer would be to restrict the damage and ameliorate the suffering caused by the evil side of human nature.

3. The Romantic Vision

The core of the romantic vision of war and violence centres around the belief in the following related concepts. Firstly, the credentials of a just cause must be seen to be established beyond dispute. This will be followed by the need for heroic sacrifices, which in turn will lead to a victory over the enemy. Variations on this theme will be found in almost every conflict and in almost all literary traditions. One classic example is the words of Horatio at the bridge:

> To every man upon this earth Death cometh soon or late.
>
> And how can man die better, than facing fearful odds,
>
> For the ashes of his father and the temples of his gods[57]

This is the basis for many of the historical explanations given by war victors for the most recent conflicts. The romantic vision of war and violence has in part grown up around the Heroic tradition, and in this sense has been created and propagated in literature by poets, story-tellers and song-writers.

The romantic myth and the revolutionary myth, were central to the glorification and justification of the role of violence. The romantic myth of violence was very much part of the culture of the First World War. It was identified by many contemporary writers and poets of the period. It can be partly summed up in Francis Ledwidge's poems:

We but war when war serves liberty and justice, love and peace.

---

[57] Lord Macaulay. *Horatius on the Bridge*. In *Exploring English J.J Carey. Dublin Gill 1967. 82*

or the classic: In Flanders Fields: by John McCrae

> Take up our quarrel with the foe:
> To you from failing hands we throw
> The torch; be yours to hold it high.
> If ye break faith with us who die
> We should not sleep, though poppies grow
> In Flanders fields.[58]

4. The Machiavellian-type Vision

The "Machiavellian-type" realist vision is as old as war itself. This type of political philosophy has become associated with the principles advocated in the modern sense with the writings of Machiavelli. It has had a considerable influence on the development of more recent political philosophies. Within this concept political power is considered nothing more than a form of pasteurised violence. In this doctrine the only legitimisation of power that is needed or understood is power itself. It is sometimes necessary to appear virtuous in the means and the ends of political power. But being virtuous or being seen to be virtuous is only necessary as it relates to the pursuit of power. Such a cynical approach must in general be covered in a veneer of contemporary respectability. Traditional moral restraints are based loosely on a belief in the unity of civilisation. The Machiavellian vision of violence is based around a much older realist vision of war; that war and violence can be used as rational instruments of national policy.

The revolutionary myths that sustained and supported the justifications for the use of political and social violence were a mixture of beliefs associated with utopianism and nationalism. There were those who, like Bertrand Russell, warned that war between the advanced industrial countries of Europe would be disastrous for the future of European civilisation. There was the hope that "reason" would prevail and that the advances in weapons technology would make war so costly and counter-productive that it would never happen. The romantic mythology

[58] Michael Wylie *The War Poets* An Anthology (London: Jarrold *1992)*.

surrounding war and the use of violence was only slowly but critically undermined in the battlefields of the First World War. Yet the lessons were not really learnt or understood. It took the developments in the technology of nuclear extermination to finally sew the seeds that would critically undermine the foundations of the romantic mythologies of violence:

> For the first time in human history, violence, that typically human way of behaving, fails to justify itself. It no longer seems feasible to contain the effects of its own logic. When the maximum possibilities of violence mean the destruction of mankind, it is not enough to demand limitations and
> control [59]

THE SEVILLE STATEMENT ON VIOLENCE

A number of attempts have been made to challenge the traditional interpretation of the relationship between the biological basis of behaviour and the function of violence in society. In 1986 a UNESCO conference produced *The Seville Statement*,[60] which caused some controversy between biologists themselves and between biology and other related disciplines. *The Seville Statement* was meant to be a very strong and almost aggressive statement that would lead to an equally strong discourse. The scientists gathered at Seville claimed the following facts to be as close to their understanding as possible:

It is scientifically incorrect to say:

1. That we have inherited a tendency to make war from our animal ancestors.

2. That war or any other violent behaviour is genetically programmed into our human nature.

---

[59] UNESCO. *Violence and its Causes* (Paris: 1981).
[60] David Adams, "The Seville Statement on Violence" *Journal of Peace Research*. Vol. XXVI. No. 2, (1989), 113-121.

3. That in the course of human evolution there has been a selection for aggressive behaviour more than for other kinds of behaviour.

4. That humans have a "violent brain."

5. That war is caused by "instinct" or any other single motivation.

The final part of this statement was equally strong. It concluded that biology does not condemn humanity to war, and that humanity can be freed from the bondage of biological pessimism. *The Seville Statement* can be seen as part of the reaction to the trend in the study of aggression which identified the biological basis as the central feature in the determination of the levels of aggression. The work of Konrad Lorenz particularly his: *On Aggression*[61] sets the agenda for much of the later approaches. In relation to the natural world; a whole range of categories of aggression have been identified ranging from territorial to maternal, from inter-male to fear-induced, and both inter-species and across species boundaries.

Within the debate on the biological basis of behaviour there is general agreement that human behaviour, in line with animal behaviour, has a genetical framework. The disagreements centre around how the genetical framework interacts with environmental and cultural factors. Anthony Storr, in his book on *Human Aggression*[62] paints a very bleak picture of human nature:

> In truth however, the extremes of "brutal" behaviour are confined to man; and there is no parallel in nature to our savage treatment of each other. The sombre fact is that we are the cruellest and most ruthless species that has ever walked the earth...[63]

---

[61] Konrad Lorenz, *On Aggression* (London: Methuen, 1966).
[62] Anthony Storr, *Human Aggression* (London: Penguin, 1968).
[63] Ibid., 9.

Storr gets even more pessimistic when he claims that the aggression he describes is a central feature of human make-up and that from a biological point of view it is the main driving force. In one sense no specific academic discipline such as biology or psychology can provide a satisfactory explanation for levels of violence or aggression in human culture. In almost all non-human conflict, violence and aggression are very specific, controlled and limited. The problem, as Konrad Lorenz pointed out is the ultimate dissociation between human violence and its consequences which has been permitted by developments in science and technology. No one can tell the eventual consequences that may arise from this dissociation as science and technology develop.

THE MYTHICAL CORE OF THE IDEOLOGY OF VIOLENCE

The culture of violence in the twentieth century has so many roots and is embedded deeply in so many world-views that any attempt to draw up an outline of its fabric must be fairly limited. The principal ideologies of the twentieth century i.e. nationalism, socialism, fascism and capitalism have produced no significant new hypothesis on the role of violence in society:

> Every scheme for the elimination of war that men have advocated since 1917 has been nothing but a copy or an elaboration of some seventeenth century programme - as the seventeenth-century programmes were copies of still earlier schemes. What is worse, those programmes are far more widely accepted as wisdom now than they were when they were first propagated. Nor is this the full extent of our stupidity.[64]

Within each ideological world-view political violence has been rationalised and justified around certain core principles. The paradox at the centre of the ideology of violence relates to the fact that the nations that developed nuclear weapons have now

---

[64] F. H. Hinsley, *Power and the Pursuit of Peace* (Cambridge: Cambridge University Press, 1963), 3.

little or no defence against them. They have rendered themselves incapable of fulfilling one of their primary responsibilities, that is the effective protection of their citizens against the threat of annihilation.

Violence in the twentieth century has certainly evolved its mythologies and cosmologies to support the cultural framework of revolutionism and conservatism. Again and again those who stand in the forefront of history have lost patience with the idea of peaceful progress. William Morris saw violence as the only way of bridging the gap between things as they are and things as they should be. But those who advocate the functional nature of violence have generally failed to face up to a number of important and far-reaching questions. In the analysis of any conflict situation three simple questions should be asked.

> Firstly, what were the aims sought in the conflict?
> Secondly, what was the price paid?
> Finally, what were the actual results obtained?

Applying these questions to any of the conflicts of the twentieth century, from Latin America to the Middle East, it becomes apparent that none of the philosophies of war give an accurate understanding of the causes and consequences of the use of violence. In many of these conflicts it was only when the use of violence was finally rejected that it was possible to make progress in resolving the fundamental issues that created the conflicts in the first instance. The philosophies of war have failed to rationalise the major disparities in almost every conflict between the aims sought, the price paid and the results actually obtained.

3

THE PHILOSOPHY OF PEACE AND THE IDEOLOGY OF WAR

Over and over again, in the past, the greatest civilisations have been destroyed or degraded by war. The fighting which Homer has taught us to regard as glorious swept away the Mycenaean civilisation, which was succeeded by centuries of confused and barbarous conflict.

Bertrand Russell

For as long as men and women have talked about war, they have talked about it in terms of right and wrong…War is a world apart…where human nature is reduced to its elemental forms. Here men and women do what they must to save themselves and their communities, and morality and law have no place. Inter arma silent leges: in times of war the law is silent

Michael Walzer

Civilisation is the conscious process of controlling aggression and regulating force on the part of man or society in the form of institutionalised conflict management and peace formation

Wolfgang Vogt

A THEORY OF PEACE

The theory of peace, like the theory of justice, has evolved different meanings and understandings in diverse cultures and historical periods. Attempts at formulating a theory of peace cover such a wide area of human experience, that a good argument can be made for the belief that no such theory can exist. *The World Encyclopedia of Peace*[1] (1986) attempts an introduction and outline of "Peace Theory". However the author acknowledges the problems of attempting to outline in any meaningful way "the peace concepts of humankind". Wolfgang Volt[2] in an anthology of peace, states his belief that there is still no comprehensive theory of peace able to muster consensus. He puts forward the idea that the theory of peace as a concept can best be identified in a theory of civilisation. In this context he attempts a clarification and comprehensive definition of civilisation:

> Civilisation is the conscious process of controlling aggression and regulating force on the part of man or society in the form of institutionalised conflict management and peace formation.[3]

He also envisages civilisation and by implication peace as a process as much as a state.

In a paper on *Peace Studies and Metanarrative* Graeme MacQueen distinguishes a number of distinct phases in what he calls the metanarrative of peace:

> My first phase begins in the Axial period of world history...A hatred and distrust of war, and even of violence generally, can be seen reaching intellectual and, in some

---

[1] Linus Pauling, et al, ed., *World Encyclopaedia of Peace*.(Oxford: Pergamon Press, 1986).
[2] Wolfgang Vogt, ed., *Frieden als Zivilisierung Sprojek*. (Baden Baden: 1995).
[3] Ibid., 21.

> cases, institutional expression in the Axial period in India, China, Greece and the Middle East. Scattered communities and individual thinkers take up the cry; now and again the cry is lost, then it is taken up again.[4]

MacQueen attempts to explain and outline the essence of the metanarrative debate. Within this framework he tries to show how such an approach can help in identifying the various developments in the history of the understanding and comprehension of peace. The second phase which he identifies in his metanarrative is associated with the various peace movements of the nineteenth century, in particular the movements towards the secularisation of pacifism and the many other groups with more secular and economic agendas for promoting the end of war and the establishment of the age of peace. This metanarrative, as outlined by MacQueen, is very limited in that it seems to ignore the great debates of St. Augustine and Aquinas and the contribution of the philosophers of the age of enlightenment. Within the debate on the theory of peace, MacQueen rejects what he terms the concepts of Western humanism, based as they are on "the hopelessly outdated notion that human beings are essentially rational?"[5]

No theory of peace has been constructed with the same authority and clarity as, for example, John Rawls' *A Theory of Justice*[6]. It may well be that a theory of peace, like the theory of justice should be related to the theory of rational choice, and that the principles of peace, like the principles of justice as outlined in Rawls, are those which rational persons would consent to as equals. Similar problems and contradictions would arise in such a theory of peace as in the theory of justice. For example, in relation to the just war theory; a theory of peace based on pacifist principles would specifically reject the just war theory. Such a theory of peace would have to address the perennial

---

[4] Graeme MacQueen, "Peace Studies and Metanarrative." *Gandhi Marg* Vol. XVI. (1995), 398-408.
[5] Ibid., 406.
[6] John Rawls, *A Theory of Justice* (Oxford: Oxford University Press, 1971)

problem of how, on the one hand, to oppose unjust regimes and on the other, how to resist unlawful revolution.
Rawls has identified the two main concepts of any ethical theory as those of the right and those of the good:

> The structure of an ethical theory is, then, largely determined by how it defines and connects these two basic notions...More precisely, those institutions and acts are right which of the available alternatives produce the most good,[7]

If it were possible to hypothesise that the good of an ethical system is peace, that peace is as essential in any system of rational choice as justice or fairness. Then this would be a help in addressing some of the problems identified by Rawls, particularly where it is seen that men take a certain pleasure in discriminating against one another, or where men seem to gain from the use of violence. Rawls is well aware of the limitations of constructing any theory of human behaviour on the basis of the principle of rationality. While there may be a warning note sounded, the concept of rationality is one of the most useful guarantees that we can adopt in the construction of any political or moral framework.

THE CONCEPT OF PEACE

The human aspiration for peace, the eternal dream, has taken many forms and has developed along many different paths down through the ages. Any attempt to comprehensively outline the various concepts of peace would be a colossal task. Professor Kende[8] confined most of his research to European society from the late middle ages onwards. He was aware that a history of the concepts of peace could be traced in Chinese, Indian, Arabic and many other cultures outside of European society. From the late middle ages onwards the concept of peace in Europe centred

---

[7] Ibid., 24.

[8] Istvan Kende, The History of Peace: Concepts and Organisations from the Late Middle Ages to the 1870's. *Journal of Peace Research*, Vol. XXVI. No. 3, (1989), 233-247. His later work has not been translated, as yet.

around a number of related idea; a federation of states, the establishment of treaties between and over nations and peoples, international courts of arbitration, the development of legal systems, to name but a few. The Enlightenment and the French Revolution were to bring about major changes in the concepts of peace. Voltaire was to reflect many of these changes in his writings:

> Permanent peace that could be established for people can only be: tolerance, the permanent peace as invented by a French abbot named Saint-Pierre was a mere dream ('chimere') which cannot exist among monarchs just as it cannot be established between elephants and rhinoceroses, between dogs and wolves...The only way to bring peace to people is to destroy all dogmas which divide them and restore verity, which would unite them; that would be permanent peace.[9]

Kende points out what he sees as a major dilemma between the English Bourgeois concepts of peace and the French Revolutionary concepts. In the English concept, peace is useful because it promotes trade and industry and allows markets to develop. The French concepts see peace as an instrument and a goal in the establishment of equality and justice. The different concepts had very different end results. The French Revolution formulated a *World Peace Declaration* (1790) which declared that the rights of war and peace belong to the nation. But the "*levee en masse" (conscription)* was to bring about a fundamental change in the nature of war and the Revolution itself was to bring about war on a scale unseen in Europe for centuries.

The evolution of the "English" concept of peace can be seen in the writings of Jeremy Bentham. The basis for the establishment and maintenance of peace had, he believed, two simple components. Firstly, the size of armies and amount of arms has to be reduced and limited on an ongoing basis to a very low level. Secondly, any territory that had been conquered, particularly colonies, must be freed. Bentham believed that

---

[9] Voltaire, *De la paix perpetuelle* 1769; quoted in Kende, 239.

these two basic components were comprehensively inter-linked. In the long term the French and English concepts were not mutually exclusive but in fact could complement each other. The age of war could give way to the age of trade and the age of trade would be the best guarantee of conditions that would establish and advance the rights of man. The French writer Saint Simon developed his ideas around some of the earlier concepts. Central to his peace plans was the concept of a "world government" with completely independent states making up its constitution. Saint Simon identified "public opinion" as a crucial factor as a contribution to the stability of such a world system.

PHILOSOPHICAL PERSPECTIVES ON PEACE

Philosophical interest in and understanding of peace has waxed and waned over the centuries. The Greek philosophers, the Roman stoic philosophers, the early Church theologians, all reflect varying philosophical thinking about the possibility and practicality of peace. Philosophical thinking on war and violence may be easier to identify than philosophical thinking on peace and non-violence. However, various different approaches can be identified in the philosophical understanding of the utility of peace and of the practicality of non-violence. Howard P. Kainz in his anthology of philosophical perspectives on peace[10] divides the perspectives into six distinct categories: see Table 2:1

Table 2:1
PHILOSOPHICAL PERSPECTIVES ON PEACE
AN ANTHOLOGY: (AFTER KAINZ)

1. Peace through World. Government.	4. Peace through Religious or Spiritual Values

[10] Howard P. Kainz, *Philosophical Perspectives on Peace: An Anthology of Classical and Modern Sources* (London: Macmillan Press, 1987).

2. Peace through International Federation.
3. Peace through. Distributive Justice.
5. Peace through Sublimation of Aggression
6. Peace through the Paradoxes of War

Each of these perspectives has a distinct historical tradition. These philosophical perspectives, as outlined by Kainz, cover some of the most important traditional interpretations of the probability and practicality of peace. The idea of peace through world government is traced by some, back to Aristotle's epistle to Alexander the Great, on the possibility of establishing a Macedonian world empire:

> When men will agree to constitute one rule and one kingdom. They will cease from wars and strife, and devote themselves to that which promotes their welfare and the welfare of their cities and countries. They will all enjoy safety and quiet, dividing their day into parts, part for rest and welfare for the body, part for education and attention to that noble pursuit, philosophy.[11]

Kainz outlines a short history of each perspective which is a useful introduction to each area and he identifies how each perspective is interrelated to each other. For example, he identifies the concept of "Peace through International Federation" with Rousseau's: *A Project of Perpetual Peace* and Kant's: *Perpetual Peace*. Within this framework he identifies the significant contribution to the understanding of peace made by the various philosophers in the age of the enlightenment. In the perspective of "Peace through the Sublimation of Aggression" Kainz identifies the works of Freud and Lorenz, among others. Kainz believes that: "elaborate and detailed philosophical thinking about peace comes to the fore primarily in the last five centuries."[12] His division of this thinking on peace into six categories is useful in identifying the different emphasis

---

[11] Ibid., 3.
[12] Ibid., x.

that have evolved in the philosophy of peace down through the ages.

While the philosophical perspectives, as outlined by Kainz, are a useful anthology they do not set the perspective of peace within the major philosophical schools that have evolved since antiquity. Being aware of the problems of over-simplification it is still necessary to set the development in the philosophy of peace within the major changes in the history of philosophy. The various developments in the history of philosophy have been outlined in different ways in numerous studies. Philosophical thinking about peace can be identified within various parts of the different traditions.

PEACE IN THE ANCIENT WORLD

In a comprehensive and critical survey of the ancient world Gerrardo Zampaglione in *The Idea of Peace in Antiquity*[13] takes a very extensive view of the concept of peace in classical philosophy. His sources range from Hesiod and Thucydides to Julian and Augustine. Zampaglione accepts that the concept of peace is often a subordinate part of more comprehensive doctrinal or literary works, but he believes that a philosophy of peace can be outlined and identified:

> In this book I have attempted to illustrate the continuity of the idea of universal peace and I have roughed out a tentative history... The results of my research have brought me to the conclusion that the problem of universal peace was posed, sometimes overtly, sometimes less so, at the centre of Classical and ancient Christian thought.[14]

In the history of *Peace in the Ancient World*,[15] the authors set out in a fairly simple way to identify some of the major peace

---

[13] Gerrado Zampaglione, *The Idea of Peace in the Antiquity* trans. Richard Dunn. (Notre Dame, Indiana: Notre Dame Press, 1973).
[14] Ibid., 15.
[15] Matthew Melko and Richard D. Weigel, *Peace in the Ancient World* (Jefferson, North Carolina: McFarland 1981).

periods from classical records. So little value had traditionally been given to peace periods that Matthew Melko and Richard Weigel start by justifying their approach:

> But surely, amidst the vent of ancient warfare, there were times of peace when trade could be carried out, when crops could be harvested, when games could be held, poets could write and philosophers could convene at the *agora (marketplace)* Surely the people of the Ancient World were not eternally preoccupied with war, or even the fear of war?[16]

It was not only a case of identifying and naming some of the major peace periods; it was necessary to challenge the assumption that peace periods were periods of stagnation and decline, that such periods saw the end of growth, creativity and vitality. It was necessary to show that peace as a concept and an idea was recognised and understood; and that long periods of peace were not seen as merely an interval between two wars.

Melko and Weigel in their study, take a more practical approach to the study of peace in the classical world; they set out to identify the practical evolution of peace in the historical process. They identify ten major historical periods of peace in the ancient world. Beginning with the Middle Kingdom peace (1991-1720 B.C.) and ending with the Hispanic-Roman peace (19 B.C.- 409 A.D.). Whatever arguments can be made for or against the periods of peace identified in Melko's study, a significant contribution is made by Melko's analysis of the criteria and definitions of the various peace periods. What common factors, if any, can be identified in the various periods studied? Are these periods ones of economic and social creativity or decline? How does the termination of the peace periods come about? Melko poses and answers many of these types of questions in his study.

The idea of peace in ancient civilisations has many roots and has taken many forms. Any serious explanation of man's place in

---

[16] Ibid., 1.

the world, whether it is based on mythological narration, religious beliefs or scientific understanding, has attempted to address fundamental questions relating to war, peace and violence and its justifications and explanations. No better example could be given than the books that make up the Old Testament of the Bible. The Warrior God stands out as almost central to the belief that the Hebrews were the chosen people. But alongside this tradition was also a very strong belief in the values of peace and justice. In the book of Genesis, it was not just the murder of Abel by his brother Cain in a fit of jealously that made the Lord despair of his creation: "And the Lord was sorry that he had made man on the earth, and it grieved him to his heart." *(Genesis 6:6)* "Now the earth was corrupt in God's sight, and the earth was filled with violence." (*Genesis 6:11*)[17] While peace is seen as a gift of God, war and violence are seen as a necessity for the safety and well-being of God's people in the hostile world in which they dwell.

The concepts of war and peace are central aspects of *The Iliad* and *The Odyssey,* two of the great classical works of European Literature. These epics reflect a culture and oral tradition that goes back generations before they were finally written down. The culture of war, the glorification of battle, the nobleness of death would seem to be central themes of this culture as reflected in its literature. But so also is the awareness of the danger and insanity of these conflicts. The very first lines of *The Iliad* warn of:

> The accursed anger which brought uncounted anguish on the Achaians and hurled down to Hades many mighty souls of heroes, making their bodies the prey to dogs and the birds' feasting.[18]

One of the central themes of *The Iliad* is the level of human suffering brought about by the vanity of the heroes. The human

---

[17] *The Holy Bible*, *Genesis* (6:6) and (6:11). Revised Standard Version. (London: Nelson 1966).

[18] Homer, *The Iliad* trans. Martin Hammond. (London: Penguin Books, 1987), 3.

cost of a disastrous war is never far from the surface of the book. In many ways the heroes are being manipulated by forces beyond their control, but in most cases it is the women, the children and the old men who have to pay the price. Bertrand Russell takes a similar view in a number of his writings. *In Justice in War-Time* he states:

> Over and over again, in the past, the greatest civilisations have been destroyed or degraded by war. The fighting which Homer has taught us to regard as glorious swept away the Mycenaean civilisation, which was succeeded by centuries of confused and barbarous conflict.[19]

FROM THE CLASSICAL TO THE CHRISTIAN WORLD VIEW

As the Greek world gave way to the Roman world and the Roman world itself was transformed by the rise of Christianity, the philosophical and theological concepts of peace underwent some dramatic changes. But at the same time the continuity of some of the basic principles associated with the concept of peace can be easily identified. The changes and transformation in the concepts of peace that took place between the time of Cicero in the middle of the first century B.C. to the time of St. Augustine in the middle of the fourth century A.D. are not as radical as first might seem. Cicero is seen by many to have played a crucial role in the transmission of Greek philosophical concepts into the Roman world; and by implication played an important part in the transmission of ideas from Greek philosophy to Christian theology. Cicero's belief in a basic natural law that governed all human activity supported his strongly held view that war was by nature fratricidal. In a number of his writings Cicero seemed to advocate a strongly pacifist position: "I cease not to advocate peace; even though unjust it is better than the justest war." In his major work *De Officiis (On Duties)* he drew back from a totally pacifist position but he believed that the only legitimate excuse for war is defensive and that all "war should be

---

[19] Bertrand Russell, *Justice in War-time* (Illinois: The Open Court, 1917).

undertaken in such a way as to show that its only object is peace."

The set of beliefs and ideas that are associated with the "Just War Theory" are the single most important contribution on the question of war and peace from classical philosophy. The just war theory as it evolved, is the example *par excellence* (*the best example)* of the marriage of Greek philosophy with Christian theology. The just war theory was brilliant in its inception and evolution because it appealed to two of the most fundamental human instincts, self-preservation and self-justification. In the first case, the theory justified war with reference to very rational concepts of human behaviour. Secondly it rationalised violence with reference to the romantic fabric of human consciousness. With these two ingredients, the just war theory was set to survive with little serious alteration from the age of St Augustine to the age of Einstein. It must be seen as astonishing that any theory so steeped in Christian theology should survive the revolutionary changes in thought that were brought about with the coming of age of the scientific world-view.

The just war theory is in many ways inappropriately named. The concepts that are associated with the just war theory are concepts that justify war. The paradox is in the belief that there may be no such thing as a just war. But that does not invalidate the concept of the just war theory. The just war theory starts with the assumption that some wars are just; in effect it sets out to identify and justify these just wars. The title of Michael Walzer's book, *Just and Unjust Wars*[20] goes some way towards identifying this paradox. The just war theory cannot be discarded because it would be:

> Nearly impossible to sustain a debate over war, peace and the use and abuse of violence without recourse to categories lodged within or emerging from the just war tradition.[21]

---

[20] Michael Walzer, *Just and Unjust Wars* (New York: Basic Books, 1977).

[21] Jean B. Elshtain, ed. *Just War Theory* (Oxford: Blackwell, 1992), 2.

St Augustine stands as a sentinel figure in the historical evolution of the philosophy of war and peace. St. Augustine was writing in one of those crucial periods of transition between the ancient world and the modern world. In the *City of God* he attempts to challenge and undermine the moral philosophy that has been handed down through the Greek and Roman worlds. He also attempts to undermine and reshape the moral cosmology of the ancient world and reconstruct it on Christian foundations:

> It is the great fascination of The City of God...that we see that two men ["the antique man of the old classical culture, and the Christian man of the New Gospel"] at grips with one another. This is what makes the work one of the greatest turning points in the history of human destiny: it stands on the confines of two worlds, the classical and the Christian, and it points the way into the Christian."[22]

The just war theory, as outlined and summarised by St. Augustine, has as a central component the legal and political definition of just war. Michael Walzer in his *Just and Unjust Wars* outlines some of the problems associated with such definitions:

> For as long as men and women have talked about war, they have talked about it in terms of right and wrong...War is a world apart...where human nature is reduced to its elemental forms. Here men and women do what they must to save themselves and their communities, and morality and law have no place. "Inter arma silent leges: in times of war the law is silent.[23]

But "Inter arma silent leges" did not fit into the theological world-view that St. Augustine was attempting to construct and reinforce. No God, and particularly not the Christian God, could opt out of moral responsibility in times of crises and war. The question that St. Augustine set himself in relation to war and

---

[22] Barker, quoted in Elshtain, 11.
[23] Walzer, 1.

violence was how to square the circle and put a Christian veneer on the classical rationalisations and justifications for war.

Walzer begins his historical analysis of the moral and ethical debate on the question of war with a study of the *History of the Peloponnesian War* by Thucydides. The central argument made by the Athenian Generals in the "Melian Dialogue" related to the realism of power:

> But you and we should say what we really think, and aim only at what is possible, for we both alike know that into the discussion of human affairs the question of justice only enters where the pressure of necessity is equal, and the powerful exact what they can, and the weak grant what they must.[24]

The *Melian Dialogue*, is according to Walzer, a classic account of aggression. The veneer of the just war has not yet been fully established. The justifications, the arguments, the excuses, the references to necessity and duress are still very rough and ready. The discourse still cannot conceal the self-deception of war. The reality of war: "strips away our civilised adornments and reveals our nakedness."[25] Thomas Hobbes translated Thucydides *History of the Peloponnesian* War and according to Walzer, Hobbes generalised its central arguments into *Leviathan*. In the new Christian world-order that St. Augustine was contemplating, the moral basis of the *Melian Dialogue* was unacceptable. In essence, war was not to be rejected as unchristian but war was to be Christianised.

THE THEOLOGY OF PEACE

The historical relationship between theology and philosophy is such that no outline of the philosophy of peace is possible without considering the theological implications. Without entering into the debate concerning the differences between

[24] Copleston, 34.
[25] Walzer, 4.

philosophy and theology, it is important to identify the theological roots of the philosophy of peace. Theological aspects of peace are influenced by the belief in a Divine Deity. This belief, however expressed, determines the basis of any analysis of the concept of peace. The concepts of good and evil, of justice and injustice are prerequisite concepts in any theological analysis and explanation of war and violence. The knowledge and understanding of the concept of peace that have evolved and developed in the great religious traditions of mankind are an important source in any analysis of the philosophy of peace. Most of the main religious traditions have attempted to construct an ethical basis of behaviour for their own followers which would also be appropriate to mankind in general.

There has been much debate concerning the value of peace and war in ancient societies. The Gods of war have in many cases been more apparent than the Gods of peace. But at the same time the concept of peace has been a central concept of all the major religions of mankind. The idea that peace is next to godliness is a common trend in most religious traditions. In this sense there is a common concern for peace which would suggest a unity in the worlds major religions. It is of course a unity in diversity, but there is no fundamental contradiction in the interpretation of the Peace relationship between God and Man: see Table 2:2

Table 2:2
INTERPRETATIONS OF THE PEACE RELATIONSHIP BETWEEN GOD AND MAN. (AFTER H. O. THOMPSON[26])

Christianity	*Blessed are the peacemakers, for they shall be called the children of God.*
Islam	*God will guide men to peace. If they will heed Him, He will lead them from the darkness of war to the light of peace.*

[26] Henry O. Thompson, "Praxis: Peace - Preachment and Practice". *International Journal of World Peace* Vol. VII. No. 1, (1990), 87-100.

Buddhism	*There is no happiness greater than Peace.*
Hinduism	*Without meditation, where is peace? Without peace, where is happiness?*
Baha'I	*War is death while peace is life.*
Confucianism	*Seek to be in harmony with all your neighbours...live in peace with your brethren.*
Jainism	*All men should live in peace with their fellows. This is the Lord's desire.*

Peace is seen as one of the divine gifts given by God to human beings and to human society. The concept of Shalom is not just the absence of war but a much more positive reflection of the divine gift. In Buddhism and Hinduism the commitment to the concepts of non-violence is more comprehensive than in the Christian tradition if for no other reason than their inclusiveness of all sentient creatures. The moral law of *karma,* of cause and effect, has no equivalent in the Christian tradition:

> In this context, killing and every kind of violence are destructive of those who commit them, and the reverse is also true; the practice of *ahimsa* is ennobling and enhancing of the future existence of the doer.[27]

Most of the world's major religions have come to the understanding that living in peace is crucial to human survival, as well as the survival of any religion, culture or people. There is a cynical approach to the study of religion and peace which is summed up in the following statement in the *World Encyclopedia of Peace*:

> If the practitioners of the world's religions would take seriously their own beliefs they could and would largely eliminate war and violence, and give new hope to those

---

[27] Monika K. Hellwig, *A Case for Peace in Reason and Faith* (Minnesota: Liturgical Press, 1992), 51.

> who survive under the shadow of disease and poverty, and bring fullness of life for all people.[28]

The comparison of peace ideas in the world's major religions is a valuable exercise within the normal restrictions of any comparative study. For example, Ferguson in his summary of peace ideas in world religions concludes:

> Of the great religions Christianity and Buddhism have been the most clearly pacifist in their origins and essence. Yet both have been deeply involved with militarism from a fairly early stage in their history...Zoroastrianism, Islam and Shinto have been the most clearly militarist in their origins and essence.[29]

Ferguson is being a little disingenuous when he states: "In a warring society religion will be more prominently associated with war, in a peaceable society with the gifts of peace." Modern Catholic social teaching on the gospel of peace and justice was clearly laid out in *Pacem in Terris*[30] *(Peace on Earth).* The prospect of order in the Universe, order among men, order between individuals and public authorities, and order between states, was set out within a Catholic framework that appealed to all men of good will. The very first statement reflects the approach taken:

> Peace on earth, which men of every era have most eagerly yearned for, can be firmly established only if the order laid down by God is dutifully observed.

In one sense the papal encyclical attempted to reinterpret the traditional confrontation in western society between secular and religious authority particularly, where this conflict touched on the issue of war and violence.

---

[28] Pauling et al, ed. Vol. II. 335.

[29] Vilho Harle, "Towards a Comparative Study of Peace Ideas." *Journal of Peace Research.* Vol. XXVI. No. 4, (1989), 342.

[30] Pope John XXIII, *Pacem in Terris* (New York: America Press, 1963).

AN ECUMENICAL THEOLOGY OF PEACE

Religious beliefs, religious differences and religious intolerance have inspired and encouraged conflict and war in almost every age of human consciousness. This reflects less on the nature of the various religious beliefs than on the ability of the human mind to rationalise any religious doctrine to accommodate and justify almost any action. In negative and destructive terms religious beliefs have compounded the destructiveness of political social and economic conflicts. In many cases it is impossible to differentiate between religious and other political and social ingredients of war and conflict and their justifications. Religious institutions by their very nature reflect the social fabric of the political environment of their respective communities. Hans Kung in his work on *Global Responsibility: In Search of a New World Ethic*[31] has attempted to outline an ecumenical approach to the theology of peace. One of his major propositions is his belief that there can be no world peace without religious peace and that an ecumenical theology of peace is an essential ingredient of this religious peace. This theology of peace would not be just a reflected watered-down version of the more traditional versions:

> For what is the use of an abstract, appellative theology of peace of the kind that is so often preached...it costs nothing…and requires nothing of its own Church, party or nation; so it remains voluntary, harmless and inefficient. [32]

The World Conference on Religion and Peace maintains a standing forum for multi-religious dialogue on issues of peace and justice. As part of its contribution to the UNESCO culture of peace programme, the World Conference has produced a "declaration on the role of religion in the promotion of a culture of peace."[33] This statement fully accepts the role and

---

[31] Hans Kung, *Global Responsibility: In Search of a New World Ethic* (London: SCM Press, 1991).
[32] Ibid., 131.
[33] Barcelona Centre UNESCO de Catalunya, *Declaration on the Role of Religion in the Promotion of a Culture of Peace*, 1994.

responsibility of the major religions of the world in their contribution to division, hatred and war. At the same time the declaration highlights the contribution that religions have made to the culture of peace. The major religions of the world commit themselves to building:

> A culture of peace based on non-violence, tolerance, dialogue, mutual understanding and justice.[34]

These declarations could be seen as very plausible but with little real significance. On the other hand, such agreement between all the major religions of the world has been almost unprecedented and should not be underestimated.

One of the most comprehensive statements on religion and peace was the declaration issued by the World Conference on Religion and Peace at Kyoto[35] in Japan. The conference represented all the major religious traditions of the world. The declaration of the conference intended to identify the fundamental beliefs that are common to all the major religions of the world: see Table 2:3

Table 2:3
SOME OF THE SHARED BELIEFS OF WORLD RELIGIONS

1. A conviction of the fundamental unity of the human family, of the equality and dignity of all human beings.

2. A sense of the sacredness of the individual person and his conscience.

3. A sense of value of the human community.

4. A recognition that might is not right, that human power is not self-sufficient and absolute.

---

[34] Ibid.

[35] Homer A. Jack, ed. "Religion for Peace: Proceedings of the Kyoto Conference," New Delhi, 1973.

5. A belief that love, compassion and unselfishness have ultimately greater power than hate, enmity and self-interest.

Hans Kung in his *Global Responsibility: In Search of a New World Ethic*[36], attempted to translate these very general shared beliefs into concepts that could be more practically applied. He produced five commandments[37] which he believed could form an ethical perspective that was common to all world religions: see Table 2:4

Table 2:4
THE FIVE COMMANDANTS COMMON TO THE MAJOR RELIGIONS OF THE WORLD (AFTER KUNG)

1. Do not kill
2. Do not lie
3. Do not steal
4. Do not practice immorality
5. Respect parents and love children

In his final analysis Kung identifies what he terms as a *Golden Rule* common to all ethical and religious beliefs. That Golden Rule is summed up in Matthew and Luke as: "Whatever you want people to do to you, do also to them." But the Golden Rule, like so many other religious beliefs, can be easily misunderstood. In much historical experience the application of the Golden Rule is the very opposite to its original meaning. In many cases it is believed that it is acceptable to do unto others what they have already done unto you. Without the additional teaching in relation to loving your enemy, the Golden Rule can encourage and justify actions that are the very opposite of the principles proposed.

---

[36] Kung.
[37] Ibid., 57.

THE SERMON ON THE MOUNT

The just war theory is only one of a number of religious traditions in relation to war and peace and violence and non-violence. There has always been a small but significant tradition in the Christian Churches that has absolutely rejected the use of force under any circumstances and promoted the idea of non-violence. The basis of this tradition is the belief that one of the most fundamental aspects of the Christian Gospel is the teaching that advocates the love of one's enemy and the exhortation to do good even to those who persecute you. One of the central questions in relation to this part of the Christian Gospel concerns the interpretation that can be given to the Sermon on the Mount. In relation to the teaching of the Christian Churches on war and violence Fr. E. C. McCarthy makes a very important point when he says:

> It is the Church's task to teach what Jesus taught, it is not the Church's task to teach what Aristotle taught or Plato, or Kant or Hume[38]

The Christian approach and the Christian arguments for peace should be centred around the belief in Jesus as God. If Jesus is the Son of God, then the Sermon on the Mount is the crucial and fundamental teaching on the relationship between violence and non-violence and good and evil.

> The Sermon on the Mount can be considered naive, but the reality is, if Jesus is whom the Church says He is, then the Sermon on the Mount is the only way to conquer evil. [39]

This is exactly where Tolstoy takes up his arguments. Tolstoy passionately believes that Christ is the Son of God and his teachings are the word of God. According to Tolstoy, in relation to the question of violence, the teaching of the Sermon on the

---

[38] Fr. Emmanuel Charles McCarthy, University of Notre Dame. *Christian Philosophy of Peace*. Lecture on RTE Radio 16th March 1996.
[39] Ibid.

Mount is very clear and unambiguous. Jesus teaches the non-violent love of friends and enemies. In this regard Tolstoy talks about seventeen hundred years of compromising the Gospel. The traditional justifications for the use of violence have generally been that an evil is being done to me and therefore I have a "right" to strike back with a fist, a thank or in court. Jesus' approach to overcome the reality of evil in the human situation is quite different: "It is by non-violently suffering the consequences of evil and explicitly returning good for evil."[40]
We may not like this message, we may think that it is Utopian, naïve, or idealistic, but: "there is no question that this is the teaching of Jesus."[41] This is the explicit direction that Jesus laid out for overcoming violence. The question then becomes who knows better how to overcome evil in the human situation - Jesus, Plato, Cicero, politicians, political scientists or academics? McCarthy believes that in the Sermon on the Mount Jesus has given us a blueprint - of universal compassion - on how to respond to violence and evil. There are many other blueprints: pagan, rational, economic, social, etc., but one act of responding to evil and violence in the way Jesus taught is better "than a thousand other ways."[42]
The Sermon on the Mount and the Beatitudes are the core concepts in the development of Christian pacifism. There has always been some debate about the meaning of peace in the New Testament. The word *eirene* is found once in Mark, four times in Matthew, twelve times in Luke and six times in John. It is also found on a number of occasions in the Acts of the Apostles and particularly in the writings of St. Paul. Almost all Pauline letters begin with the words: "Grace to you and peace from God our Father."[43] More important than any statistical analysis of the New Testament is the wider context of the message that was being preached:

> You have heard that it was said, 'You shall love your

---

[40] Ibid.
[41] Ibid.
[42] Ibid.
[43] Herman Hendrickx, *A Time For Peace: Reflections on the Meaning of Peace and Violence in the Bible* (London: Claretian, 1986), 23.

> neighbour and hate your enemy.' But I say to you, love your enemies and pray for those who persecute you, so that you may be sons of your Father who is in heaven; Mt. 5. 43-45.

Again and again Jesus turns the teaching of the Old Testament on its head in relation to how people should react to violence and wrongdoing:

> You have heard that it was said, 'An eye for an eye and a tooth for a tooth.' But I say to you do not resist one who is evil. But if any one strikes on the right cheek, turn to him the other also; and if any one would sue you and take your coat, let him have your cloak as well; Mt. 5.38-40.

The seventh beatitude is a direct call to the peacemakers "Blessed are the peacemakers, for they shall be called the sons of God."[44] From time immemorial mystics, saints, revolutionaries and many ordinary people have been inspired by this preaching. The Christian Church itself as it evolved as a corporate structure was less and less willing to face up to the implications that this message actually meant what it said. There are many passages in the New Testament that can and have been used to justify the use of violence, one of the most quoted is found in Luke 12.51 and Matthew 10.34, "Do you think that I have come to give peace on earth? I have not come to bring peace, but a sword." Mt. 10.34. The Old Testament itself is full of passages that can be, and have been used morally and religiously to justify the role of violence and the concept of just wars.

[44] The Holy Bible. Matthew 5.9. RSV.

4

THE ENLIGHTENMENT AND THE PROBLEM OF WAR

War was stupid. It was irrational. It was neither glorious nor necessary.
Those who conducted it were worthy not of admiration but of contempt.

War was a mask behind which governments could extend their powers over their subjects, since once war was declared, then all the affairs of the state are at the mercies of the appetites of the few

Princes who wished to display their power and glory, would be better employed, developing the welfare of their own kingdom, rather than extending their boundaries at the price of untold suffering

Desiderius Erasmus (1466-1536)

WAR AND THE LIBERAL CONSCIENCE

Another important influence on the shape of this study was a series of lectures given as the George Macaulay Trevelyan Lectures at Cambridge by Professor Michael Howard and published as *War And The Liberal Conscience* in 1981.[1] As a background to his analysis Professor Howard accepts and identifies that there has always been a Christian tradition that totally rejects war. But he believes that this tradition since the time of Constantine had been a very minor tradition in the Christian world; he summarises the views of many in a few words:

> The teachings of the Gospels were sufficiently ambiguous and the policy of the Church sufficiently flexible for Christianity to become, and to remain for a thousand years, one of the great Warrior Religions of mankind.[2]

Professor Howard starts his study in the early part of the sixteenth century with this view:

> The mediaeval ideal, that force could be justly used only by Christian chivalry for the defence of Christendom and for the maintenance of God's justice within its borders was virtually dead. The modern concept of force as a necessary instrument in preserving an orderly system of states was only beginning to appear - in the work of Machiavelli.[3]

The first lecture in this study covers *'The Growth of the Liberal Conscience 1500-1792.* Professor Howard starts by identifying the critical attitude of the philosopher Desiderius Erasmus[4]

---

[1] Michael Howard, *War and the Liberal Conscience* (Oxford: Oxford University Press, 1981).
[2] Ibid., 13.
[3] Ibid., 16.
[4] M. M. Philips, *Erasmus And His Times* (Cambridge: Cambridge University Press, 1967).

towards the institution of war and the principles on which war had been traditionally justified. In the arguments put forward by Erasmus, Howard identifies the rational arguments against war, which were to become central to the debate on war and peace as it evolved up to the present day. Erasmus rejected the principles of the just war theory, he rejected the idea of war as a romantic adventure of feudal knights:

> Erasmus despised the profession of arms with a scorn that generations of intellectuals were to inherit...War was stupid. It was irrational. It was neither glorious nor necessary. Those who conducted it were worthy not of admiration but of contempt.[5]

Erasmus also strongly believed that war was unnatural:

> Whoever heard of a hundred thousand animals rushing together to butcher each other, as men do everywhere?[6]

More importantly for later arguments, Erasmus came to believe that those in authority started wars for reasons much different than the reasons stated in public:

> If a claim to possession is to be reckoned sufficient reason for going to war, then in such a disturbed state of human affairs, there is no one who does not possess such a claim.[7]

Among princes and soldiers Erasmus wrote bitterly:

> The one who conducted himself with the most savagery is the one who is thought to be captain in the next war.[8]

The ideas expressed by Erasmus on the function of war in society have rightly been put forward by Howard as the beginning of a critical change in the analysis of war and violence

[5] Howard, 14.
[6] Philips, 107.
[7] Howard, 15-16
[8] Ibid., 14-15.

and the philosophies on which they had been traditionally justified. Erasmus rejected the just war theory as unworthy of rational analysis. While Erasmus put forward many criticisms of war and the war-fighting traditions of mediaeval Europe, he was not very clear about alternatives or possible future peaceful developments. In contrast, Professor Howard looks at the work of Thomas More, a friend and contemporary of Erasmus, who took an entirely different approach to the problem of war. More accepted:

> As thinkers for the next two hundred years were to accept, that European society was organised in a system of states in which war was an inescapable process for the settlement of differences in the absence of any higher common jurisdiction.[9]

Howard believes that the major differences in the approach to war between More and Erasmus lay in the fact that More had actually exercised political power in real terms and saw the problem in all its complexity. In his *Utopia,* which he finished in 1516, More puts forward a very practical approach to war: "While the 'Utopians' are practically the only people on earth who fail to see anything glorious in war,"[10] and while they absolutely loathe war, they are prepared to fight and will fight to the finish for what they consider a just *casus belli (reason for war)*

In the early part of his chronology Professor Howard identifies and traces the initial development of a number of theories that were to have important and influential effects on the debate on war and peace in the age of scientific reason. For example, he identifies the idea of a 'United Nations Assembly to settle international differences by compulsory arbitration' which was put forward by Emeric Cruce in a work published in 1623. He traces the debate as it was picked up by the "Enlightenment philosophies" over the next two centuries, and identifies some of the key concepts as put forward by Jean-Jacques Rousseau in his

---

[9] Ibid., 18.

[10] Thomas More, *Utopia* trans. Paul Turner, (London: Penguin, 1965), 109.

various writings and in particular in *Judgment on Perpetual Peace* and *A Lasting Peace through the Federation of Europe*[11]. He also identified other philosophers who took up the debate on war and peace such as Immanuel Kant in his *Perpetual Peace*[12]. In the final analysis, Professor Howard states that:

> The original view of the eighteenth-century philosophies, that international disputes could be settled without violence, by reasoned discussion and agreement between men of goodwill, has remained the basis of most liberal Western thinking about international relations.[13]

The historical analysis put forward by Professor Howard was very interesting and stimulating. He identified some of the major conflicts of interest in the debate on the nature of man and his social systems and the role of war and peace in that relationship. As the debate evolved it was dominated by two competing paradigms, - one based on the principles of *idealism*, and the other on the principles of *realism.* The idealist paradigm describes human interaction in terms of reason, justice, freedom and progress. While the realist paradigm, by contrast, describes the human condition in terms of passion, power, determinism and constancy.[14]

It is in the analysis of the developments in the twentieth century that Howard has left a lot to be desired. His analysis of the conflicts of the twentieth century and their probable causes is excellent, but it would seem from this analysis that no new development or original ideas on the philosophy of peace were produced in this century.

---

[11] Jean-Jacques Rousseau, *Judgement sur la Paix Perpetuelle* (1756), trans. C. E. Vaughan. (New York: 1915).

[12] Hans Reiss, ed. *Kant Political Writings* (Cambridge: Cambridge University Press, 1991).

[13] Howard, 32.

[14] Torbjorn Knutsen, "Re-reading Rousseau in the Post-Cold War World" *Journal of Peace Research*, Vol. XXXI. No. 3, (1994), 247-262.

PERPETUAL PEACE AND THE GROWTH OF ENLIGHTENMENT

The so called "religious wars" that swept over Europe in the sixteenth and seventeenth centuries gave an important new urgency to the study of war and peace. The debate on the nature of war and peace has taken many paths and has followed many philosophical trends throughout the centuries. Desiderius Erasmus and Emeric Cruce have been identified by Howard[15] as two of the most important individuals in the early evolution of the logical analysis of war and peace. Erasmus[16] formulated very strong views against the ignorance and fanaticism which he believed were the foundations for the justifications of war and the use of violence. At the time of warrior popes and the traditional belief by princes that war was their only true vocation, Erasmus's opinions on war were not very popular and it was, as he realised himself, dangerous to push such opinions too far. Erasmus declared:

> That war was stupid and irrational, it was neither glorious nor necessary. Those who conducted it were worthy not of admiration but of contempt.[17]

Erasmus's views on war are important in that they can be seen as early attempts at formulating arguments for and against war which are still being debated today. There are three major points in Erasmus's arguments which are interest for later developments. Firstly, Erasmus believed that the just war theory only excused war-making and legitimised the violence associated with war. He felt that war should be rejected totally, particularly by men of learning. He rejected the just war theory and believed that in most cases: "an unjust peace is preferable to a just war".[18] Secondly, Erasmus believed that war was a mask

---

[15] Michael Howard, *War and the Liberal Conscience* (Oxford: Oxford University Press, 1981).
[16] M. M. Phillips, *Erasmus and his Times* (Cambridge: Cambridge University Press, 1967).
[17] Howard, 14.
[18] Ibid., 16.

behind which governments could extend their powers over their subjects: "since once war was declared, then all the affairs of the state are at the mercies of the appetites of the few".[19] Thirdly Erasmus held very strong views on Princes who wished to display their power and glory, he felt that they would be better employed, developing the welfare of their own kingdom, rather than extending their boundaries at the price of untold suffering.

Almost one hundred years after Erasmus had formulated his theories Emeric Cruce published "*Nouveau Cynee*" in 1623 which contained a proposal for a United Nations assembly to settle international differences by compulsory arbitration. Cruce believed that war arose from the twin vices of arrogance and brutality and he also rejected in the strongest terms the idea of a just war. More importantly for later analysis, Cruce developed some original ideas about the causes of war. "He was one of the first scholars to realise that the incidence of war might be connected with the social structure of society"[20] and from this he speculated that one way of reducing the amount of war would be by changing the social structures. This idea that the incidence of war might be directly related to the vested interests of the ruling elite is the basis of much more recent analysis on the causes of war and the conditions of peace.

Hugo Grotius in his *The Rights of War and Peace* (1625)[21] reflects many of the worries of contemporary philosophers. Montaigne in his: *Essays* made frequent references to the cruelties and hatreds associated with the new wars of religion. It was generally believed by contemporary thinkers that the more traditional feudal and mercenary type wars were far less cruel and much more limited in their nature and scope. It was also believed that the centralised moral authority of Rome, however ambiguous in relation to violence, had been a significant restraining factor on the limits of violence that were acceptable. When religious beliefs themselves became a central factor in the

[19] Ibid., 15.
[20] Ibid., 19.
[21] Hugo Grotius, *The Rights of War and Peace* (1623) trans. A. G. Campbell (London: Universal Classics Library, 1901).

causes of war then these restraints were removed or became very much less significant as a factor in reducing the levels of brutality associated with armed conflict. In fact the opposite was more likely to be the case. The religious elements were now used as a justification for brutality and savagery. Within this context many of the contemporary theologian-philosophers started to look outside of the traditional Christian moral theology for a more rational analysis of the causes and functions of war.

Grotius and many of his contemporary philosophers believed that the wars which had taken place in Europe before the Reformation were limited in the level of brutality and the extent to which atrocities were committed against civilians. The Christian consensus on war had been eroded by the division of Christian Europe and what was needed now was a new consensus on the limits of war which would hold under the new religious and political climate. The concept of limited war under generally agreed restraints if not actual rules was not very new. The concept itself was associated with the romantic images of the code of chivalry dating to pre-feudal times. How far the romantic image of chivalrous warfare was an actual historical fact or a figment of the European imagination is still open to debate.

In his detailed analysis of natural law and the development of his concept of natural right, Grotius came to the conclusion that war was not only natural but in many cases in accordance with the principles of natural justice. He believed that the logical analysis used by the Greeks and the Romans had a strong basis in natural law. He believed and accepted that wars which are fought in the defence of a people against attempts to destroy or enslave them are just wars. His analysis goes even further:

> So far from any thing in the principles of nature being repugnant to war, every part of them indeed rather favours it. For the preservation of our lives and persons which is the end of war and the possession of or acquirement of things necessary and useful to life is most suitable to those principles of nature, and to use force if necessary, for

> those occasions, is no way dissonant to the principles of nature,[22]

What Grotius hoped to find were the natural and rational limitations on war. Wars according to Grotius could be waged with moderation with the minimum of killing and destruction. He was well aware of the savagery of the religious wars and the hatreds and exterminations associated with them. He hoped for the restoration of the form of limited war that he and many of his contemporaries believed had been a central part of Christian European history for such a long period of time.

THE PROJECT FOR PERPETUAL PEACE

In any attempt to outline the developments in the philosophy of peace in the seventeenth and eighteenth centuries a number of the more important individuals and their ideas have been identified. The concepts of *Perpetual Peace* associated with Jean Jacques Rousseau and Immanuel Kant are key developments in the evolution of the debate. In historical terms, the ideas put forward by the Abbe de St. Pierre are of significance because of the direct influence they had on the political philosophy of Rousseau and Kant.[23] The Abbe de St. Pierre was one of the first of the philosophers of the enlightenment to attempt to tackle the problem of war in a rational way. He was not content with condemning war as morally wrong or seeing it as endemic to human nature. The editorial work undertaken by Rousseau on the Abbe's work resulted in the publication of the *Project for Perpetual Peace* and Rousseau's: *Judgment* on it.[24] The *Project for Perpetual Peace* suggested a confederation of European Heads of State with a common interest in promoting peace and preventing war. In his judgment, Rousseau acknowledged that such a confederation was from a rational and logical point of view a very good idea. But he pointed out that the interest of princes and the decisions of those in power are not always made on a

---

[22] Ibid., Chap 2, Sec. 1.

[23] John Hope Mason, *The Indispensable Rousseau* (London: Quartet, 1979).

[24] Ibid., 103-109.

rational basis. There are according to Rousseau, a number of important factors which encourage princes and rulers to reject peace and make war.

There were, of course, other voices that saw war and the function of war from different perspectives. By the beginning of the eighteenth century: "political thinkers in general thus saw war as a necessary evil arising from a social organisation which itself was necessary to keep in check yet greater evils."[25] Hegel was one of those philosophers who saw the function of war as beneficial and necessary for the stability of the social order. Hegel states quite clearly his belief that war is essential to the health of the state:.

> Just as the blowing of the wind preserves the sea from foulness which would be the result of long calm, so also corruption in nations would be the product of prolonged, let alone perpetual peace[26]

One of the central paradoxes of the tradition of the enlightenment is the realisation that rational analysis leads to the conclusion that man is primarily a non-rational animal. Man is a rational animal only under certain circumstances and over a limited time period:

> Although the quest for a rational explanation of war has for centuries been the favourite exercise of thinkers and philosophers in the service of states, it is mainly during the last four hundreds years that the Western world has developed its own doctrine of war, its causes and effects. This philosophy owes much to the birth of nationalism."[27]

KANT'S PERPETUAL PEACE

Immanuel Kant has been accorded a relatively prominent place in the history of political thought. *Perpetual Peace A*

---

[25] Howard, 21.
[26] G. W. F. Hegel, The Philosophy of Right. (1821).
[27] Zampaglione, 2.

Philosophical Sketch was first published in Konigsberg in 1795.[28] In this work Kant attempted to identify the:

> Philosophical principles on which a just and lasting internal order and world peace could be based. He wanted to provide a philosophical vindication of representative constitutional government, a vindication which would guarantee respect for the political rights of all individuals.[29]

Kant's: *Perpetual Peace*, both for its time and even today, is still a masterly work of political thought. The six Preliminary Articles, the three Definite Articles, the two Supplements and the statements in the appendix, contain within them the outline of a fundamentally new framework on which international relations could be built. The basis for this shift in the paradigm of international relationships was the acceptance by Kant and other philosophers of the enlightenment that peace was not just to be a period of time between wars, but that peace was the ultimate indication that Man had reached the age of reason from which there was no going back. While wars would still occur, Kant believed that once the principles outlined in *Perpetual Peace* were applied to ancient historical conflicts, then these conflicts would be solved in such a manner as not to give rise to further conflicts. The first preliminary article identifies this vital problem. A peace treaty should end all hostilities and not lay the foundation for future conflicts. Kant was being ironical when he states that:

> A conclusion of peace nullifies all existing reasons for a future war, even if these are not yet known to the contracting parties, and no matter how acutely and carefully they may be pieced together out of old documents.[30]

---

[28] Immanuel Kant, *Gesammelte Schritten* Vol. VII. (Berlin: 1900), 121.
[29] Hans Reiss, ed. *Kant Political Writings* trans. H. B. Nisbet. (Cambridge: Cambridge University Press, 1991), 4.
[30] Ibid., 93.

In the third of the preliminary articles Kant is quite clear about the role of armies in war and peace: "They constantly threaten other states with war by the very fact the they are always prepared for it."[31] One of his main arguments related to the dangers of standing armies which he believed should be gradually abolished altogether. On the function and the costs of standing armies Kant had some very clear views:

> They spur on the states to outdo one another in arming unlimited numbers of soldiers, and since the resultant costs eventually make peace more oppressive than a short war, the armies are themselves the causes of war of aggression which set out to end burdensome military expenditure."[32]

In the final of the six preliminary articles Kant looks at the problem of *bellum internecinum* (*wars of extermination*). Wars of this kind, he believes, must be absolutely prohibited. It is easy enough to be critical of Kant's logic in: *Perpetual Peace.* He did not attempt to reject Christian theology totally but to move away from that part of the traditions that he felt were based on prejudice and superstition. While he set out to move away from the traditional theories of the "just war" his logic is set firmly within the pre-Machiavellian world-view. He states in article six: "For it must still remain possible, even in wartime to have some sort of trust in the attitude of the enemy."[33] This statement reflects the problems that Kant himself identified in his appendix: "On the disagreement between morals and politics in relation to Perpetual Peace." In his attempts to reason out the relationship between morality and politics Kant analyses the abstract concepts of morality and duty in relation to the constitution of civil society and international order. In his final analysis, Kant states: "it is not just an empty idea that Perpetual Peace will eventually replace what have hitherto been wrongly called peace treaties, (which are actually only truces)".[34]

---

[31] Ibid., 94.
[32] Ibid., 94-95.
[33] Ibid., 96.
[34] Ibid., 130.

In his earlier writings Kant had attempted to formulate rational principles of politics on which all men could agree. Kant attempted to set out the basic philosophical principles on which a just and lasting internal order and world peace could be based. He developed some of the principles that had already been outlined in the work of the Abbe de St. Pierre. He believed that the fundamental element of any republican constitution should take account of these ideas:

> We have to admit that the greatest evils which oppress civilised nations are the result of war, not so much of actual wars in the past or present, as of the unremitting, indeed ever-increasing preparation for war in the future. All the resources of the state, and all the fruits of its culture which might be used to enhance that culture even further, are devoted to this propose.[35]

THE PACIFIST TRADITION

The ideals and principles associated with the modern concept of pacifism have many historical roots. The historical tradition of the rejection of war and violence can be identified in various forms in all the great religious traditions, and many of the indigenous cultures of mankind. The developments in the early Christian Church, based on the teachings of Jesus, gave a new impetus to the belief in the possibilities of non-violent action. A belief in the unconditional rejection of war and violence has been seen by many theologians as a central, if not a primary aspect of the early Christian Church. The period from the execution of Jesus to the granting of official status to the Christian religion by the Emperor Constantine in the year 313 A. D. is the period where much of the debate is centered around. Initially, the early Church: "was not compelled to deal directly with the question whether its members could carry out the duties of a magistrate or serve the state with arms."[36] But after the

---

[35] Kant, Vol. VII. 121.

[36] Peter Brock, *A Brief History of Pacifism from Jesus to Tolstoy* (Toronto: Syracuse University Press, 1992), 10.

granting of official status the "Soldier Question" became a major issue for Christian theologians.
Many of the early Christians felt that there was a fundamental incompatibility between the teachings of Christ and the support of state institutions such as the Roman army. The ambiguity of the Gospels was such that it was possible for the realist arguments to win out so that: "From 438 A. D. on, the imperial army came to be recruited exclusively from Christians."[37] Many individuals such as Tolstoy see the abandonment of the pacifist principles as the "fall of Christianity". Over the next few hundred years the just war theory was to evolve as the dominant social philosophy of the Church in relation to war. Under the just war theory the Christian Church was to become one of the great Warrior Religions of mankind.

The question of how so many of the great religions of mankind have contributed so much to the causes of war and violence has baffled many philosophers. In the western tradition Christianity became not only compatible with war and violence but directly responsible for much of the conflict. Religious beliefs in many cases increased the barbarous nature of the conflict. The religious wars of the sixteenth and seventeenth centuries are a classical example which must rank with the crusades in their level of religiously inspired barbarism. The military mystique, the romance of war, the attractions of the hero have never gone totally unchallenged in western society. It was not only theologians and philosophers but also statesmen and soldiers who, from time to time, questioned the necessity and rationality of the use of violence. Even those who professed a purely utilitarian vision of human destiny felt the need to undermine the arguments put forward by the various pacifist traditions.

While the just war theory became the central Christian philosophical response to the problem of war and violence; there always remained within the Christian tradition small groups that were either officially exempted from this belief or unofficially rejected this teaching. "The rise of the monasteries represented an effort by some men and women to live according to the

[37] Ibid., 13.

Gospel in a world where these ideals were not widely upheld."[38] The monastic movement kept alive the spirit of non-violence. The Celtic monastic Church on the fringe of the Roman world would seem to have upheld the pacifist principles for hundreds of years after its rejection in the rest of the Christian world.

The history of the pacifist tradition is normally associated with small religious sects that arose from time to time in various parts of Europe. These groups were generally led by individuals who were attempting to construct a social philosophy based on their religious beliefs but which would be very different to the existing social consensus. At the end of the twelfth century the Waldenses was one such group that developed in the southern part of France. On the other side of Europe some of the followers of John Hus (burnt at the stake in 1415) adopted the principles of non-violence. Peter Chelcicky expounded strong pacifist views in his masterpiece: *Net of Faith,* the message preached by Jesus was the "Law of Love", those who claimed to be Christian must accept this law. "The temporal order of force and Christ's way of love are far removed from each other."[39] As the fortunes of the Czech Brethren waxed and waned, other groups took up the message of pacifism in its different forms and beliefs.

The birth of the Anabaptist movement in Zurich in the early part of the sixteenth century and the developments brought about by Menno Simons are important milestones in the history of pacifism. In England, George Fox began attracting followers from around the year 1650. The developments in the beliefs and ideals of the Quakers on both sides of the Atlantic are significant factors in the history of pacifism. Many of the religious groups who, for religious reasons rejected the use of force also found themselves refusing to support the civil institutions of the local state. In times of religious and social unrest this was a doubly dangerous position to take. Many of the pacifist sects were

---

[38] Gerard Vanderhaar, *Nonviolence in Christian Tradition* (London: Pax Christi, 1983), 10.
[39] Peter Chelcicky, *Net of Faith*, quoted in Brock, 15. There is no English translation of *Net of Faith*.

forced to make compromises or face almost certain extinction. The central dilemma faced by St. Augustine is the same dilemma faced by pacifists from whatever tradition down through the ages. How can a legally constituted and morally supported state defend itself from an aggressive enemy? Does the state have a right or a need for a different set of ethics from the individual?

In a number of his writings Aldous Huxley attempted to outline a theory of pacifism and construct a coherent philosophy of pacifist beliefs.[40] Huxley believed that he did not have the ability or the dedication to set forth a comprehensive philosophy of pacifism but his writings on what he termed "the intellectual justification for pacifism" can still be seen as a major contribution to the debate on pacifism. Huxley concentrates his arguments on the central issue of the relationship between means and ends.

> Now, all experience seems to show that means determine ends. Particular ends can be realised only by appropriate means; if the means are inappropriate the ends realised will be quite different from the ends proposed.[41]

This according to Huxley is the central dilemma that the military-minded theologians and philosophers who had invented the various justifications for war had failed to answer.

Abraham J. Muste wrote a number of important studies on the question of pacifism.[42] Muste challenged what he termed "bourgeois pacifism" which hoped that war could be abolished without fundamental changes in the economic and social structures. But he argued passionately against those who used violence to bring about social and economic change. He believed that war is: "the greatest single obstacle to social

---

[40] Aldous Huxley, *Pacifism and Philosophy* (London: Peace Pledge Union, 1994).
[41] Ibid., 10.
[42] Abraham J. Muste; *Non-Violence in an Aggressive World.*(New York: Harper, 1940).

change"[43]. He criticised the radicals who sought to bring about profound change in society without challenging the ideology of war and violence. According to Muste the use of violence only perpetuates the social injustices that many high-minded revolutionaries try and transform. One of the major reasons for this lies in the nature of the individual. Muste's Christian pacifism led him to believe that the problem of evil in mans nature was the key to understanding war and violence.

THE QUESTION OF CIVIL DISOBEDIENCE

In one sense Henry David Thoreau's essay on *Civil Disobedience*[44] has had an influence on later developments out of proportion to its content. Thoreau's importance would seem to be his attempt to explain the relationship between the individual and the State in a modern context within an ethical framework. Thoreau attempted to rationalise the individual's right to withdraw support for a government that is believed to be acting in an unjust way. Such an explanation opens up a whole range of related questions about the role of government and the interpretation given to the concept of justice. The essay on *Civil Disobedience* has been cited by Gandhi, King and numerous other peace activists. This essay was printed under the title *Resistance to Civil Government*[45] and, more significantly, at one stage it was entitled *The Duty of Civil Disobedience*.

Thoreau set the agenda that many pacifist thinkers were to adopt into the twentieth century. He saw the state as the enemy, but he did not attempt to overthrow it by force. He simply refused allegiance to it and withdrew himself as much as possible from any contact with it. Thoreau does not fit into the classical anarchist tradition; his refusal to associate with or obey the state was based on purely moral grounds. The state puts itself forward as the upholder of law and the arbitrator of justice. Thoreau would accept none of this:

---

[43] Ibid., 98

[44] Henry David Thoreau, *Walden and Civil Disobedience* (London: Penguin, 1983).

[45] Ibid., 429

> Law never made men a whit more just; and, by means of their respect for it, even the well disposed are daily made the agents of injustice.[46]

His ideas and beliefs developed along the lines already set out in the writings of Tom Paine and Thomas Jefferson. Thoreau quotes Jefferson in the very first line of *Civil Disobedience* "That government is best which governs least" and sharpens its meaning by changing it to: "That government is best which governs not at all."[47] According to Thoreau, government by its very nature would corrupt those involved in its processes. When you become involved in government either governing or being governed you can lose all sense of your inherent humanity. One example Thoreau gives is related to the army:

> Visit the Navy-Yard, and behold a marine, such a man as an American government can make, or such as it can make a man with its black arts, a mere shadow and reminiscence of humanity, a man laid out alive and standing, as one may as, buried under arms with funeral accompaniments, though it may be,[48]

UTOPIA AND THE PHILOSOPHY OF PEACE

No outline of the historical unfolding of the philosophy of peace would be complete without some information on the concepts of those who have put forward Utopian visions of the future. Thomas More sets the agenda in his description of what the Utopians think about war:

> They say it is quite a subhuman form of activity. Although human beings are more addicted to it than any of the lower animals.[49]

---

[46] Ibid.
[47] Ibid., 385.
[48] Ibid., 386-387.
[49] Thomas More, *Utopia*. Trans. Paul Turner. (London: Penguin, 1965), 109.

In a very practical way More faces up to the problems of defence, the promotion of interests that any country must face. He is able to side-step the issue of defence by describing Utopia as a country with only one secure entrance and harbour. This entrance is extremely dangerous without a very experienced pilot, and would be almost impossible for a foreign power to enter in force. Within the nation both sexes are trained in the art and science of military combat so that they will be able to defend themselves if they ever have a need to do so:

> In fact, the Utopians are practically the only people on earth who fail to see anything glorious in war.[50]

More gives us an outline of the Utopian concept of a just war. The Utopians:

> Hardly ever go to war, except in self-defence, to repel invaders from friendly territory, or to liberate the victims of dictatorship-which they do in a spirit of humanity, just because they feel sorry for them.[51]

He then lists many other reasons why the Utopians who dislike war so much will still go to war. To support friendly powers and make reprisals on their behalf, to protect trade, or for any reason they believed was an adequate *casus belli.* Later writers have taken a more radical approach to the question of war and violence in their Utopias. William Morris in his *News from Nowhere*[52] paints a picture of a post-war society that only came about after a war to end war almost destroyed the human race. The importance of Utopian concepts in the framework of the philosophy of peace is in the context of what the writing of Utopia reflects in human society. According to Kumar, Utopia can be seen as a perennial philosophy, a basic habit of mind, part of the human social imagination:

---

[50] Ibid., 109.

[51] Ibid.

[52] William Morris, *News from Nowhere* ed. Krishan Kumar. (Cambridge: Cambridge University Press, 1995).

> It may even be the product of some 'instinctual principle of hope' in the individual human psyche.[53]

The use of Utopia to imagine a better and more peaceful world has had a long tradition and the Utopians have contributed in a very positive way to the debate on a more peaceful social system. There are some problems with equating Utopias with the concepts of peace, but that should not take away from the importance of their contribution. Oscar Wilde wrote:

> A map of the world that does not include Utopia is not worth even glancing at, for it leaves out the country at which Humanity is always landing. And when Humanity lands there, and, seeing a better country, sets sail. Progress is the realisation of Utopias.[54]

The basic assumption found in some of the earlier nineteenth century Utopias involved the hope that technical and scientific progress would have such an improving effect on man and his social institutions that war and the need for war would just wither away.

Other literary traditions challenged in various ways the absurdities of war and violence. Jonathan Swift's corrosive satire is one good example of this tradition. In the land of Lilliput Swift goes into some considerable detail about the causes of their deep routed conflicts. Within the kingdom of Lilliput most of the violence related to a bitter historical dispute between the *Tramecksan* and the *Slamecksan.* The main point of contention revolved around the use of high or low heels on one's shoes. The animosities between these two parties was so strong that they could not consider talking or meeting with each other:

> His majesty hath determined to make use of only low heels in the administration of the government, and all

---

[53] Krishan Kumar, *Utopianism* (Milton Keynes: Open University, 1991) 43.
[54] Oscar Wilde, "The Soul of Man Under Socialism" (1891), in *De Profundis and Other Writings*, ed. Hesketh Pearson. (Harmondsworth: Penguin, 1973), 34; quoted in Kumar, 95.

> offices in the gift of the Crown, as you cannot but observe; and particularly, that his Majesty's Imperial heels are lower at least by a drurr than any of his court.[55]

The major international conflict was with the Kingdom of Blefuscu; this conflict went back generations and involved numerous wars and revolutions and the deaths of thousands of people on both sides, including at least one Emperor. The cause of this conflict, according to Swift, concerned the misinterpretation of a sacred document in relation to which end of an egg was the correct end to break before eating. The Big-Enders had been outlawed in Lilliput and were treated as traitors:

> Many hundred large volumes have been published upon this controversy; but the books of the Big-Endians have long been forbidden[56]

Swift was a genius in the use of satire in order to lampoon and ridicule the sacred beliefs of contemporary European civilisation. His detailed analysis of the causes of the bitter conflicts in Lilliput reflect quite accurately the rational explanations for similar conflicts in Ireland and in Europe at the time. No one in contemporary European society could misunderstand the type of human behavior that Swift was being so critical of.

---

[55] Jonathan Swift, *Gulliver's Travels* (London: Penguin, 1994) 43
[56] Ibid.,44

5

LEO TOLSTOY: FIVE PROPOSITIONS

We must take the Sermon on the Mount to be as much as a law as the Theorem of Pythagoras

With amazing effrontery, all governments have always declared, and still go on declaring, that all the preparations for war, and even the very wars themselves, that they undertake, are necessary to preserve peace

There can be only one permanent revolution - a moral one: the regeneration of the inner man.

Leo Tolstoy

TOLSTOY: THE PROPHET OF PEACE

There is one major problem with what Tolstoy is saying in relation to war and violence. If what Tolstoy is saying, if his analysis of how society works or what makes individuals act is correct, then almost everyone else is wrong right back to Plato and Aristotle. As Tolstoy is writing from a Christian perspective, he traces this "Perversion of Truth" as he calls it, right back to: "That scoundrel the Emperor Constantine". Tolstoy believes that the very basic analysis of the traditional approach of rationalizing cause and effect are faulty, or as Tolstoy puts it "they are full of childish absurdities." Tolstoy accepted that legal and reasonable excuses have been made for every form of violence, but he believed that no infallible standard has ever existed by which to measure or justify the worth of these excuses.

Tolstoy believed that what he calls, "The Law of Violence", which has been a central part of the framework of the traditional analysis of the human condition is faulty and the actual law that makes human society work is what Tolstoy identifies as the "Law of Love". As Tolstoy himself said: "We must take the sermon on the Mount to be as much a law as the theorem of Pythagoras". He accepts that the: "Law of Violence" is so deeply ingrained in the modern world-view that it will be very hard to get people to see a different reality, which is the "Law of Love". In relation to the "Law of Violence" Tolstoy asks: "how is it possible, for people endowed with reason and conscience to be deceived by arguments so manifestly irrational and directed by the self interest of the privileged few?" Tolstoy answers this question by saying that our very belief in reason has been deliberately undermined by the attempt to support the "Law of Violence" and this is where the real debate on war and peace and violence and non-violence should be studied.

TOLSTOY AND LENIN

Given the major role that Lenin and his ideology subsequently played in Russian and world history, his voracious criticism of Tolstoy's philosophy is of more than purely historical importance. There could be no greater contrast in any philosophy of human affairs than that between Tolstoy and Lenin. In one sense these two world-views represent polar opposites of cause and effect, and of ends and means. Lenin, like most of Tolstoy's critics, recognised Tolstoy's ability as a great novelist but totally rejected his understanding of historical forces and repudiated his ideas of how progressive change might be brought about in society or in man. There was absolutely no meeting of minds in their understanding of how the relationship between man and society works or is supposed to work. In 1908 on the occasion of Tolstoy's eightieth birthday Lenin published one of his very critical essays on Tolstoy. Lenin accepted that in his many works, Tolstoy as an artist had painted an outstanding picture of the Russian system of capitalist exploitation; of the violence of government, of the farce of the courts and of the poverty and brutalisation of the system. Against this what does Tolstoy offer? According to Lenin, Tolstoy offers: "one of the most abominable things on earth - religion."[1] Lenin described Tolstoy as:

> The washed out, hysterical cry-baby known as the Russian intellectual, who publicly beats his breast and cries: I do not eat meat any more and now feed only on rice patties.[2]

Lenin criticised almost every aspect of Tolstoy's basic values:

> Tolstoy is ridiculous as a prophet who has discovered new recipes for the salvation of mankind - and therefore the foreign and Russian "Tolstoyans" who desire to transform what is actually the weakest aspect of his teaching into a

---

[1] Leo Tolstoy. *War and Peace*. The Maude Translation. Essays in Criticism.Ed. By George Gibian. (New York. Norton. 1966) 1393.
[2] Ibid.

> dogma are absolutely contemptible.[3]

Lenin believed that Tolstoy's ideas of the forces that were at work in Russian society were completely misconceived and out of date. The principles set out by Tolstoy in what has been described as: "Christian Anarchism"[4] were, according to Lenin, totally unrelated to the historical forces that were driving the peasants to inevitable revolutionary action. Lenin's view was that:

> Tolstoy reflected the immaturity of day-dreaming, lack of political training, and revolutionary spinelessness.[5]

If Lenin could be identified with any character in Tolstoy's novels it would be with Napoleon in *War and Peace*, that is, with the man of destiny, the man of vision, the man of force. But Tolstoy believed that these men, "the heroes of history" who believe themselves to understand and to be controlling historical forces, are fooling themselves and everyone else:

> The primeval conception of a cause was the will of the Gods, succeeded later by the will of those who stand in the historical foreground - the heroes of history.[6]

Tolstoy, more than most other authors, understood that the human capacity for self-delusion cannot be underestimated. This capacity for self-delusion becomes extremely dangerous when it is associated with the contagion of self-righteousness. It does not only lead to the loss of critical thinking, it creates the belief that ideas based on fanaticism and intolerance are rational beliefs. Tolstoy, for all his preaching and all his self-righteousness, never lost his capacity to doubt his own ideas.

But Tolstoy also believed that the human capacity for love, for good, for justice, was not just a dream, but was an essential part

---

[3] Ibid., 1394.
[4] Ibid.
[5] Ibid., 1169.
[6] Leo Tolstoy, *War And Peace*, trans. Rosemary Edmonds. (London: Penguin, 1982), 1168.

of reality. Individuals like Lenin who attempted to construct a reality or to explain existing reality while ignoring these human capacities were according to Tolstoy building their theories on false foundations.

In the years after Lenin wrote his criticism of Tolstoy, the revolutionary forces that swept over Russia would seem to confirm that Lenin had a better grasp of reality than Tolstoy. Lenin saw Tolstoy's idea of "non-resistance to evil" as one of the most serious causes of the defeat of the first revolutionary campaign of 1905. But the hope for the emancipation of mankind through political revolution as expressed by Lenin and rejected by Tolstoy, had lost nearly all of its justifications by the end of the twentieth century. Almost one hundred years after this debate the total collapse of the system of government brought about by Lenin's revolutionary forces has raised the ghosts of this debate.

TOLSTOY'S WORLD-VIEW

Tolstoy's life history has been recorded in detail by many of his biographers and in his own diaries and writings.[7] Tolstoy's aristocratic family background, the loss of his mother at such an early age, and his childhood at his grandfather's house at Yasnaya Polyana are just some of the more important influences on his early childhood. Tolstoy was born in 1828, seven years after the death of Napoleon. The campaigns of Napoleon and the French revolutionary armies, and the type of changes they had brought about throughout Europe, were to dominate much of contemporary thinking in the society in which Tolstoy developed his ideas and his outlook. The Russian state, with all its faults, had eventually defeated Napoleon's army. But the great revolutionary ideas of Liberty, Equality, and Fraternity were to continue to challenge the very basis of the Russian society and its *Ancien Regime.*[8] *(Old Order).*

---

[7] Aylmer Maude, *The Life of Tolstoy* (Oxford: Oxford University Press, 1929; reprint, 1987).
[8] A.N. Wilson, *Tolstoy* (London: Hamish Hamilton, 1988; reprint, London: Penguin Books, 1989).

Tolstoy himself was no stranger to war and military service. His family had proudly produced its fair share of generals and colonels, and his father, Nikolai Tolstoy, had served in the war against Napoleon. Tolstoy saw active service in a number of campaigns in the Balkans, in the Caucasus and in the siege of Sevastopol in the Crimea. During Tolstoy's lifetime Russian society came under intense pressure for change and transformation. At every level of Russian society, economically, politically and socially, the forces of change were undermining the traditional structures of the social order of the *Ancien Regime.*

There are ninety volumes of Tolstoy's work in the standard edition of *The Complete Works of Tolstoy* by Chertkov.[9] There have been numerous other English translations of Tolstoy's work; the best known and the ones most reflective of the originals are those by Louise and Aylmer Maude.[10] Professor Christian is recognised as an important source for his translations of Tolstoy's letters and diaries.[11] Given so much material, it is not surprising that much of Tolstoy's work would seem to be full of inconsistencies and contradictions. The paradoxes in his life and in his writings are numerous. Even in his latter "doctrinal" writings it is possible to identify views that are critically inconsistent. Many of Tolstoy's critics and biographers have identified and debated these contradictions.

In his old age Tolstoy was described as a "pacifist anarchist" and these labels reflect some of his most important beliefs. His solutions to both the great problems of the nineteenth century and to the personal problems of individual existence can be outlined in a number of words such as pacifism, vegetarianism, self-sufficiency, reading the Gospels and anarchism. Tolstoy not only attempted to preach these ideals but he tried to practise

---

[9] David Egan and Melinda A. Egan, *Leo Tolstoy, an Annotated Bibliography of English-language Sources* (London: Scarecrow, 1979).

[10] Leo Tolstoy, *War and Peace* trans. Louise Maude and Aylmer Maude. (New York: Norton, 1966).

[11] R. F. Christian, ed. and trans. *Tolstoy's Diaries*, (London: The Athlone Press, 1985; reprint, Flamingo, 1994).

them as well. The picture painted by Tolstoy's biographers of his drinking, gambling and whoring in his earlier years reflects accurately the life of a typical young nobleman of his time in Imperial Russia. When Tolstoy came to write and publish: *Why Do Men Stupefy Themselves* (1891), he was well able to utilise much of his own earlier experience. Tolstoy's strength and his greatness lie in his ability to portray so accurately the ordinary feelings of so many different 'real' people, and to see through the sham of things that most people accepted as inevitable. Throughout his life it has been said that Tolstoy: “had been troubled by a conflict between an unyielding, intellectual rationalism and a passionately religious temperament."[12]

TOLSTOY'S PHILOSOPHY OF PEACE

In many ways Tolstoy had numerous philosophies. There were the philosophies of life interwoven into his great novels, there were the philosophies of life recorded in his diaries and the philosophies preached in his doctrinal writings. Whatever one critic might write about some aspect of Tolstoy's philosophy another might with legitimacy write something quite different. Tolstoy can be seen as a philosopher in the classical sense of the term. He sought to find or to produce: "a universal explanatory principle"[13] which would help to define and explain the predicament of mankind. Like most other philosophers he hoped to discover an indestructible core of knowledge which would produce a set of unifying principles by which man must live. Most of his critics would say that Tolstoy failed to discover any such principles; some would say that no such principles exist. But Tolstoy himself believed that he had rediscovered the basic principle of life in the uncorrupted message of Christ in the Gospels.

Every so often in Tolstoy's writings, in his great novels, in his shorter writings and in his letters and pamphlets, we get a

---

[12] Leo Tolstoy, *Resurrection* trans. Rosemary Edmonds. (London: Penguin, 1966), 11.

[13] Henry Gifford, ed. *Leo Tolstoy A Critical Anthology* (London: Penguin, 1971), 256.

glimpse of what can be called Tolstoy's: "fundamental conception of existence."[14] Many of Tolstoy's critics have identified and attempted to create some understanding from these sources. Dr. Steiner, in his study of the contrasts between Tolstoy and Dostoyevsky says: "The art of Tolstoy is anti-Platonic,"[15] but then Dr. Steiner goes on to say that he believes that Tolstoy's philosophy was fundamentally rationalist and that Tolstoy himself believed that common sense and the "inner light" would indicate to him or to anyone else the inherently true meaning of the gospels.

Tolstoy prided himself on the fact that his ideas challenged the basic assumptions about power and violence on which human culture has traditionally rested. Throughout his life he was known as a person who never feared to incur the wrath of the Church, the State, the revolutionary groups or any of the power elites who tried to use him. In attempting to identify Tolstoy's fundamental conception of existence, Dr. Steiner outlines two opposing sets of principles which help to illuminate two contrasting views. On one side there are the liberals:
Who distrust final solutions and believe that some measure of injustice and absurdity in human affairs is unavoidable.[16]

On the other side can be seen the Tolstoys of this world who believed that a just and peaceful arrangement of society - the Kingdom of God - can be established on earth. Within this framework were the fundamentalists, the enemies of the open, free, and by implication, imperfect society - some of whom believe that the kingdom of God must be established on earth whatever the cost.

Such a basic picture is in many ways unfair to Tolstoy, because Tolstoy would never have seen himself as an enemy of an open and free society. In fact, he saw himself as the enemy of the type of closed society that had traditionally been experienced in Russian culture. Tolstoy never saw the western type of liberal

---

[14] G.W. Spence, *Tolstoy the Ascetic* (Edinburgh: Oliver and Boyd, 1967), 117.
[15] Spence, 118.
[16] Ibid.

society as any sort of panacea. His avid reading of Dickens and his own experience in London would have given him a critical insight into the liberal society that some of his contemporaries advocated for the future of Russia. Tolstoy was not too impressed with such a possibility. In the view of Isaiah Berlin, Tolstoy's philosophy springs from:

> A bitter inner conflict between his actual experience and his beliefs, between his vision of life, and his theory of what it, and he himself, ought to be, if the vision was to be bearable at all; between the immediate data which he was too honest and too intelligent to ignore, and the need for an interpretation of them which did not lead to the childish absurdities of all previous views.[17]

The beginning of this inner conflict appeared in Tolstoy's earliest literary work, it did not, as some of his critics believed, appear suddenly in later life; it was central to what made Tolstoy such a great novelist.

THE LAW OF LOVE VERSES THE LAW OF VIOLENCE

The fabric of Tolstoy's philosophy of peace is scattered throughout most of his writings. It is to be found in his major works such as *War and Peace, Anna Karenina,* and *Resurrection*, but also in his lesser known works. Tolstoy's letters and correspondence and the writings in his diary are also an important source which reflect the changes in his ideas and beliefs over time. Taking his writings in chronological order, it is possible to get some picture of how his philosophy of war and peace developed and matured over time. However *What Then Must We Do?* (1886) and *The Kingdom of God is Within You* (1893) are the two classical works within which Tolstoy himself sets out to explain the driving forces which underline his own philosophy and upon which he was to construct his philosophy of peace. These two works bristle with Tolstoy's critical analysis of society and are central in his attempt at producing an

---

[17] Isaiah Berlin, *The Hedgehog and the Fox* (London: Weidenfeld, 1953), 35.

alternative set of moral values. In the publication of: A Confession (1879), Tolstoy clearly sets out his views on non-violence and puts himself forward as an apostle of non-resistance. Many of Tolstoy's contemporaries saw this development as a dramatic conversion of ideas associated with a mid-life crisis. Tolstoy himself felt that it was:

> The climax of a long process of spiritual fermentation, of growing discontent with orthodox religion and with the aristocratic society of which hitherto he had been a member.[18]

Tolstoy re-read and interpreted for himself the teachings of the New Testament and was particularly influenced by the Sermon on the Mount. Tolstoy came to believe that Jesus had taught:

> Non-resistance to evil as part of a broader philosophy of non-violence that contemporary civilisation denied in all its activities.[19]

In: *The kingdom of God is Within You,* Tolstoy tried to explain in some detail how the application of the message of non-resistance might work in practical terms. The central message of non-resistance is that which Christ taught - it is wrong to return evil for evil. Many people who do not understand this message believe that non-resistance requires people to offer no resistance to evil. The message of the New Testament was not, "resist not evil." Tolstoy believed that the very opposite to this was the true message, evil should be resisted by all means except by the use of evil. He quotes the catechism of Adin Ballou, an American who had preached and practiced non-resistance throughout his life:

> Q. Are we to understand the word "non-resistance" in its broad sense, that is, as meaning that one should offer no resistance to evil whatsoever?

---

[18] Peter Brock, *A Brief History Of Pacifism From Jesus To Tolstoy,* (New York: Syracuse University Press, 1992), 72.
[19] Ibid.

> A. No, it should be understood literally as Christ taught it - that is, not to return evil for evil. Evil should be resisted by all lawful means, but not by evil.
>
> Q. From what does it appear that Christ gave that meaning to non-resistance?
>
> A. From the words which he used on that occasion. He said "Ye have heard it hath been said, an eye for an eye, and a tooth for a tooth. But I say unto you, That ye resist not evil: but whosoever shall smite thee on thy right cheek, turn to him the other also..."[20]

For Tolstoy and for many others the ultimate message of non-resistance, is the refusal of returning evil for evil. Christ's gospel is based on the principle of returning only love for evil. For Tolstoy this message is the central message of the crucifixion. The message of Christ's crucifixion can only be fully understood within the gospel of love and non-resistance. What is the crucifixion of the Son of God if it is not the ultimate act of non-resistance and love? Tolstoy's monumental work: *The Four Gospels Harmonised and Translated,* was written between 1881-1882 when Tolstoy was going through his near suicidal mid-life crisis. The work on this book, according to Sampson:

> Played an important part in the development of his belief that the teaching of Jesus is absolutely opposed to violence of any kind.[21]

Tolstoy eventually believed that in human society there were two fundamentally opposing forces: the Law of Love and the Law of Violence. The laws which govern the Law of Love are set out clearly in the Sermon on the Mount and these laws must be seen according to Tolstoy: "as much a law as the theorem of Pythagoras." Tolstoy accepts that the Law of Violence is so

---

[20] Leo Tolstoy, *Writings on Civil Disobedience and Nonviolence* (Santa Cruz: New Society, 1987), 297.
[21] Leo Tolstoy, *What Then Must We Do?* Trans. Aylmer Maude. (London: Green Books, 1991), vii.

deeply ingrained in the modern world-view that it will be very hard to get people to see a different reality which is the Law of Love. In relation to the Law of Violence Tolstoy asks, how is it possible:

> For people endowed with reason and conscience to be deceived by argument so manifestly irrational and directed by the self-interest of the privileged few?[22]

Tolstoy answers this question by saying that our very belief in reason has been deliberately undermined by the attempt to support the Law of Violence and this is where the real debate on violence and love should be studied. The fundamental principle underlining the development of Tolstoy's philosophy of peace was his firm belief that the Christian principles as taught by Christ were the highest religious principles known to man. Tolstoy believed that these Christian principles were opposed to all forms of violence and that they preached love as the highest law of the universe.

TOLSTOY AS PROPHET

Tolstoy's life history is sometimes seen as falling into two quite distinct halves. Some time after the publication of *Anna Karenina*, the first installment of which was published in 1875, Tolstoy underwent what can best be described as a religious conversion: "He began to read the Gospels, deeply and attentively, and this reading had a revolutionary effect upon his life."[23] From then on Tolstoy's mind and energy concentrated on the essence of the Christian Gospel -the Sermon on the Mount, - where Christ teaches the Gospel of love:

> You have heard that it was said, 'You shall love your neighbour and hate your enemy. But I say to you love your enemies and pray for those who persecute you'.

---

[22] Ibid., x.

[23] Wilson, 300.

Tolstoy tried to do what many other saints and sinners had done before him, to strip away the dogma of the institutional Church and get to the central moral teaching of Christ *the Son of God.* He believed that the institutional Churches had deliberately perverted and distorted the simple message of the Gospel. Tolstoy called this the perversion of religion and is very clear about how this perversion happened (see proposition one: the perversion of religion).

By 1885 Tolstoy had become a vegetarian, a teetotaler, and had given up smoking and hunting. Many of Tolstoy's literary critics are very cynical about this particular phase of his life. Wilson says:

> It is also possible to read the next thirty years as an extraordinary demonstration of the fact that the Sermon on the Mount is an unlivable ethic, a counsel of craziness which, if followed to its relentless conclusion as Tolstoy tried to follow it, will lead to the reverse of peace and harmony and spiritual calm.[24]

Tolstoy himself felt that the critics who had praised his earlier works had praised them for the wrong reasons and had not understood the central message contained in them. In a letter to M. P. Pogodin he says:

> These are not casual thoughts. These thoughts are the fruit of all the mental labour of my life and are an integral part of my view of life, which I worked out with a labour and a suffering that God alone knows.[25]

SOCIETY AND LITERATURE:

Tolstoy's analysis of Russian society was very similar to the analysis put forward by contemporary revolutionaries and reformers of various political backgrounds. Tolstoy believed that most of the social problems of poverty, degradation and violence arose directly out of the corruption of the traditional

---

[24] Ibid., 300-301.

[25] Leo Tolstoy, *War And Peace,* the Maude translation, 1362.

social structures of Russian society. These traditional structures; i. e., the monarchy, the aristocracy, the Church, the courts and the military, were, according to Tolstoy, corrupted beyond reform. Many of the revolutionaries and reformers looked to other more liberal European countries and hoped for similar changes in Russian society. Not all of the reformers looked west; others looked to a golden age in Russian history and hoped that Russia could reform itself using the strength of its own cultural traditions. Tolstoy, Dostoyevsky and Turgenev were all caught up in this conflict. Turgenev in: *Fathers And Sons* painted a very realistic picture of the:

> Profound and bitter conflicts between Slavophile nationalists and admirers of the West, conservatives and liberals, liberals and radicals, moderates and fanatics, realists and visionaries, above all between old and young.[26]

Because of the conservative nature of Russian political society the importance and significance of literature was far greater than in any western society. Literature was the battle ground on which the central social and political issues of life were fought out. Isaiah Berlin said that after Belinsky:

> No Russian writer was wholly free from the belief that to write was, first and foremost, to bear witness to the truth: that the writer, of all men, had no right to avert his gaze from the central issues of his day and his society.[27]

In *Resurrection,* Tolstoy describes in glaring detail the terrible brutalities and injustices imposed by the system of courts, prisons and deportations. One of the political prisoners sums up his life's work as an attempt to: "destroy the established order of

---

[26] Isaiah Berlin, " 'Fathers and Children' the Romanes Lecture," (Oxford: Oxford University Press, 1972), in *Fathers and Sons* by Ivan Sergeyevich Turgenev, (London: Penguin, 1965; reprint, 1972), 10.
[27] Ibid., 14.

things which made possible what he had seen"[28] the cruelties, the brutalities, the injustices etc. In *Resurrection*, Tolstoy outlines an "Alice in Wonderland" version of reality, black is white and white is black. The "Old General," the pillar of the social system who had more medals than his uniform could hold at any one time, had certain duties to carry out which he considered very important. These duties:

> Consisted in keeping political prisoners of both sexes in casemates, in solitary confinement and in such conditions that half of them perished within ten years, some of them going out of their minds, some dying of consumption, others committing suicide by starving themselves, cutting their arteries with bits of glass, hanging or setting fire to themselves.[29]

Tolstoy used the general as one of the many examples of the hypocrisy and the double standards of the social system. The general not only knew the cruelties of the system: he was part of that system and was proud of his part in the system. The general believed himself to be a highly honourable pillar of society. Everyone else in 'society' had to believe the same thing or else dangerous doubts which could undermine the very foundations on which the whole system was built would take hold. Another general only wore one medal which was a very important White Cross and Tolstoy contemptuously explains how the general got this medal in the Caucasus. Because under the general's command:

> Close-cropped Russian peasants killed more than a thousand men who were defending their liberty, their homes and their families. Later on he served in Poland, where he again compelled Russian peasants to commit all sorts of crimes, and got more orders and decorations for his uniform.[30]

---

[28] Leo Tolstoy, *Resurrection* trans. Rosemary Edmonds. (London: Penguin, 1966), 485.
[29] Ibid., 345.
[30] Ibid.

Resurrection, not surprisingly, was ruthlessly cut by the Russian censor. Chapter after chapter disappeared in the final, politically correct version. Only Tolstoy's personal standing both at home and abroad saved him personally from more direct action by the authorities. The moral sentiments contained in *Resurrection* reflect the evolution in Tolstoy's moral understanding. As Rosemary Edmonds his translator points out in her introduction to *Resurrection*:

> The essence of all that Tolstoy had thought and suffered since his spiritual change is crammed into its pages. There is no place for the lies which would cheat us into the belief that wrong may sometimes be right through passion, or genius or heroism.[31]

THE PHILOSOPHY OF WAR AND PEACE

Tolstoy's epic novel *War and Peace* has given rise to more than its fair share of critical examination. The critical schools can be divided into any number of groups. Turgenev, a contemporary of Tolstoy, sums up many of the critical trends when he states of War and Peace:

> There are tens of pages which are absolutely magnificent, first class - all the descriptive parts, the stuff of everyday life...But the historical addition, which is precisely the part which enraptures the reader, is a sham and charlatanery.[32]

It is precisely where Tolstoy has given rein to his various theories of history, to his attempt at painting a picture of the psychology of personality and to the development of many of his philosophical theories that the critics have gathered like vultures. Boris Eykhenbaum has said about *War and Peace* that: "this 'novel-chronicle' became a new genre that grew out of combining novel-like action and historical material with philosophical reasoning."[33] In addition, Tolstoy, during the

---

[31] Ibid., 11.
[32] Tolstoy, *War and Peace,* the Maude translation, 1430.
[33] Ibid., 1442.

course of writing the book in the 1860s began to feel that he: "was a historian and publicist teaching his contemporaries and dictating the truth to them."[34] Tolstoy certainly weaves his philosophy of history throughout the story of *War and Peace.* Within the structure of the novel Tolstoy also develops some of his psychological theories of personality and in the final chapters of the book, particularly in the epilogue, he develops his historical theories to the full.

Anatol Rapoport in his introduction to Carl Von Clausewitz's *On War:* outlines three distinct philosophies of war which show Clausewitz and Tolstoy propounding two diametrically opposed doctrines. Clausewitz views war as a rational instrument of national policy. Tolstoy, on the other hand, sees war as a cataclysm that afflicts humanity and believes that wars are caused by unknown historical forces. Tolstoy believes that:

> The decisions of princes or the manoeuvres of generals to be irrelevant to either the outbreaks or outcomes of wars.[35]

According to Tolstoy's philosophy of war, no one person can be held responsible for war and in particular no-one person can gain from war. Tolstoy's description of the events which were taking place in France before the revolution reflects his cataclysmic view of historical forces:

> At the end of the eighteenth century there has gathered in Paris a couple of dozen persons who began talking about all men being equal and free. Because of this, over the length and breadth of France men fell to slaughtering and destroying one another.[36]

Tolstoy had no sentimental feelings about war. In the words of Prince Andrei in *War and Peace* the view of war is very rationalistic:

---

[34] Ibid., 1443.
[35] Carl von Clausewitz, *On War* ed. Anatol Rapoport. (London: Penguin, 1968), 16.
[36] Tolstoy, *War and Peace* the Maude translation, 1402.

> War is not a polite recreation but the vilest thing in life, and we ought to understand that and not play at war. Our attitude towards the fearful necessity of war ought to be stern and serious. It boils down to this: we should have done with humbug, and let war be war and not a game. Otherwise, war is a favourite pastime of the idle and frivolous..:[37]

In a contemporary essay on the publication of the fifth and sixth volumes of *War and Peace,* the Russian critic Nikolai Strakhov asked the question: "What is the meaning of War and Peace?" He expresses his answer in the words of the author himself: "There is no greatness where there is no simplicity, goodness, and truth."[38] According to Strakhov one of Tolstoy's central messages of *War and Peace* is to show that true greatness is far superior to false greatness at every level of human endeavour, whether in the individual, the family, or the nation. Tolstoy believes that European culture has confused the issues of true greatness and false greatness and has lost the ability to differentiate between the true and the false. European culture puts forward Napoleon as a great leader. Tolstoy's view of the great men of history was unequivocal; Napoleon was a disaster for the people of France and the people of Europe: "Napoleon brought six hundred thousand men to Russia and captured Moscow; but afterwards he suddenly ran away from Moscow."[39] It would, as Tolstoy said, be a mistake to think that this description is a mere irony or a caricature of history.

In the characterisation of Napoleon and General Kutuzov, Tolstoy outlines the classic differences between what he considers the measure of true greatness as against false greatness. False greatness is represented by the worst passions, vanity, self-love, envy, hatred and many more of the negative aspects of human nature. True greatness is represented by simplicity, goodness, truth, love and many more of the positive aspects of human nature. At the end of *War and Peace*,

---

[37] Ibid., 922.
[38] Ibid., 1382.
[39] Ibid., 1403.

characters like Pierre and the families that have survived, along with the Russian nation itself, have in Tolstoy's opinion, been purified, strengthened and enlightened by suffering. Tolstoy's central message of *War and Peace* is that these forces of simplicity and truth can defeat every false and untrue force.

Tolstoy was by his birth and by his nurture a Russian. He was a Russian with a small "r," but nevertheless he was a Russian in the nature of his soul and in the outlook of his mind. In one sense *War and Peace* could not have been written by a French author in the sympathetic way that it paints the Russian cause. As much as any author can, Tolstoy attempted to be impartial and objective in the production of his art. In the structure and content of *War and Peace* there can be seen a conflict between Tolstoy as a Russian whose homeland has been invaded and Tolstoy the author depicting impartially the military campaign of invasion and defence. R. F. Christian in his study of Tolstoy's *War and Peace* identified some of these problems but states:

> All this does not alter the fact that for Tolstoy war is an unmitigated evil, and the battle of Borodino as senseless and wicked as that of Austerlitz or any other battle not on Russian soil. ...On both sides in the struggle there is cruelty; on both sides magnanimity; on both sides muddle and confusion.[40]

One of the main differences between the French and the Russians as contrasted by Tolstoy was in their military leadership. On one side there is the Emperor Napoleon who believes that he alone is controlling the historical events and the general, Kutuzov, who acknowledges that these historical events are too powerful for anyone to control. The result, according to Tolstoy, is two opposing sets of philosophies which produce two opposing sets of strategies, one which leads to disaster for the Emperor and victory for the general:

> Structurally speaking the arrangement of the war material in *War and Peace* follows the lines not of a just and unjust

[40] Ibid.1462

> cause, but of "good" and "bad" men:[41]

The historical details of this analysis may lack some confirmation and Tolstoy has been criticised for such a simple classification; those who criticise this picture may paint their own picture which may or may not be more valid than Tolstoy's:

> And what is war? What makes for success in warfare? What are the morals of the military world? The aim and end of war is murder; the weapons employed in war are espionage, treachery and the encouragement of treachery, the ruining of a country, the plundering and robbing of its inhabitants for the maintenance of the army, and trickery and lying which appear under the heading of the art of war.[42]

THE LAW OF LOVE VERSES THE LAW OF VIOLENCE

In order to focus in on some of Tolstoy's more specific ideas relating to the culture of violence it is intended to select a number of statements that reflect some of the central aspects of his philosophy of peace. While these statements are chosen on an arbitrary basis, it is hoped that they will reflect in a reasonably accurate fashion some of the lines of reasoning used by Tolstoy. When Isaiah Berlin called his famous essay on Tolstoy *The Hedgehog and the Fox* he had in mind the saying "The fox knows many things, but the hedgehog knows only one big thing." Berlin believes that Tolstoy:

> Has told us more about himself and his views and attitudes than any other Russian, more almost than any other European writer.[43]

Berlin goes on to say that there are no dark corners in his universe. He explains himself with greater clarity than most

---

[41] Ibid.
[42] Ibid., 922.
[43] Isaiah Berlin, *Russian Thinkers* ed. Henry Hardy and Aileen Kelly. (London: Penguin, 1978), 23).

other writers. As to the question of whether Tolstoy was a hedgehog or a fox, the answer Berlin gives is that he was a bit of both. Tolstoy was by nature a fox but he believed that the solution to many problems was the solution of the hedgehog. This reflects the conflict between what Tolstoy was and what he believed he was. In any analysis of a historical or contemporary culture, the perversion of ethical beliefs must be seen as a central issue. Tolstoy's passionate belief in the Christian message of non-violence was only matched by his passionate animosity to those who, he believed, perverted the fundamental message of the Gospel. For Tolstoy, the manipulation of the concept of obedience reflected a central aspect of this perversion.

PROPOSITION ONE: THE PERVERSION OF RELIGION

> The government, in order to have a plausible basis for its domination of the people, has to pretend that it holds the highest religious teaching known to man. (i.e. the Christian). That (Christian) teaching however, is in its nature opposed not only to murder, but to all violence, and therefore, the government in order to dominate the people and to be considered Christian, had to pervert Christianity and to hide its true meaning from the people. This perversion was accomplished long ago, in the time of that scoundrel the Emperor Constantine, who for doing it was enrolled among the saints.[44]

Within this statement there are contained a number of important principles and criticisms which re-occur in much of Tolstoy's later writings. Similar principles can be identified in the work of different philosophers throughout the ages. Part of this question concerns the role of ethical values, however defined in the moral structures of any society. Equally important for Tolstoy was the interpretation of those values by contemporary ruling elites. Tolstoy eventually came to believe that Christian ethical values were continuously manipulated by those in authority to create

---

[44] Tolstoy, *Civil Disobedience*, 160-161.

the ethical norms that were required to maintain them in their positions of authority. The contention is that there is a truth which has been revealed by Christ or Buddha or Muhammad or within other systems of beliefs. The recognition of that truth has evolved at different levels in different cultures over time. Tolstoy believes that, within the Christian world, this truth has been deliberately misinterpreted by the various ruling elites in order to help them keep their dominance in society.

Tolstoy eventually came to believe that all the true religions of the world held the same basic principles and were moving towards the recognition of the fundamental "Law of Love". This Law of Love was, according to Tolstoy, the direct opposite of the Law of Violence which was the prevailing dominant law of society.

Tolstoy's criticism of the contemporary moral values of his society were compounded by his belief that "Law of Violence" was concealed and preached as the "Law of Love." It was not simply a question of ambiguity about moral values; it was, for Tolstoy, a deliberate perversion of basic moral principles. Tolstoy believed that the message of the Gospel had not only been misinterpreted, but that it had been turned completely around and now it was being used to support principles which were the very opposite of those from which it sprang.

One of the fundamental principles underlining the development of Tolstoy's philosophy of peace was his firm belief in the incompatibility of Christian teaching and the making of war. His refusal to accept the idea of the just war theory was the foundation of his philosophy of peace. The changes that took place over time in Tolstoy's philosophy revolved around these principles:

> It was through (Tolstoy's) reinterpretation of Christian ethics that pacifism achieved a status as a significant, if not fully developed, social philosophy of contemporary

> civilisation.[45]

As Tolstoy once said: "the most fearful evil in the world is hypocrisy"[46] and the biggest hypocrisy of our time is the hypocrisy of governments and their preparations for war. And even worse than this, men who are intelligent and well-meaning fail to see through this hypocrisy and support it with all their might.

PROPOSITION TWO: THE QUESTION OF OBEDIENCE

> It is not sinful to kill people when ordered to do so by the authorities, but that it is sinful to disobey the authorities.[47]

For Tolstoy, the manipulation of obedience was one of the greatest deceptions that have ever been contrived by those who would be in authority. It is the central structural framework of any government or any form of authority that the people obey that authority. There can be no power in human society without obedience. That obedience can be brought about in a number of different ways; either through voluntary association, through manipulation or through fear and the use of force. Most societies would experience a combination of these factors with one dominating over the others at any particular time, but still dependent to some extent on all the factors combining.

Tolstoy, through his experience in the autocratic Russian society, did not give much credence to voluntary association. His opinion of the more liberal western system was not very sympathetic. He believed that the western model of liberal democracy was really just another form of manipulation under the guise of freedom, which made it even more deceptive than the autocratic systems of control. Tolstoy's arguments against the falsity of most organised religion has a similar foundation to

---

[45] Irving L. Horowitz, *War And Peace In Contemporary Social And Philosophical Theory* (London: Condor 1973), 69.
[46] Tolstoy, *Civil Disobedience*, 143.
[47] Ronald Sampson, *Tolstoy on the Causes of War* (London: Peace Pledge Union, 1987), 24.

the uneasiness he felt about the structures of liberal democracy. The Liberal system, as much as any other system of government, was designed to manipulate people, in this way:

> People's very sense of the existence of truth is confused or undermined, so that they are as putty in the hands of the authorities...[48]

Tolstoy saw this manipulation not as an isolated political phenomena, but that it:

> Is part and parcel of a whole system of closely interwoven deception to which people are subjected throughout their education from early childhood.[49]

In one sense Tolstoy's analysis of the philosophy of violence can be said to be simplistic. In many of his analyses of the use and justification of violence Tolstoy gives way to his anarchist tendencies and concentrates his criticism almost entirely on the institutions of the state and the state itself. Men, according to this analysis, are corrupted and led into mistaken beliefs by outside influences such as the state and all its apparatus, the army, the legal system and the school system. The Church and its traditions are seen by Tolstoy to be even more corrupted than these institutions because the Church has deliberately corrupted the message of Christ. Tolstoy put all his faith in those individuals uncorrupted by power and privilege; they, the peasants, were the only ones who could hear plainly the message of Christ.

Tolstoy relentlessly identified and criticised the type of deceptions built into the state structure, and the hypocrisy of the Christian Churches in their attitudes to war. These authorities had come to confuse morality with obedience so were able to teach that:

> It is not sinful to kill people when ordered to do so by the

---

[48] Ibid.

[49] Ibid.

> authorities, but that it is sinful to disobey the authorities.[50]

But fear is very much a secondary tool of control that can be used at certain times for certain purposes. Real power and control lie in the manipulation of obedience.

PROPOSITION THREE: ON WAR

> With amazing effrontery, all governments have always declared, and still go on declaring, that all the preparations for war, and even the very wars themselves, that they undertake, are necessary to preserve peace.

Tolstoy compared the abolition of war with the movement for the abolition of slavery. The idea that human society could exist without slavery was very slow to develop. As Tolstoy pointed out, the Greek philosophers Plato and Aristotle could not even conceive of societies without the institution of slavery. Thomas More could not imagine an *Utopia* without the use of slavery. Tolstoy saw that the abolition of the institution of slavery came about less than one hundred years after the "first clear expression that mankind can live without slavery."[51] In relation to the institution of war Tolstoy believed that:

> Even now the question (of war) stands solved in the human conscience, and with every day, every hour more and more men come to the same conclusion.[52]

The problem that Tolstoy now saw with the question of war was what he termed the problem between the awakening conscience and the inertia of the old condition:

> At first the inertia is so powerful, the conscience so weak, that the first attempt to escape from error is met only with

---

[50] Sampson, 24.
[51] Tolstoy, *Civil Disobedience*, 17.
[52] Ibid., 18.

> astonishment.[53]

This astonishment then turns to contempt for the new idea, and then subterfuge and trickery to try and undermine the new truth. Tolstoy is convinced that conscience will continue to grow and become stronger:

> And there shall not pass away another hundred years after the clear utterance of the idea that mankind can live without war, before war shall cease to be. Very likely some form of armed violence will remain, just as wage-labour remains after the abolition of slavery; but at least, wars and armies will be abolished in the outrageous form, so repugnant to reason and moral sense, in which they now exist.[54]

Tolstoy addresses the realists' argument which accepts that while war is an evil, it is a necessary evil, "while mankind is still so bestial, abolition of armies will do more harm than good."[55] But Tolstoy sees this argument as the same type of argument put forward by so-called realists for upholding the institution of slavery.
In relation to governments and their justifications for war Tolstoy had many strong opinions:

> With amazing effrontery, all governments have always declared, and still go on declaring, that all the preparations for war, and even the very wars themselves, that they undertake, are necessary to preserve peace.[56]

Tolstoy does not necessarily believe in a conspiracy theory by governments; he believes that the forces at work are much more subtle than a deliberate and calculated plan:

> The fact is that they are deceitful with no wish to deceive

[53] Ibid.
[54] Ibid., 17.
[55] Ibid., 19.
[56] Ibid., 155.

> but because they cannot be otherwise. They deceive with no consciousness of their deceit and usually with the naive assurance that they are doing something excellent and elevated.[57]

Tolstoy expressed himself astonished at the cynical nature of the Franco-Russian festivities of 1893 and 1894, which culminated in the visits of the French fleet to Russia and the Russian fleet to France. Tolstoy felt that everything that was being written and said by the "experts" about these developments was a great pantomime of parody. The ministers, the generals, the newspapers and informed public opinion, all talked about a great love that had suddenly developed between the countries of France and Russia. This development of friendship was considered so important and significant because it *would* bring peace and stability to Europe.

Tolstoy felt that, in reality, the opposite was the actual truth; France and Russia were drawn together in order to better be able to prepare to fight Germany. When the Russian fleet arrived in France they were wined and dined by the French authorities and media interest was so great that even the menus were published in detail on the same level as the speeches. Tolstoy in his cynicism wrote:

> The menus were more varied than the speeches. The latter, without exception, always consisted of the same words in different combinations.[58]

All the speeches without exception talked of peace, no one was allowed to mention the real purpose of this new alliance - the problem of Germany. - Tolstoy stated that he had seen all this before, just before the Turkish war, when the Russian people suddenly found an undying friendship for their Slavonic brethren.

Tolstoy identified how the process works, and he predicted quite accurately how a war with Germany would eventually come about. Government ministers from both countries would get

---

[57] Ibid., 61.

[58] Ibid., 57.

together, wine and dine and talk nonsense to one another, but never mention the real business: the problem of Germany. The government functionaries would buzz about full of possibilities. The military authorities would hurry hither and thither and increase their importance. The manufacturers of weapons would become excited. The idle crowds of wealthy people would have something different and exciting to do. The press would goad itself on by publishing stirring articles. Even the Churches would get involved and the whole episode would be made to appear as God's will. And finally the peasants would follow and accept that the "enemy" must now be Germany. Tolstoy summed up the role of the peasants as the following:

> The truth is not - as in all countries is stated on all the war memorials - that he voluntarily gave his life for freedom or love for his country. The truth is that while killing others out of fear of punishment or disgrace, he unavoidably put his own life at risk.[59]

Tolstoy put little faith in well-meaning international organisations and their attempts to find a solution to the international conflicts that bring about war:

> Thus also with these false and refined scientific means of abolishing war, such as international tribunals, arbitration, and similar absurdities with which we occupy ourselves.[60]

Tolstoy was very critical of what he called: "the enlightened friends of peace" who believed that: "the misunderstandings which arise between governments will be settled by tribunals or arbitration."[61] Tolstoy believed that this opinion only supported the deceit practiced by government: "Governments do not at all desire the settlement of misunderstandings. On the contrary, if there be none they invent some."[62]

---

[59] Ibid.
[60] Ibid., 129.
[61] Ibid., 130.
[62] Ibid.

Tolstoy believed that the problem of war was not a difficult problem to solve, and only needed the deluded people - who support or acquiesce in war - to free themselves from the delusion of war. The way to free oneself from the delusion of war had, according to Tolstoy, been preached from earliest times by Christian writers such as Tertullian and Origen and can be found in their successors, the Mennonites and Quakers. But Tolstoy probably underestimated the strength of the delusion of war on men's minds.

PROPOSITION FOUR: ON HUMAN NATURE

> We must take the Sermon on the Mount to be as much a law as the theorem of Pythagoras.[63]

Tolstoy's views on human nature were changed considerably by his experiences in the poverty-stricken areas of Moscow. During his time in Moscow after he moved there in 1881 Tolstoy came face to face with the most appalling poverty. He had seen and was aware of the effects of rural poverty but the poverty he saw in Moscow was, on his own admission, beyond his belief. Tolstoy was also aware of the enormous wealth that existed in Moscow and the luxurious life followed by the gentry. Tolstoy felt guilty because he believed that the two conditions of absolute poverty and luxurious wealth were related to each other: "I could not escape the thought that these two things were connected and the one resulted from the other."[64] Tolstoy got the idea of using the census that was due to take place as a means of co-ordinating a massive campaign against the worst areas of poverty and degradation. He published an article about his philanthropic idea, appealing for help, and talked to the richest people he knew. He describes very accurately the negative response he got from every quarter, even from those who were known for their philanthropic works:

> I felt all the time in the depth of my soul that it was not the

---

[63] Tolstoy, Civil Disobedience, xv.
[64] Leo Tolstoy, *What Then Must We Do?*, trans. Aylmer Maude. (London: Green Books, 1991), 9.

> right thing, but, as often happens, reasoning and imagination stifled that voice of conscience.[65]

His actual experience with taking the census dramatically changed his views on the causes and the cures of the poverty and degradation of the inhabitants of Lyapin Free Night-Lodging-House or Rzhanov House, or any of the slum areas of Moscow. In relation to his attempt to 'save' one young person from the poverty of Moscow - he offered this young boy a chance to go to the country and be adopted by, and work with, a peasant family. Tolstoy was initially surprised when the young person in question refused to be saved:

> I did not then understand that such men can only be helped by changing their outlook on life; and to change another man's outlook one must oneself have a better one and live in accord with it; [66]

Tolstoy's analysis of human nature reached its conflictual heights in *Resurrection.* The story of *Resurrection* is based around the conflict in the mind and soul of the main character Prince Dimitri Nekhlyudov:

> Every man bears within him the germs of every human quality, and now manifests one, now another, and frequently is quite unlike himself, while still remaining the same man.[67]

Tolstoy paints his picture of Nekhlyudov as the picture of everyman:

> In Nekhlyudov, as in all of us, there were two men. One was the spiritual being...but there was also the animal man...[68]

---

[65] Ibid., 10.
[66] Ibid., 25.
[67] Tolstoy, *Resurrection*, 252-253.
[68] Ibid., 80.

Tolstoy is probably describing his own youthful experience when he describes the experience of Nekhlyudov in St. Petersburg: "at this time the animal nature prevailed completely, suppressing the spiritual man in him."[69]

Tolstoy's depiction of human nature is not a very reassuring one, particularly for those people who see themselves as "good" people and who can reassure themselves that they can identify those people who are not "good." According to Tolstoy one of the commonest and most generally accepted delusions is that every man can be qualified in some particular way - said to be kind, wicked, stupid, energetic, apathetic and so on:

> People are not like that. We may say of a man that he is more often kind than cruel, more often wise than stupid, more often energetic than apathetic or vice versa; but it could never be true to say of one man that he is kind or wise, and of another that he is wicked or stupid.[70]

Within all of Tolstoy's writings, questions of morality and ethical values play a significant part. Tolstoy's vision of morality is at its best when it is subtly interwoven into the characters of his novels. In *Resurrection* as in *War and Peace* Tolstoy paints a picture of morality which cuts through the superficiality of the characters and their own opinions of themselves. In *Resurrection*, Tolstoy attempts to redefine the concepts of "good" and "bad." He does this by developing each character and their conception of themselves within the structure of thesis, antithesis, and synthesis. In most of Tolstoy's novels this process is brought about in individuals through a baptism of fire.

PROPOSITION FIVE: THE QUESTION OF REVOLUTION

> There can be only one permanent revolution - a moral one: the regeneration of the inner man.[71]

---

[69] Ibid.
[70] Ibid., 252.
[71] Ibid.

Tolstoy believed in the possibility of revolutionary change and progress but not in the traditional social, or military sense of revolutionary change. A real revolution, Tolstoy believed, would have to challenge the fundamental ethical and moral structures of society. He believed that this revolution of morality would create more positive change than would be attained by:

> All the efforts of the revolutionists during centuries, even were complete power within their hands.[72]

The secret of this revolution lay in the possibility of people being able to see through the propaganda of their governments and of the institutions that support these government: "If people would only believe that strength is not in force but in truth,"[73] Tolstoy believed that many people in government understood where the foundations of real strength and authority in society lay, and that is why control of education, control of religion, and control of the press was so important to those in government:

> They know that strength is not in force, but in thought and in clear expression of it, and, therefore, they are more afraid of expression of independent thought than of armies;[74]

Tolstoy also believed that the real power in any society lay with those who were in a position to, or were capable of, manufacturing the moral and ethical environment, which justified their positions. Especially in an autocracy like Czarist Russia, this was the key to power and control. He believed that the greatest changes in society would be brought about by individuals refusing to accept the power structures which had been artificially created to support the authority of the rulers over the ruled:

> No feats of heroism are needed to achieve the greatest and most important changes in the existence of humanity:

---

[72] Tolstoy, *Civil Disobedience*, 116.
[73] Ibid.
[74] Ibid., 117.

> neither the armament of millions of soldiers, nor the construction of new roads and machines...[75]

Most of Tolstoy's later political writings were unmercifully critical of governments and of the organisations and interests groups that make up government. But he was also very critical of the revolutionary organisations that just wanted to replace the Czarist form of government with their own version. Tolstoy was voracious in his criticism of the functions of government. There was little or no trace in Tolstoy's writing of the tradition of government, of the people, by the people, for the people. Many of Tolstoy's contemporaries dismissed his ideas on how change could be brought about in society, even those critics who sympathised with him dismissed his political analysis:

> What is valuable in Tolstoy, to my mind, is his power of right ethical judgments, and his perception of concrete facts; his theorizings are of course worthless. It is the greatest misfortune to the human race that he has so little power of reasoning.[76]

Later experience in Russia showed that Tolstoy had as good a grasp on political reality as any of the professional revolutionaries:

CONCEPTIONS OF UNIVERSAL PEACE

In the final analysis, Tolstoy may have seen himself as a prophet crying in the wilderness. He believed himself to have found the prophet's stone, which would lead to the advancement of mankind towards God's kingdom on earth. At times he believed that the truth that he had rediscovered was older than Christianity itself:

> Once men have acknowledged Christianity, or at least the perception of human equality and respect for human

---

[75] Ibid., 115.

[76] Bertrand Russell, *The Autobiography of Bertrand Russell 1872-1914* Vol. I. (London: George Allen and Unwin), 188.

> dignity which flow from Christianity... [77]

These two concepts, the perception of human equality and the respect for human dignity, are the two central concepts of Tolstoy's philosophy. Tolstoy's perception of these concepts was shaped by what he believed were the highest principles known to man.

Tolstoy believed that, in order to get a better understanding of the world in which we live and the forces that act upon that world, there are three sources of information that we must refer to. Firstly, what he calls the collective wisdom of the greatest teachers that have gone before us. Secondly, by reference by each person to his own reason and conscience; and finally, by the opening up of each person to the feelings in their own heart, in which the highest aspirations of human nature are to be found. Any institution, any set of beliefs, any form of government that took away from the strength of these fundamental principles, was seen by Tolstoy as flawed and beyond repair.

Tolstoy accepted that legal and reasonable excuses have been made for every form of violence, but he believed that no infallible standard has ever been found by which to measure or judge the worth of these excuses. Tolstoy's critical analysis of the institution of war and his critique of the traditional moral justifications for violence are distinctly relevant to the same issues today. The doctrine of non-resistance as taught by Christ was for Tolstoy the only genuine way forward that had been clearly sanctioned. The people who said that the present day, because of our particular problems, is not suitable for the application of this doctrine; or that this doctrine of non-resistance need not be followed in all cases - these people are totally misguided:

> A being that breathes one day and vanishes the next receives one definite, indubitable law to guide him through the brief term of his life; but instead of obeying

[77] Leo Tolstoy, *Civil Disobedience*, 176.

> that law he prefers to fancy that he knows what is necessary, he decides that he and other people should temporarily abandon the indubitable law given to one and all...[78]

Tolstoy as a moralist can seem overbearing, arrogant, out of touch with reality. In the final analysis, Tolstoy bases his faith and his hope on changing the individual, the regeneration of the inner man; rather than trying for revolutionary change of the state or the social system. How far these two forces can be separated, or how far they are interrelated remains partly unanswered in Tolstoy's analysis. Tolstoy continually examined and criticised the social and economic roots of human misery. He believed that he had rediscovered the roots of violence and aggression in the soul of Man; for him, the Christian message bearing these truths had been distorted and lost over time and were only now being rediscovered. Even the people who, for cultural and historic reasons were not Christian, or the people who could not accept Christianity, these people could acknowledge: "the perception of human equality and respect for human dignity which flow from Christianity".[79] Tolstoy believed with all his heart that the problems of social injustice and the conditions of human misery were manifestations of the weaknesses inherent in human nature. For any real improvements to be made in the human condition, changes must be made in the consciousness of man. For Tolstoy, the prime human function was the progressive changing of consciousness.

[78] Ibid., 246.
[79] Ibid., 176.

6

BERTRAND RUSSELL:

THE POLITICAL FOUNDATION

The absurd assumption...that if one side is to blame, the other must be innocent

In order to support this belief in the peculiar wickedness of the enemy, a whole mythology of falsehood grows up, partly through the deliberate action of newspapers and governments, but chiefly through the inherent myth-making tendencies of strong collective emotions

All considerations of humanity and liberty were subordinated to the great game...and the patient populations, incited cynically by lies and claptrap, were driven on to the blind work of butchery

They loved democracy because they hated Germany; but they thought they hated Germany because they loved democracy

So long as hate and fear and pride are praised and encouraged, war can never become an impossibility

Bertrand Russell

JUSTICE IN WAR-TIME

Bertrand Russell stood firmly against the passions of war. His initial stand against the madness of the First World War was the foundation of his philosophy of peace. He applied his logical analysis to the First World War and found that this war failed the test of logical justifications. The First World War, according to Russell, was not rational in any scientific sense and could not be justified in any philosophical sense. Russell believed that, whoever won, "the results would be disastrous to civilisation, probably for 100 years." In 1956 Russell re-affirmed that he was unshaken in this belief:

> We owe to the first war and its aftermath Russian Communism, Italian Fascism and German Nazism. We owe to the first war the creation of a chaotic unstable world where there is every reason to fear that the Second World War was not the last.[1]

In 1916 Russell believed that he could, by the use of logic, identify certain factors that contributed towards the causes of war and the conditions for peace. He believed that wars were caused by x, y, and z factors and he set out to define these factors and their relationship with each other. In this sense Russell's objective appraisal and critical analysis of the causes and possible consequences of the war are among some of his best work. If Russell had been struck down at this stage and if he had never written another word about war or peace we would still have a reasonably clear picture of his ideas and beliefs on this subject. But Russell wrote on war and peace in every decade of the twentieth century right up to 1970. He wrote for newspapers, magazines, journals and books. He wrote in great depth and off the top of his head. Russell said that: "he never

[1] Richard A. Rempel et al., ed. *Prophecy and Dissent 1914-1916,* Vol. XIII. *The Collected Papers of Bertrand Russell.* (London: Unwin Hyman, 1988), xiii.

rewrites anything" and as Jager says: "there is evidence that he seldom rereads what he didn't re-write."[2]

Russell was never a pacifist in the traditional sense. Russell attempted to apply his mathematical logic to the institution of war. It is not surprising that his x, y, z, of 1916 were at times contradicted, rejected, redefined; and at other times changed completely. In 1916 Russell believed above all else in the power of human reason to resolve human conflict without resorting to brutish violence. He believed that it was almost suicidal for the advanced industrial nations of Europe to go to war against each other. One of the major criticisms that can be levelled against Russell at this stage was that he under-estimated the complexity of human motives that are in the balance for war or peace for violence or non-violence. Like so many other liberals Russell's logic of human nature, according to his critics, was built on a false idealism, a failure to recognise the possibility of evil.

RUSSELL'S PHILOSOPHY OF PEACE

In relation to Russell's philosophy of peace the fundamental principles were set out in his publication of *Justice In War-Time* published in 1916, and the various other articles and books published prior to and during the period of the First World War. The framework in which Russell constructed his analysis of the causes of the First World War can be seen as the foundation of his later attempts at formulating and augmenting a philosophy of peace. The ethical and philosophical basis for Russell's opposition to war and violence is clearly outlined in *Justice in War-Time* (1916). From the publication of *German Social Democracy* (1896) right up to works such as *War Crimes in Vietnam* (1967), there is no easily identifiable pattern which could be recognised simply as a philosophy of peace. What can be identified in Russell's writing is a series of questions, of doubts, of problems with the existing moral philosophy which rationalised a justification for violence and in particular for the violence of war.

---

[2] Ronald Jager, *The Development of Bertrand Russell's Philosophy*. London: Allen @Unwin, 1972. 25.

The questions and doubts that Russell raised about the utility and morality of war and the use of violence produced no simple answers. The rational arguments that Russell and his contemporaries put forward against the First World War were not as easily applied against the Second World War. Russell's ideas of how people could best live in peace and freedom changed considerably between the publication of *Roads to Freedom* (1916) and *Which Way to Peace* (1936). However it is possible to identify a number of questions which are central to understanding the developments in Russell's philosophy of peace. In this context the first set of questions which Russell set his mind too concerned the question of *Why Do Men Fight*? and related to this *Why Do Nations go to War?* Russell's arguments on these and related questions were set out clearly in *The Principles of Social Reconstruction* (1916) and *Justice In War-Time* both of which were published during the First World War.

A second set of questions which also reflects much of Russell's thinking on a philosophy of peace, concerns how peace might actually be brought about. The publication of *Which Way to Peace?* outlined many of the ideas which Russell had already developed and some of the ideas he was to reject at a later stage. A number of critics have rightly pointed out the contradictions that can be found in any analysis of Russell's ideas on peace and war issues. Some of these contradictions would seem to be very fundamental, but in a lifetime that spanned from the Boer War to the Vietnam War it would be more surprising if there were no contradictions. Russell sets his arguments initially within the traditional framework of the liberal/socialist world-view of the early part of the twentieth century. Firstly, he looks at the nature of Man and the questions that arise out of the interpretation given to that nature. Secondly, he looks at the structure of the social systems and raises questions about how these systems legitimate and perpetuate violence. Finally, he looks at the system of international relations and examines alternatives that have been proposed for the anarchy that has traditionally passed for law in international relations.

In reading *Justice in War-Time* it is easy to understand the strength of feeling against Russell by those who reluctantly supported the war. Russell's criticisms hit at the very foundations of the moral high ground and the rational justifications on which this moral high ground rested. Russell in effect was attacking the establishment who supported the war at the very foundation of that support. The government could easily play down the pacifist arguments. It could grudgingly accommodate the concept of conscientious objection, but people like Russell who disputed the very fundamental question of what was actually at stake between Britain and Germany were of much more trouble. In the early pages of: *Justice in War-Time* it is possible to see clearly where Russell was aiming his arguments. It was at the men of learning on both sides, who should have known better, that Russell aimed his sharpest criticism. There is, as Russell said:

> No reason to expect an unusual degree of humane feeling from professors, but some pride of rationality, some unwillingness to let judgments be enslaved by brutal passions, we might have hoped to find. But we should have hoped in vain.[3]

Russell is at his sharpest when he criticises his contemporaries who support the war:

> In modern times, philosophers, professors, and intellectuals generally undertake willingly to provide their respective governments with those ingenious distortions and those subtle untruths by which it is made to appear that all good is on one side and all wickedness is on the other.[4]

As well as criticising the role of professors and intellectuals Russell was also very aware of the role of the mass media in popularising the war for people generally:

---

[3] Bertrand Russell, *Justice in War-Time,* (Illinois: The Open Court, 1917), 11.
[4] Ibid., 1.

> In order to support this belief in the peculiar wickedness of the enemy, a whole mythology of falsehood grows up, partly through the deliberate action of newspapers and governments, but chiefly through the inherent myth-making tendencies of strong collective emotions.[5]

In *Justice In War-Time* Russell sets out his ideas on the causes of war and the ethical issues raised by violence. Russell identified and examined what he considered were the social and psychological causes of war. He analysed the moral and ethical arguments which lay behind the state's justification of war. Many of Russell's arguments reflect a time when it was still generally believed that science and the scientific approach would show how irrational war was as a means of resolving conflicts.

RUSSELL ON THE CAUSES OF WAR

Russell's explanation and analysis of the origins and the causes of the First World War are set out in many of the articles and pamphlets written at this time. The *Tribunal*, the fortnightly magazine of the No-Conscription Fellowship (NCF), has over fifty articles by Russell. At the same time he wrote for other publications such as the *Labour Leader, Atlantic Monthly, International Journal of Ethics* and many more. Russell's initial attitude to the war:

> Was like that of many liberals and radicals; he could not believe that anything so foolish was happening.[10]

Like many of his contemporaries he saw the origins of this war in the area of international relations. The colonial rivalry of the Great Powers and the failure of the statesmen to preserve the balance of power in Europe were seen as central to the emergence of war. Russell was particularly critical of British foreign policy of the period from 1904. The criticism of Russell by Professor Murray in his *The Foreign Policy of Sir Edward*

---

[5] Ibid., 4.
[10] Alan Ryan, *Bertrand Russell: A Political Life* (London: Penguin, 1988), 57.

Grey, 1906-1915 led to a major response by Russell under the title *The Entente Policy 1904-1915* which became the longest chapter in *Justice In War-Time.* Russell believes that Murray, like so many others who seek justification for the war, has:

> Fallen into the absurd assumption...that if one side is to blame, the other must be innocent.[7]

Russell believed this assumption had no logical foundation. He viewed this war as a lunatic enterprise in which victory for either side would be a disaster. Many of the statesmen of both sides also believed that the war would be a disaster but they felt that they were unable to prevent it no matter what they did or did not do. Where they would diametrically disagree with Russell was what alternatives there might be, and on the results of the outcome. Russell states:

> The fundamental irrational belief, on which all the others rest, is the belief that the victory of one's own side is of enormous and indubitable importance, and even of such importance as to outweigh all the evils involved in prolonging the war.[8]

Russell goes on to state that:

> This war is trivial for all its vastness, no great principle is at stake, no great human purpose is involved on either side. The supposed ideals for which it is being fought are merely part of the myth.[9]

Russell recognised that the people who supported the war and who attempted to put forward rational arguments to justify the necessity of this war had many good reasons for their beliefs. What should any country do if threatened by an invasion from another? What if one country is threatened with economic blackmail by another? Many people believed that the British

---

[7] Russell, *Justice,* 120.
[8] Ibid., 11.
[9] Ibid., 13.

way of life was threatened by German ambitions, and more importantly that British and German interests were incompatible. Some people believed that the war was a colossal struggle between good and evil, in the case of British perception, the good being the British interests and the evil being the German intentions.

Russell accepted that many of these arguments in favour of supporting the war were not easily answered. These are the questions that arise whenever the arguments for and against war are debated. However, Russell felt that many of these arguments were standard arguments that could be used to support any and every war, and these particular arguments would not stand up to rational analysis.

> Russell was able to see through many of these arguments and was annoyed when colleagues whom he felt should have known better were not. Side by side, in the pages of Scientia, are to be read articles by learned men, all betraying shamelessly their national bias, all as incapable of justice as any cheap newspapers, all as full of special pleading and garbled history.[10]

Russell's war typology was very basic and in many ways very problematic at this stage. For the purposes of classification he identified four different kinds of war, (1) Wars of Colonisation; (2) Wars of Principle; (3) Wars of Self Defence; (4) Wars of Prestige. Russell attempts to analyse each of these war-types as objectively and as scientifically as possible. But the results of this analysis are not very illuminating. Russell concludes that wars of type one and two can fairly often be justified, and he gives a number of examples which do not seem to have been thought out very well. The general basis of his justification is that: "if we are to judge by result, we cannot regret that such wars have taken place."[15] Russell was at this time basing his arguments within a very Eurocentric world-view. Under this view European civilisation and the benefits of that civilisation

---

[10] Ibid., 1.
[15] Ibid., 27.

could be seen as a rational justification of the wars of colonisation.

THE GOD OF REASON

The Principles of Social Reconstruction was written as a series of lectures during 1915 and first published in 1916. In this series of lectures Russell outlines a philosophy of politics on which he bases his analysis of the causes of war. He had hoped to spend some time re-writing these lectures before publishing, but under pressure of time was unable to carry out much editing. He sets out in the initial chapter "The Principle of Growth" to outline the basis of his own philosophy of politics. Russell believed that he was able to stand outside the cycle of beliefs and passions which make war seem necessary[12]. He believed that by identifying a fundamental flaw in the basis of the philosophy of politics, he would be able to contribute to a more rational analysis of the self-destruction that was being carried out by supposedly rational men with rational minds.

> My aim is to suggest a philosophy of politics based upon the belief that impulse has more effect than conscious purpose in moulding men's lives.[13]

Russell states his belief that all human activity springs from two sources, impulse and desire.[14] He believed that almost all, political philosophy, has traditionally been based on the belief that reason as manifested in "desire" is the source of all human actions. In what he calls ordinary human nature, Russell put forward the argument that in the more basic instinctive part of our nature "impulse" is far stronger than "desire" as a driving force for our actions. Those who believe that man is a rational animal, driven by rational desires have greatly underestimated the influence of instinctive impulses in influencing our course of action. Russell believes that what in many cases is put forward

---

[12] Bertrand Russell, *Principles of Social Reconstruction* (London: George Allen and Unwin, 1916), 9.
[13] Ibid., Preface.
[14] Ibid., 10.

as "reason," is "instinct" dressed up as reason to suit the particular situations that we find ourselves in.

> Whole philosophies, whole systems of ethical valuation, spring up in this way; they are the embodiment of a kind of thought which is subservient to impulse, which aim at providing a quasi-rational ground for the indulgence of impulse.[15]

It is within this framework that Russell analyses the rational arguments that were being put forward to support the First World War which, he said, were not rational in any truly objective sense. Even if they were rational, Russell believes that reason itself is not sufficiently strong to control the passions.

> Only passion can control passion, and only a contrary impulse or desire can check impulse. Reason, as it is preached by traditional moralists, is too negative, too little living, to make a good life. It is not by reason alone that wars can be prevented, but by a positive life of impulses and passions antagonistic to those that lead to war. It is the life of impulse that needs to be changed, not only the life of conscious thought.[16]

Russell accepts the sincerity of the people who support the war. To a certain extent he accepts that the "logic" and "reason" that are being used to justify the war have some firm basis in rational argument. But Russell believed that the conclusions drawn from the rational arguments had been turned on their heads.

> The impulse of resistance to Germany made them value whatever was endangered by the German attack. They loved democracy because they hated Germany; but they thought they hated Germany because they loved democracy.[17]

---

[15] Ibid., 13.
[16] Ibid., 11.
[17] Ibid., 16.

He felt that many of the people in Britain and France who now talked so much about saving democracy were the very people who before the war would do anything to prevent the extension of democracy in any form. When the war was over and when the German threat was dealt with these people would soon lose their love for democracy.
Russell believed that the war was generally being justified on two basic "impulses," the impulse to aggression and the impulse of resistance to aggression; what annoyed him most was that these impulses were being masqueraded as reason.

> The war has grown, in the main, out of the life of impulse, not out of reason or desire. There is an impulse of aggression, and an impulse of resistance to aggression. Either may, on occasion, be in accordance with reason, but both are operative in many cases in which they are quite contrary to reason.[18]

In relation to the ongoing war Russell identified two main causes that reflected the main opposing views. The view held by the majority of British people and the nearest to the official view was that: "the main cause of the present war could be traced in principle to the wickedness of the Germans."[19] This belief, according to Russell, was based: "on a firm conviction of the superior excellence of one's own group."[20] Such a belief is seen as a fundamental part of the traditional world-view of most national groups. This, according to Russell, justifies the feeling that: "only the good and evil of one's own group is of real importance."[21] Only a small minority of people saw the war from an alternative perspective. From this point of view the war had been caused by a catalogue of mistakes made by diplomats, politicians and generals. The war was seen as a potential disaster for everyone involved. If the political will was found these mistakes could be undone and the catastrophe averted.

---

[18] Ibid., 15-16.
[19] Ibid., 10.
[20] Ibid., 16.
[21] Ibid.

THE ETHICS OF WAR

The question of whether war can ever be justified was one of the central questions raised by Russell in the debate on the ethics of war. Russell admitted at the very start of the debate that: "I cannot believe that war under all circumstances is a crime."[22] More importantly for our debate was the logic used by Russell in constructing his arguments on the ethics of war. Russell believed that the:

> Opinions on such a subject as war are the outcome of feeling rather than thought. The fundamental facts in this as in all ethical questions are feelings; all that thought can do is to clarify and harmonise the expression of those feelings.[23]

The rational justifications given by those who supported the First World War were based in part on what Russell called the principle of "judicial justification." A particular country was seen to break a certain treaty, or proceed in a fashion that was seen to be unfriendly towards the interests of another country. The rationale as Russell saw it was that a Great Power was considered unscrupulous if it went to war without a judicial justification. There were some exceptions to this rule; a Great Power did not consider it needed justifications when it was dealing with colonial interests or small countries who had no other Great Power backing.

Russell attempted to demolish the judicial justification arguments by saying that this type of justification was not appropriate for the international relations of states. Russell believed that judicial justification was one of the foundations of the rule of law, where the rule of law existed, that is, within a civilised state. But in the international arena no such state existed. There was a body of conventions called "international law," but the conventions and treaties that made up this international law were quite different in character from the rules

---

[22] Russell, *Justice,* 19.
[23] Ibid.

that made up the law within a state. Russell considered that: "the real justification for any war must be in the balance of good which it is to bring to mankind."[24], and not just in its paper justification. In order to obtain some sense of this balance of good, Russell outlines what he believes are the most obvious evils associated with war. Even assuming, as Russell does, "the utmost possible humanity in the conduct of military operations,"[25] the evils associated with the First World War both directly and indirectly, far outweigh the supposed benefits.

To begin with, Russell identifies the evils associated with military operations, especially the killing of large numbers of young men who are usually the most courageous and physically fit of their generation. Apart from those killed, before they can make any real contribution to the welfare of their countries, there are the large numbers of young people who are physically maimed. Most significantly of those that survive Russell believed that: "many will be brutalised and morally degraded by the fierce business of killing,"[26] and also that the culture of society will be brutalized and degraded by war. Russell believed that the evils produced by war outside of the direct military operations were even more serious because they were far more widespread and would become deeply entrenched in all aspects of society. One example that he gives is related to the sympathy shown to the problems of Belgium. The misfortunes of Belgium were seen by many in England as a reason in favour of war. Russell felt that this belief was a "tragic delusion" and that the opposite was the truth. "Our sympathy with Belgium should make us hate war rather than Germany."[27]
War and the fear of war, according to Russell had a double effect in retarding social progress. The economic damage inflicted by war was far greater than was generally realised or admitted. Some people were in a position to gain economically from war, but most people who were concerned with the basic

---

[24] Ibid., 22.
[25] Ibid., 24.
[26] Ibid., 23.
[27] Ibid., 24.

economic necessities would lose out. Throughout the Napoleonic wars, Russell believed that:

> While the land owners of England continually increased their rent-rolls, the mass of the wage-earning population sank into greater and greater destitution.[28]

It was only afterwards, according to Russell, during the long period of peace that the economic damage done to so many people could slowly be rectified.
Russell, as a socialist, believed that war was used as a means of distracting mens' minds from the claims of social justice:

> Everywhere the well-to-do, and the political parties which represent their interests, have been the chief agents in stirring up international hatred and in persuading the working man that his real enemy is the foreigner.[29]

For Russell, as the utilitarian liberal, brought up by his grandmother with a deep awareness of fundamental Christian morality; war was seen as one of the great evils that afflict mankind:

> But of all the evils of war the greatest is the really spiritual evil: the hatred, the injustice, the repudiation of truth, the artificial conflict.[30]

THE ATTRACTIONS OF WAR

In one of the early chapters in *Justice in War-Time* Russell addresses the question *Why Nations Love War*, His object was to:

> Analyse and try to understand this widespread enjoyment of war - a phenomenon, as I think of the very greatest

---

[28] Ibid., 25.
[29] Ibid.
[30] Ibid.

> importance[31]

Russell had the feeling that among even those who objected to the war there was an underlying feeling of enjoyment and excitement at the prospects of the forthcoming struggle. Russell was aware of a general feeling that with the outbreak of war people felt more alive, happier and suffered less from minor complaints than in times of peace. He criticised people like H. G. Wells who claimed that this war was a "war to end war," Russell felt that this argument was being used as a justification for the war by people who had traditionally seen themselves as being against war. Russell claims that, in the days preceding the outbreak of war, every nation in Europe went:

> Through a certain instinctive development as definite as falling in love, though much more complex.[32]

It had been expected by many socialists and liberals that people who were going to suffer most from the war would put pressure on their various governments to look for diplomatic solutions. But as Russell pointed out, that what in fact occurred:

> Was exactly the opposite: every government became increasingly popular as war drew nearer.[33]

The feeling for war had grown to such an extent that if a diplomatic solution had been found at the last moment a number of governments would probably have fallen.

The First World War was seen both by those who experienced it and by later historians to have some unique characteristics. David Thomson, writing in the late 1950s, said that:

> This was the first general conflict between the highly organised states of the twentieth century, able to command the energies of all their citizens, to mobilise the productive capacities of modern industries...New resources of

---

[31] Ibid., 58.
[32] Ibid., 59.
[33] Ibid.

> economic and even psychological warfare were tapped; for, since it was the first war of the masses, industrial production and civilian morale became of great importance.[34]

Russell tried objectively to analyse the forces that were pushing people towards a desire for war. He centred his argument around the instinctive desire of man as an animal:

> To co-operate with members of his own herd and to oppose members of other herds...an instinctive dislike of men who are different, who are felt as foreign...and with this…an impulse to co-operate for defence and attack.[35]

Round this basic primitive feeling Russell identified a number of other human desires which attracted people to war. The desire for excitement, the desire for triumph and honour, the need for heroism and sacrifice. These are very important emotions and desires, the importance of which Russell himself felt that he could not fully comprehend. Besides these motives Russell looked at what he termed as an almost religious passionate devotion to the State or the ideal of the State. This passionate devotion gives rise to a desire for self-sacrifice, an impulse for heroism that can be identified in so much of European culture and literature.

At the beginning of the century and right up to the early part of the First World War there was a dominant view that war promoted moral qualities in the young men who fought in them. War, according to this view, promoted self-sacrifice, heroism and the more admirable qualities of patriotism. War was seen as a character forming experience. As the war dragged on and the number of young men being killed grew out of all proportion, this argument was heard less and less. Russell led the attack from an early stage on these perceptions:

> Our newspapers, parsons, and professors prate of the

[34] David Thomson, *Europe Since Napoleon* (London: Pelican, 1986), 547.
[35] Russell, *Justice,* 59.

> ennobling influence of war.[36]

Russell conceded that some of these desires and emotions were to be seen as the noblest of motives. The willingness to sacrifice oneself for the nation could be seen as essentially a religious experience on the same level as martyrdom.
Russell understood the strength of the emotions that were pulling people towards war, and the relative weakness of the alternatives that might pull people towards peace. In the case of nationalism, and in particular in the form of militaristic nationalism that was dominant at this time, the antidote as seen by Russell was the development of internationalism. But Russell knew that the strength of emotions and feelings that could be aroused by nationalism were far stronger than those that could be aroused by some form of internationalism. He believed that major changes in the standard of values of nationalism would be the key to reducing the attractiveness of war to the individual. He did not believe that this was a totally Utopian idea:

> The day may come when we shall be as proud of Shakespeare as of Nelson[37]

Russell looks at the possible substitutes that would replace some of the attractions of armed national conflict. He puts most of his faith in the possibility of changes in the standard of cultural values which nations set themselves. The highest values which motivate patriotism do not necessarily have to involve armed conflict between nations. Civilised nations, according to Russell, had inherited standards from a barbarous past, which must now be put aside in the interests of all. This could be done through a process of popular education and a gradual change in the standard of values which are accepted as civilised.

---

[36] Russell, *Justice*, 107.
[37] Ibid., 63.

REFLECTIONS ON VIOLENCE: THE NATURE OF MAN

One of the main contemporary critics of Russell's attempt to construct a philosophy of peace which would undermine the rational justifications for the First World War, was T. E. Hulme. Hulme, writing a number of articles in the *Cambridge Magazine* early in 1916, accused Russell of "faded Rousseauism" and he believed that Russell had an entirely false concept of the nature of man. In this debate on the nature of man Hulme was heavily influenced by Sorel's: *Reflections on Violence*. Hulme believed that Russell, like other Liberals, was chronically deluded by the belief that man was naturally good and would develop into a free and rational creature if not manipulated by other forces. The debate concerning the nature of Man is one of the central questions in any philosophical debate about the causes of war. The framework in which Russell attempted to develop his analysis was certainly influenced by the ideas of Rousseau, among others; and the belief that man is naturally good, and if left to develop without manipulation, would be a free and rational creature.

But Russell examined both sides of the contemporary debate which reflected the two opposing views of human nature. On the one hand, the idea that man is naturally pacific and co-operative and on the other that man is naturally warlike and aggressive. Russell rejected such a simple division and he adopted the position taken by others in the anti-war movement. He accepted the belief that mankind has some natural tendency to fight but that this tendency might remain completely latent unless aroused by deliberate manipulation. Russell accepted the contemporary Marxist interpretation that this manipulation is brought about directly as a result of the interests of capitalism. Not least among these capitalist "warmongers" were the arms manufacturers who would turn a tidy profit in the build-up of an arms race between the Great Powers or in the event of a little war breaking out here or there. The Marxist interpretation also suggested that the capitalists who manufactured the weapons were also able to control and manipulate the media, and this was one of the points that Russell picks up on a number of occasions. Russell believed more strongly than many of his contemporaries that an important element in the causes of war was the unsatisfactory nature of modern industrial society.

PACIFISM

Most pacifists believed that the main causes of the war could be traced to the diplomatic tangles that were caused by the over-ambitious diplomacy of the governments involved, including the British government. Russell sets out this argument in some detail in *The Entente Policy 1904-1915:*

> If our foreign policy in recent years had been conducted with more courage, more openness, and more idealism, there is a likelihood that the present European war would never had occurred.[38]

The central thrust of Russell's argument in this case was to challenge what he believed was the "absurd assumption" that if one side is to blame then the other side must be innocent. This sort of confused logic was, to Russell, a recipe for future disasters:

> Germany's guilt is no proof of our innocence. And if we remain to the end wrapped in self-righteousness, impervious to facts which are not wholly creditable to us, we shall, in the years after the war, merely repeat the errors of the past, and find ourselves, in the end, involved in other wars as terrible and destructive as the one which we are now waging.[39]

It is possible, given this belief, to understand why Russell was so passionately against the First World War. The people like Russell who stood firmly against supporting the war were accused of all sorts of villainy. Their motives were seen by many as treachery and their reasoning was dismissed as

[38] Ibid., 118.
[39] Ibid.

emotional and immature. Russell felt that he had to defend his own position and to defend the position of people who thought like him. He never wavered in his belief that there was no moral justification for the war, that the lives being lost were being lost in vain, and more importantly that results of this war would create future wars.

RUSSELL ON NON-RESISTANCE

In *Justice In War-Time* Russell examines the case for and against non-resistance as a possible alternative to the use of violence. The term "non-resistance" is the term used by Russell in the sense of an alternative to the use of military force, as a means of defending the interests of any particular country. He started this analysis by looking at the tradition which totally rejects the use of force; represented by the small religious movements such as the Quakers and by individuals such as Tolstoy. This tradition rejects the so-called 'right to self-defence' and with it the whole philosophy of the 'just war' theory. Russell attempted to build a bridge between the tradition which totally rejects the use of any sort of force and what he would see as a more moderate stance. Russell accepted that the 'right to self-defence' as an argument to justify the use of force has been used almost without exception by every side in every war. He attempted to put some realistic meaning into the argument for self-defence as a justification for the use of force:

> I think the use of force is justifiable when it is ordered in accordance with law by a neutral authority, in the general interest and not primarily in the interest of one of the parties to the quarrel [40]

Russell outlines an interesting scenario in relation to the possible use of organised non-resistance. He gives as his example the possibility of England being overrun by Germany, and he goes into some detail of what might happen in such a situation. Some of the examples he gives relates to different groups in society

---

[40] Ibid., 39.

refusing to co-operate with any imposed administration. The civil servants, the transport workers, the teachers, etc., would all refuse to carry out any instructions from the new administration. More recent studies by Gene Sharp,[41] among others, have shown that this is almost exactly what happened in Norway during the German occupation of the Second World War. In Norway, a minority of Norwegians fully co-operated with the Germans and formed the Quisling government, but even so, non-cooperation was widely practiced by the majority of Norwegians. One of the best examples of this was set by the teachers in Norway who refused to co-operate with the new administration. Over one thousand teachers were arrested and sent to camps, even so the teachers held firm and the Quisling government withdrew their attempt at control and released the teachers within a few months. There were two other considerations which Russell addressed in relation to German military domination. Firstly, German military domination would rob England of its empire; and secondly, Germany could use military might to impose economic blackmail on England and other countries. In the first question Russell approaches the argument from a different perspective when he says:

> They could take away those parts of our Empire which we hold by force, and this would be a blow to our pride; the oppression of subject races is one of the chief sources of patriotic satisfaction, and one of the chief things for which Germany envies us.[42]

Many of the arguments put forward by Russell could be seen as academic arguments about the use of reason, and influence of passions on mens' motives. But again and again Russell brings the debate around to criticism of the war and those who have been responsible for creating the conditions which have led to the war. The Germans, Russell said:

> Cherish a desire to own African swamps, of which we

---

[41] Gene Sharp, *The Politics Of Nonviolent Action,* 3 vols., (Boston: Porter Sargent, 1973).
[42] Russell, *Justice*, 48.

> have a superfluity. No one in England benefits by the possession of them, except a few financial magnates, mostly of foreign origin. If we were reasonable, we should regard the German desire as a curious whim, which we might gratify without any real national loss. Instead of that, we regard the German desire as a crime, and our resistance to it as a virtue.[43]

These arguments did not go down very well with the conservatives who believed so much in the pre-ordained role of the British Empire. It would seem to Russell and to others, in the contemporary peace movement, that many of the things that the British diplomats were accusing the Germans of, were exactly things that the British themselves were guilty of.

IS A PERMANENT PEACE POSSIBLE?

In an article which was published in the *Atlantic Monthly* (March 1915) entitled *Is a Permanent Peace Possible"* Russell criticises the fallacies associated with the "great game" of diplomatic manoeuvering which he believed had led directly to the First World War. His criticisms of the Great Power politics are sometimes not very convincing but he does identify many of the absurdities of the game as it developed from the Anglo-French *entente* of 1904:

> All considerations of humanity and liberty were subordinated to the great game...and the patient populations, incited cynically by lies and claptrap, were driven on to the blind work of butchery.[44]

Russell believed that the diplomatic manoeuvres are so complicated and so full of treachery that a mere peace treaty will only bring about a short stoppage in the war until it starts again.

At this stage Russell puts forward three steps which he feels must be taken simultaneously with a peace treaty for any chance

[43] Ibid., 53.
[44] Ibid., 82.

of a lasting peace. These ideas were not entirely novel and had already been debated by peace societies and individuals involved in the various peace movements. In: *Which Way to Peace?* Russell develops and expands some of these ideas. The first of these steps is that the conditions for peace must be established which go far beyond the signing of a peace treaty. Secondly, that some better machinery capable of resolving international disputes must be established. Thirdly, a more sane public opinion that is not so easily led by jingoism, would need to be established throughout Europe from an early stage of the war Russell was very sceptical about the type of peace conference that might emerge after the conflict. Russell believed that any peace conference would have to be judged on the following principles:

> That no nation should make such great gains as to feel that it was worth while going to war, and that none should suffer such humiliating losses as to be impelled to revenge.[45]

When Russell wrote this he was thinking of the settlement of 1870, the basic faults of which were to be repeated in reverse after 1918. In 1870 the Germans were encouraged by the success of their militarism, the French were to be humiliated by their military failure and sought another chance for their militarism to prove itself. Russell believed that:

> The only men who will desire to prolong the present system are statesmen, sensational journalists, and armament makers - the men who profit by slaughter, either in credit or in cash, without running any risk of being slaughtered themselves.[46]

Russell knew that these were the very people who would control the peace conferences that were sure to come at the end of the war. In order to get around this he hoped that the peace conferences would be held in the United States and that

---

[45] Ibid., 92.
[46] Ibid., 93.

President Wilson would have a major part in any settlement. Russell accepted that whatever form of International Council was set up after the war, the task of preventing future wars would be very complicated. Would the council itself have the capability of armed intervention to enforce its mandate? If it did have this ability would it just succeed in creating more wars? Russell felt initially that in the settling of international disputes moral authority would be more important than the threat of military intervention.

The third step that Russell felt was essential in bringing about the conditions which might make peace possible, related to the question of public opinion. In the last resort, Russell believed that: "peace can only be preserved if public opinion desires peace in most of the great nations."[47] Russell felt that recent experience had shown that public opinion could be easily manipulated by a resort to national jingoism. Russell wished that in the period immediately after the war there would be a natural anti-war reaction, and this would be the time to educate public opinion against war. The first thing that public opinion should be made aware of is that modern warfare between the industrialised countries cannot secure the type of national advantages that were traditionally associated with warfare.
Russell believed that it was vitally important to change the perception of two very basic concepts, "glory" and "patriotism." Such a change in perception would have to begin in the classrooms with school history textbooks. This fundamental change in the perception of such ideas as "glory" and "patriotism" would have to take place not only in the schools but also in the press and among politicians:

> So long as hate and fear and pride are praised and encouraged, war can never become an impossibility.[48]

RUSSELL'S CONTRIBUTION TO THE PHILOSOPHY OF PEACE

---

[47] Ibid., 98.
[48] Ibid., 100.

The Philosophy of Bertrand Russell published as volume V in the Library of Living Philosophers contains articles from over twenty different contributors. These articles concentrate on various aspects of Russell's philosophy. There are papers on Russell's philosophy of religion, his philosophy of history, his philosophy of education, his political and economic philosophy and many other aspects of his ideas and principles. Bertrand Russell said, on reading these essays, that his greatest surprise was that of the twenty one contributions, over half of their authors had not understood him.[49] It is surprising, given all his writings and commitment to the issues of war and peace, that his philosophy of peace was not identified at this stage as worthy of a separate study. Aspects of Russell's philosophy of peace are certainly contained in a number of the papers in this anthology, but they have to be fished out from many different areas. In the final analysis Bertrand Russell did not produce a study of peace that would rank alongside such works as: *Principia Mathematica (Principle of Mathematics).* Russell has left no *Magnum Opus (Major Work)* on peace but by his own definition he addressed the peace issue as one of the fundamental philosophical issues. He summed up his own approach to the study of philosophy in the following terms:

> The business of philosophy, as I conceive it, is essentially that of logical analysis, followed by logical synthesis...the most important part of (philosophy) consists in criticizing and clarifying notions which are apt to be regarded as fundamental and accepted uncritically[50]

One good description of the problems involved in understanding the developments in Russell's philosophy is given by Jager (1972):

> Under the microscope Russell's philosophy is technical, piecemeal, frequently cross-purposed. In the telescope it is a continuous zigzag movement, a veritable armada of

---

[49] Paul Arthur Schilpp, ed. *The Philosophy of Bertrand Russell* (Illinois: Open Court,1944; revised edition, 1971), xiii.

[50] Bertrand Russell, *Logic And Knowledge* ed. Robert C. Marsh. (London: George Allen and Unwin, 1956), 34.

> ideas; it tacks into contrary winds, it lists with a ballast of undiscarded half-forgotten doctrines.[51]

Russell's family background, his educational experience and the social environment into which he was born and raised, have all helped in various ways to shape his world-view. Russell's family was firmly part of the British upper class aristocratic tradition, but the family also had strong radical and liberal beliefs. The fact that the great liberal economist John Stuart Mill was chosen by Russell's parents to be his godfather, gives some indication of where their political sympathies lay. Partly because of his family background, but also because of his own intellectual ability, Russell became part of quite an exceptional circle of men during his student days in Cambridge. As a young man, and through his contacts with Lady Ottoline Morrell he became part, but was very much on the fringe, of the Bloomsbury group. Before the build-up to the First World War few of his colleagues or friends could be considered to be pacifists; but there was a general belief among the Cambridge and Bloomsbury sets that war between the industrialised nations was a thing of the past. It would seem inconceivable to many of them that "civilised man would again take arms against civilised man."[52]

From the broad political spectrum Russell's beliefs were set firmly within the liberal tradition. see table: 6:1

Table 6:1
LIBERAL PRINCIPLES FOR PROMOTING PEACE

1. A fair distribution of economic and political power

2. A belief in negotiation rather than force

3. A belief in the rule of law based on justice

---

[51] Ronald Jager, *The Development of Bertrand Russell's Philosophy* (London: George Allen and Unwin, 1972).
[52] Jo Vellacott, *Bertrand Russell and the Pacifists in the First World War* (Brighton: Harvester Press, 1980), 1.

These principles underlined by the power of reason:

1. To promote progress

2. To resolve conflict

3. To develop tolerance

Within that tradition he was drawn very much to the left wing of the great liberal beliefs. The failure of Liberal governments to deliver the expected reforms did not weaken his beliefs in liberal principles. Russell above all else believed in the power of reason to bring about progress, to resolve conflict and to develop toleration. In writing his autobiography Russell summed up his beliefs:

> Three passions have governed my life, the longing for love, the search for knowledge, and the unbearable pity for the suffering of mankind.[53]

Russell's privileged educational background and his early knowledge of utilitarianism, liberalism and socialism were to have important influences on the developments of his ideas on war and violence. But the war that began between the Great Powers in 1914 was to have the most significant influence on the developments of Russell's ideas. The War of 1914-1918 changed everything for me...I changed my whole conception of human nature."[54]

---

[53] Bertrand Russell, *The Autobiography of Bertrand Russell 1872-1914 Vol. 1.* (London: George Allen and Unwin, 1967), Introduction.
[54] Christopher Farley and David Hodgson, *The Life Of Bertrand Russell in Pictures and His Own Words* (Nottingham: Spokesman, 1972), 39.

7

MAHATMA GANDHI: THE SPIRITUAL FOUNDATION

I have nothing new to teach the world. Truth and non-violence are as old as the hills

Non-violence is the greatest force at the disposal of mankind. It is mightier than the mightiest weapon of destruction devised by the ingenuity of man

We are constantly being astonished these days at the amazing discoveries in the field of violence. But I maintain that far more undreamt of and seemingly impossible discoveries will be made in the field of non-violence

The method of violence gives no greater guarantee than that of non-violence. Millions sacrifice themselves in war without any guarantee that the world will be better as a result or even that the enemy will be defeated

I have been practicing with scientific precision non-violence and its possibilities for an unbroken period of over 50 years. I have applied it in every walk of life domestic, institutional, economic and political. I know of no single case in which it has failed

Mahatma Gandhi

GANDHI'S PHILOSOPHY

The name of Mahatma Gandhi will be forever associated with the concept of non-violence. However, Gandhi himself believed that the concept of non-violence that he identified and promoted was in many ways completely misunderstood. This misunderstanding was not just a matter of the terms used in English, although the term non-violence was seen by Gandhi to be very misleading. *Ahimsa* was, to Gandhi, a fundamental law of nature. If it was not, then he believed that the human race would have self-destructed at a very early stage. Gandhi believed with all his soul that:

> Non-violence is the greatest force at the disposal of mankind. It is mightier than the mightiest weapon of destruction devised by the ingenuity of man.[1]

He looked forward to significant developments in the science of *ahimsa:*

> We are constantly being astonished these days at the amazing discoveries in the field of violence. But I maintain that far more undreamt of and seemingly impossible discoveries will be made in the field of non-violence.[2]

Gandhi believed that there could be identified in historical terms a progressive *ahimsa* and a diminishing *himsa*. He believed that:

> Man as animal is violent, but as Spirit is non-violent. The moment he awakes to the Spirit within he cannot remain violent.[3]

---

[1] Kripalani, 350.
[2] M. K. Gandhi, *All Men are Brothers* Compiled and edited by Krishna Kripalani. (Ahmedabad: Navajivan Trust, 1960), 114.
[3] Ibid., 112.

J.B. Kripalani, in his attempt to produce an integral approach to Gandhian thought, has made a number of important observations. In western culture there is a tradition that authors, philosophers and scientists claim originality for themselves and believe themselves to be the first in the field of discovery of a particular truth. Contrary to this J. B. Kripalani states that:

> The great men of India have rarely claimed originality for themselves.... Every thought and institution according to them was *puratana* and *sanatana*, old and eternal.[4]

In this sense:

> The Indian genius has been pre-eminently constructive. It does not reject; it builds without destroying. Destruction is left to the corroding action of Time, which eliminates the worn-out, the useless and pernicious.[5]

Any attempt to understand Gandhi's philosophy of peace must be aware of, and appreciate, the uniqueness of this Indian cultural tradition.

In the scientific world-view, theories must be formulated in terms of cause and effect, and the effect must inevitably flow from the cause. Gandhi did not follow this method of proving his propositions. For Gandhi, in human affairs, the relationship between cause and effect was not as rational or as scientific as many people hoped:

> The Indian effort has always been to resolve apparent contradictions through a dialectical process of its own. This does not require destructive revolutions to eliminate the thesis and the antithesis and establish on their destruction a temporary and unstable synthesis.[6]

---

[4] J. B. Kripalani, *Gandhi His Life and Thought* (New Delhi: Publications Division, Ministry of Information and Broadcasting, Government of India 1970; reprint, 1991), 321.

[5] Ibid., 322.

[6] Ibid., 317.

Gandhi was pre-eminently a man of action, not an intellectual in the modern academic sense of the term. The books and articles written by Gandhi were not written in a philosophical attempt to rationalise a system of beliefs. Gandhi did not attempt to produce a rationally justified and logically argued philosophy of non-violence. Gandhi rarely quotes authorities and he made no systematic study of the subjects he dealt with. Gandhi believed that philosophies and creeds have a tendency over time to become rigid, fixed and formal, and to lose most of their meaning. One of the problems in attempting to understand Gandhi's philosophy of peace is that

> The trends in his thinking on the many subjects he discussed are scattered throughout his writings...His ideas need to be systematised, co-ordinated and correlated.[7]

Gandhi himself never attempted a systematisation of his thoughts. He set out to establish to his own satisfaction basic principles and values which can be used as a guide to action. This is not very satisfying for an age limited by science and rationality. Gandhi's philosophy of peace developed in that frontier land where rational thought, with its roots in scientific principles, challenged the very foundations of religious beliefs and the moral authority built upon them.

Gandhi accepted that the scientific approach challenged and undermined the theological approach wherever the two clashed. For Gandhi the dismantling of the oppressive domination of organised religion was a liberating factor. The concept of God was challenged but also liberated by the scientific revolution. The basic principles of the moral order would have to be re-defined in this context, and this is where Gandhi made his major contribution. Gandhi was not the only person to attempt to re-define man's role in the world in the light of progressive scientific knowledge. "Economic Man" and "Rational Man" were invented as possible working models. Gandhi believed that: "Moral Man" was the essential framework that shaped the very foundations of the other models.

---

[7] Ibid., 316.

One of the difficulties to understanding Gandhi is that:

> He cannot be neatly pigeon-holed into any one of the convenient categories into which we divide people and ideas to make them more understandable; or into any of the numerous cultural traditions of thought and action which impose a quiltwork pattern on humanity.[8]

Gandhi did not write a *Das Capital* of non-violence, in the traditional sense of a systematic thesis setting forth his views on the world. He believed himself to be engaged in experiments out of which a blueprint for a philosophy of non-violence might be established.

> If Gandhi had sat down to write a comprehensive treatise on his unique doctrine - Truth and *Satyagraha* - the product would have been a valuable addition to our libraries, but no more.[9]

But Gandhi's life experience was the experiment. Gandhi was constantly growing and changing in his thought and ideas and in his outlook on the world. Gandhi's experiments were set within a life of active politics combined with a life of never-ending contemplation. In relation to the concept of peace and non-violence in various cultural traditions, Gandhi attempted to bring about a synthesis of these traditions and to identify a guiding concept for dynamic social change.

The key to Gandhi's understanding was his belief in the power of change from within each individual. Gandhi sought to understand how the individual could be awakened to change and how this change could be brought about in the best interests of the individual and society. The foundation of Gandhi's philosophy is his fundamental belief in the spiritual nature of man. The fundamental concepts of *satya* and *ahimsa*, i.e. truth and non-violence, are to be found in the major religious and philosophical traditions of mankind. Gandhi's unique

---

[8] Manmohan, Choudhuri, *Exploring Gandhi* (New Delhi: The Gandhi Peace Foundation, 1989), 1.

[9] Malcolm S. Adiseshiah in Choudhuri, xii.

contribution was the way he fused these concepts both in theory and in practice, and his impassioned belief that in every area of human experience *ahimsa* was a far greater force than *himsa*. In personal, social or political experience *ahimsa* has a greater and deeper impact than the use of violence. For Gandhi believed that the use of *ahimsa* tapped into the immortal soul-force of the universe. Louis Fisher who spent some time with Gandhi and wrote a biography of Gandhi: *The Life of Mahatma Gandhi*[10] summed up much of Gandhi's contribution to the future in one statement:

> In the evolution of civilization, if it is to survive, all men cannot fail eventually to adopt Gandhi's belief that the process of the mass application of force to resolve contentious issues is fundamentally not only wrong, but contains within itself the germs of self -destruction.

INFLUENCES ON GANDHI'S THINKING

The major sources of influence on the development of Gandhi's philosophy of peace can be divided into at least four distinct areas of importance. According to Gandhi's own autobiography each of these areas had a distinct influence on his character and on the development of the principles on which he based his beliefs and philosophy. Firstly, there was the cultural and religious experience that Gandhi received from his background in India and from the fabric of the society in which the family lived. The second major source of ideas was the strength of the religious beliefs held by his own family, particularly his mother, which Gandhi became aware of and sensitive to from an early age. These experiences helped to shape his very open approach to different religious beliefs and his very broad definition of religion. The third area which can be identified separately is the books and philosophers which Gandhi read and studied. Fourthly, and probably the most important, was the way Gandhi used his own personal life-experiences to interpret and to put into practice the wisdom and understandings he found in these

---

[10] Louis Fisher. *The Life of Mahatma Gandhi*. London. Grafton Books. 1988

various sources. His experiments in Truth were guided and directed from his various readings and meditations, and also from the experience gained from his religious and cultural influences.

According to Duncan "most of (Gandhi's) early influences had been Western in origin."[11] But this must be qualified in that the most important influences on Gandhi's early life were his family and the strong beliefs that made up the religious and social culture in which his family lived. Gandhi himself identified in his autobiography and other writings the philosophers and the ideas that had a great influence on him. Some of the most important of these could be called western in origin. Gandhi was strongly influenced by writings from Socrates to Thoreau and from Tolstoy to Ruskin. Gandhi identified in particular with Henry David Thoreau and his essay on *Civil Disobedience;* John Ruskin in the ideas set forward in *Unto This Last* and Leo Tolstoy, particularly in the principles and beliefs set forward in: *The Kingdom Of God Is Within You.*

From shortly after he arrived in London, Gandhi became aware of Theosophy, and in his second year in London he went to Blavatsky Lodge and was introduced to Madame Blavatsky. His reading of: *The Key to Theosophy* encouraged in him: "the desire to read books on Hinduism."[12] In London, when some friends from the Theosophy Society had invited Gandhi to read with them: *The Song Celestial*, the book with translations by Sir Edwin Arnold, he had to admit that he himself had not at that time read the *Gita* in any great detail. In his writings down through the years, Gandhi identified and paid tribute to the individual authors and books that had influenced him most. Gandhi had a gift for abstracting the essential or core concepts and ideas from the books he was studying. From the *New Testament*, Gandhi identified the *Sermon on the Mount* as the

---

[11] Duncan, Ronald. (ed) *Selected Writings of Mahatma* Gandhi.London. Fontana. 1972. 26.

[12] Raghavan Iyer, ed. *The Essential Writings of Mahatma Gandhi* (Ahmedabad: Navajivan Trust, 1990; reprint, Delhi: Oxford University Press, 1994), 67.

teaching that went straight to his heart. Gandhi, on his own admission, was able to re-define the concepts that he was studying and to bring them into line with his own experience to date. All of these writers and the various influences only helped Gandhi to see more clearly the ideas and beliefs that had already formed in his mind. One example of how cosmopolitan Gandhi's readings were can be seen from his time in prison in South Africa in the early part of 1908. While in prison he read the: *Gita* in the morning and the: *Koran* in the afternoon. In the evening he used the Bible to teach English to fellow prisoners.

THE BHAGAVAD GITA

According to Professor Dhawan: "Of the books that have moulded Gandhi, the *Gita (The Bhagavadgita or Sacred Song. One of the most important Hindu Texts).*"[13] Although Gandhi only read the *Gita* for the first time when he went to London in 1888-1889, it was the book that he read almost daily for the rest of his life. He endeavoured to live by the influence of its teachings from that time on. Gandhi was very aware that the *Gita* was: "not a treatise on non-violence, nor was it written to condemn war."[14] But he believed that the: "logical outcome of the teaching of the Gita is decidedly for peace at the price of life itself. It is the highest aspiration of the human species."[15] In effect, Gandhi's experiments in truth put a new interpretation on the whole meaning of the *Gita* and his beliefs re-emphasised the role of one of the traditional aspects of the spirit of Hinduism - its non-violence.

Gandhi believed that the *Gita* was the book *par excellence* for the understanding of true knowledge.

> The *Gita* contains the gospel of *karma* or work, the gospel of *bhakti* or devotion and the gospel of *jnana* or knowledge. Life should be a harmonious whole of these

---

[13] Gopinath Dhawan. *The Political Philosophy of Mahatma Gandhi*. Delhi: Gandhi Peace Foundation. 1990 11.

[14] Duncan, 40.

[15] Ibid., 40-41.

three.[16]

But Gandhi's message was also very uncompromising at times, addressing students in Tiruppur, he explained that for a proper understanding the Gita must be approached within a certain framework. This framework was summarised by Gandhi in five principles; *ahimsa* (non-violence), *satya* (truth), *brahmacharya* (celibacy), *aparigraha* (non-possession), and *asteya* (non-stealing).

HENRY DAVID THOREAU

There has been some controversy over the development of Gandhi's ideas of non-violence and Civil Disobedience and their relationship to the ideas put forward by Thoreau in his essay on *Civil Disobedience*[17]. But Gandhi himself wrote that his resistance to civil authority in South Africa: "was well advanced before I got the essay of Thoreau on *Civil Disobedience*."[18] The movement that Gandhi was leading against the South African authorities was then known as a movement of "Passive Resistance." Gandhi was not happy with this name so, when he read and studied Thoreau's *Civil Disobedience,* he began to use this name because he felt that it was more appropriate than "Passive Resistance." Gandhi was still not satisfied with the name "Civil Disobedience" and he adopted the phrase "Civil Resistance." Eventually Gandhi used the term "Non-violent Resistance." At this stage Gandhi had already coined the word *satyagraha* for his Gujarati readers; his problem was with a suitable English translation.

Gandhi called Thoreau's: *Civil Disobedience* a masterly work and admitted that it had left a deep impression on him. It is interesting to note that Thoreau had studied the *Bhagavad Gita* and some of the sacred Hindu *Upanishads*. Thoreau wrote in his journal:

---

[16] Iyer, 69.

[17] Henry David, Thoreau *Walden and Civil Disobedience*. (London: Penguin 1983).

[18] Fischer, 115.

> Every morning I bathe my intellect in the stupendous and cosmogonal philosophy of the Bhagavad Gita, in comparison with which our modern civilisation and its literature seem puny and trivial.[19]

Thoreau hated slavery, and not just Negro slavery, but the individual's slavery to the State, to the Church, to Property, to Customs, and to Traditions. Much of what Thoreau did at Walden Pond, Gandhi did at a later stage. Thoreau built with his own hands the hut that he was to live in, he grew his own food and became as self-sufficient as possible. Thoreau and Gandhi were just following a long tradition of individuals and groups who felt the desire to go outside society as much as possible in order to be independent enough to criticise that society.

JOHN RUSKIN

Gandhi had never read Ruskin until 1903 when he was given a copy of *Unto this Last* at the start of a train journey from Johannesburg to Durban, a journey at that time of about 24 hours. In his autobiography Gandhi said about reading Ruskin's book:

> The train reached there in the evening. I could not get any sleep that night. I determined to change my life in accordance with the ideals of the book."[20]

Ruskin urged people to live as simple a life as possible, he preached the dignity of manual work and he identified above all else the danger to the human spirit from the modern economic system. These were the ideals that had already began to dawn on Gandhi and he was very excited to see them put so clearly in Ruskin's books.

---

[19] Henry David Thoreau, from his journal, in A. C. Bhaktivedanta Swami Prabhupada. *Bhagavad-Gita As It Is.* (Los Angeles: Bhaktivedanta Book Trust, 1981), xliii

[20] Gandhi, *Autobiography,* 274.

Unto This Last: Four Essay's on the First Principles of Political Economy was one of Ruskin's most important works. In its publications, Ruskin declares that:

> Riches are a power like that of electricity, acting through inequalities or negation of itself

He preached that:

> Men should seek not greater wealth but simple pleasure; not higher fortune but deeper felicity; making the first of possessions, self-possession.[21]

It is almost as if Gandhi himself could have written these very words. The ideals put forward by Ruskin were in many ways the very same principles that Gandhi was evolving through trial and error. In a lecture given by Gandhi in 1916 entitled: "Does economic progress clash with real progress?" Gandhi's very strong feelings on this subject reflected much of what Ruskin had already preached. Gandhi stated:

> I hold that economic progress in the sense I have put it is antagonistic to real progress. Hence the ancient ideal has been the limitation of activities promoting wealth...Western nations today are groaning under the heel of the monster-god of materialism. Their moral growth has become stunted. They measure their progress in £. s. d.[22]

Ruskin explains the title of *Unto This Last* by saying that:

> The rich should abstain from luxuries until all, the poorest too, shall have enough, until the time come and the kingdom, when Christ's gift of bread and bequest of peace shall be unto this last as unto thee.[23]

---

[21] Fischer, 91.
[22] Iyer, 97.
[23] Fischer, 91.

Gandhi identified and substantiated these principles:

> The test of orderliness in a country is not the number of millionaires it owns, but the absence of starvation among its masses."[24]

Gandhi did not have any romantic illusions about poverty; he answers his critics on this by stating clearly that:

> No one has ever suggested that grinding pauperism can lead to anything other than moral degradation.[25]

His view on economics was even more moralistic than either Thoreau's or Ruskin's. Gandhi said of economic theory:

> I venture to think that the scriptures of the world are far safer and sounder treaties on laws of economics than many of the modern text-books."[26]

GANDHI AND TOLSTOY

Gandhi and Tolstoy never met in person, but Gandhi always acknowledged the importance of Tolstoy in the formation of his ideas and as an example to be followed. Gandhi came to be aware of Tolstoy's ideas through the published writings of Tolstoy and in particular: *The Kingdom of God Is Within You.*[27] Gandhi's first personal contact with Tolstoy was in the form of a long letter, written in English and sent from London, dated the first of October 1909. This letter was sent by Gandhi to inform Tolstoy of the problems that the Indians were encountering in the Transvaal and the type of action that Gandhi was offering as a direct response. Gandhi's second letter to Tolstoy contained a copy of his book on; *Indian Home Rule.* "As a humble follower

---

[24] Iyer, 94.
[25] Ibid.
[26] Ibid., 95.
[27] Leo Tolstoy, *The Kingdom of God Is Within You.* Published in 1894 See *Writings on Civil Disobedience And Non-Violence.*(Philadelphia: New Society1987), 285-347.

of yours," Gandhi wrote: "I send you herewith a booklet which I have written." Tolstoy wrote in his diary: "the book and the letter (of Gandhi) reveal an understanding of all the shortcomings of European civilisation and even of its total inadequacy."

One of the clearest statements on Tolstoy's beliefs can be seen in the last letter that Tolstoy wrote to Gandhi. The letter was dated 7th of September 1910 - Kotchety, Russia; and it outlines in very definite terms some of Tolstoy's strongest beliefs. He identifies the ideals associated with passive resistance:

> That which is called passive resistance, but which is in reality nothing else than the teaching of love, uncorrupted by false interpretations. That love, i.e. the striving for the union of human souls and the activity derived from this striving, is the highest and only law of human life, and in the depth of his soul every human being (as we most clearly see in children) feels and knows this; he knows this until he is entangled by the false teachings of the world This law was proclaimed by all, by the Indian as by the Chinese, Hebrew, Greek and Roman sages of the world. I think this law was most clearly expressed by Christ, who plainly said that "in this only is all the law and the prophets."[28]

This letter from Tolstoy must have delighted Gandhi, because it confirmed the very ideals that Gandhi believed were fundamental to the foundations of his belief in passive resistance. The Christian message from the gospel of Christ was clearly a message of love, but this message of the Law of Love had been corrupted almost from the very beginning of the Christian Gospel. As Tolstoy said in his letter "so lived Christian humanity for nineteen centuries."

In this letter of just over one thousand words Tolstoy outlines to Gandhi his very clear perception of what he believes is the most fundamental law of life - the Law of Love-,

---

[28] Duncan, 62.

> The use of force is incompatible with love as the fundamental law of life, that, as soon as violence is permitted, in whichever case it may be, the insufficiency of the law of love is acknowledged, and by this the very law is denied.[29]

What Tolstoy was saying about the: Law of Love was not appreciated by many people, but Gandhi identified Tolstoy's view on the Law of Love as of crucial importance to his own developing beliefs. Tolstoy's letter repeated in a number of different forms his views on the Law of Love and the Law of Violence.

> In reality, as soon as force was admitted into love it was no more, and there could be no love as the law of life, and as there was no law of life, there was no law at all except violence - i.e. the power of the strongest.[30]

GANDHI'S PHILOSOPHY OF PEACE

Gandhi's philosophy of peace, in so far as it can be described or analysed, is best described in Gandhi's own words as: "the story of his experiments with truth." Gandhi himself was weary of those who attempted to set his beliefs within an ideological or philosophical framework:

> I do not know myself who is a Gandhian. Gandhism is a meaningless word for me. An ism follows the propounder of a system. I am not one hence I cannot be the cause of any ism.[31]

According to Gopinath Dhawan, the core of Gandhi's philosophy is his: "unshakable faith in God, his insistence on the primacy of spirit."[32] In this sense Gandhi's: "political philosophy and political technique are only corollaries of his religious and

---

[29] Duncan, 62.
[30] Ibid.,
[31] Iyer, 62.
[32] Dhawan, 39.

moral principles."[33] If Gandhi's philosophy of peace can be described in any meaningful sense, it can best be described as a philosophy of non-violence. The core ingredients of this philosophy were Gandhi's unique contribution to the understanding of *ahimsa* - the power of moral force in human society, the power of moral non-violence. And his contribution to the identification and understanding of *satyagraha*- the truth force and its importance in human affairs. Gandhi did not attempt to put forward a philosophy in the traditional western sense of the term:

> I have nothing new to teach the world. Truth and non-violence are as old as the hills.[34]

Gandhi attempted to re-define and re-interpret the essence of the philosophy of non-violence as it manifested itself in the religious traditions of mankind. In his "experiments" with truth Gandhi made an unique contribution to the understanding of the philosophy of non-violence.

In the introduction to the: *Selected Writings of Mahatma Gandhi*, Ronald Duncan, writing some years after his meetings with Gandhi, identified what he believed was the most important contribution that Gandhi had made to twentieth-century thought. Gandhi had identified the ethical structure of the relationship between religion in its broadest sense, and politics in its broadest sense to social and economic action. Gandhi believed that this relationship was the key factor in the moral progress of mankind:

> Every act has its spiritual, economic and social implications The spirit is not separate. It cannot be so.[35]

Many other philosophers down through the ages had identified the crucial importance of this relationship. But Gandhi made the

---

[33] Ibid., 38.
[34] Iyer, 384.
[35] Duncan, 19.

constitution of this relationship the basis of his philosophical vision.

In any understanding of Gandhi's philosophy of peace a number of core concepts have to be identified and comprehended. Gandhi's understanding and development of the concepts of *satyagraha* and *ahimsa* are of crucial importance. Gandhi's search for truth through the way of non-violence is the framework on which his philosophy of peace is built. In essence, Gandhi put forward the ideology of truth as the basis of his interpretation of the dialectical process of history. Gandhi, more than most other philosophers, accepted the equal validity of all other cultures. He did not believe that anyone could produce an universal culture that would dominate the existing sub-cultures.

One of the most important aspects of Gandhi's *Experiments in Truth* is the contribution that he has made to the understanding of the complexities of human nature and the dynamics of social structures. Gandhi, like other revolutionaries before him, attempted to re-define the methodology of social and political transformation. For Gandhi there were two basic ways of resolving conflicts and of bringing about social change, either by violence or non-violence. Gandhi had little or no faith in the power of violence. He did not believe that violent revolutions could or would ameliorate human misery and mass deprivation He was convinced that non-violence would generate a more lasting and more fundamental transformation of society than violence, regardless of the ideological framework. Gandhi's message on this was very clear; he believed that injustice can only be removed through truth, non-violence and purity of means. The alternative way to right an injustice is by violence, hate and war. This, according to Gandhi, only leads to a cycle of yet more injustice *ad infinitum* (without end). Gandhi hoped for the spiritual enlightenment of humanity, and believed that political enlightenment without spiritual enlightenment would not stand the test of time. Within this context one of the central components of Gandhi's philosophy of peace, was his attempt to re-interpret the relationship between the means and the ends, particularly in relation to the problem of how to challenge fundamental issues of injustice and security both for the individual and for society.

THE LAWS OF VIOLENCE AND NON-VIOLENCE

Gandhi accepted that non-violence would bring about less dramatic social change than violence. But if you take away the ideological propaganda, most revolutions only succeed in replacing one set of ruling elite with another set; and replacing one set of ideological justifications with another. At another level while Alexander Herzen was afraid of those who wanted to oppress him, he was more afraid of those who wanted to liberate him:

> If only people wanted, instead of liberating humanity, to liberate themselves, they would do much better for the liberation of man.[36]

Gandhi's understanding of human nature and the potential of revolutionary change in the social structures were much closer to Herzen's than to Marx's:

> The Constructive Programme could slowly build upon every success whilst leaving the future open to bold experimentation, in which there are invariably errors, but errors that do not undermine the benefits.[37]

Central to the Law of Violence is the belief that:

> The method of violence gives no greater guarantee than that of non-violence. Millions sacrifice themselves in war without any guarantee that the world will be better as a result or even that the enemy will be defeated.[38]

---

[36] Alexander Herzen, in Isaiah Berlin *Russian Thinkers* (London Penguin1978), 200.
[37] Iyer, 15.
[38] Fischer, 435.

While Gandhi believed that reason and science were essential to progress, he warned that they were disastrous without ethics and morality. Gandhi accepted that it was easy to identify the oppressive domination of organised religion. This oppressive domination is a characteristic of any institution that establishes its view of reality as infallible, but he felt that his approach rejected this tradition:

> I have no desire to carry a single soul with me, if I cannot appeal to his or her reason. My unconventionality I carry to the point of rejecting the divinity of the oldest *shastras* (scriptures) if they cannot convince my reason.[39]

In order to get some understanding of the core concepts that are central to Gandhi's philosophy of peace it is necessary to give some analysis and explanation to the concepts of *ahimsa* and *satyagraha.* Gandhi himself said that:

> I have not put anything new before India; I have only presented an ancient thing in a new way. I have tried to utilise in a new field. Hence my ideas cannot be appropriately called Gandhism."[40]

THE PHILOSOPHY OF AHIMSA

How can Gandhi's principle of *ahimsa* be best understood? Much of what Gandhi said about violence and non-violence can be and has been misunderstood. Any critic who wants to identify contradictions in Gandhi's beliefs and principles will have no problems finding them. One of the most important decisions in attempting to analyse and understand Gandhi's concept of *ahimsa* is the framework in which such an analysis is made. Gandhi attempted to establish a theory of human relations based on the foundation of non-violence, or the force of moral persuasion. It is within this critical framework that any

---

[39] M. K. Gandhi,*The Collected Works of Mahatma Gandhi,* 90 vols. Vol. XIX. (New Delhi: Publications Division of the Government of India, Navajivan, 1958-1984), 45.
[40] Ibid., 384.

serious analysis of Gandhi's beliefs must be developed. Gandhi was:

> No doctrinaire, nor a starry-eyed believer in non-violence, he was keenly aware of the nature of the world and the problems in it he had to contend with.[41]

The concept of non-violence that Gandhi outlined did not make people incapable of self-defence. Gandhi was very critical of people who confused this issue either deliberately or un-intentionally. Gandhi was very clear about this:

> I do believe that, where there is only a choice between cowardice and violence, I would advise violence.[42] But he goes on to say quite clearly I believe that non-violence is infinitely superior to violence.[43]

While Gandhi put love at the centre of his beliefs, he did not exclude such important considerations as human dignity. An essential part of human dignity involves the ability of the individual to stand against some thing that is harmful to his interests. What Gandhi was attempting to do was to establish a way of restructuring human relations that would enhance the dignity, freedom and humanity of everyone involved in any particular interaction whether conflictual or not.

One good example of the understanding of the effectiveness of Gandhi's approach was given by Rabindranath Tagore a contemporary of Gandhi's who won the Nobel Prize for Literature in 1913. For Tagore, the unarmed defiance of Gandhi's volunteers at the Dharasana Salt Works was a turning point. Out of this one example of the moral courage *ahimsa,* Tagore said that:

> Europe has completely lost her former moral prestige in

---

[41] Choudhuri, 51.
[42] M.K. Gandhi. *All Men Are Brothers*. Ahmedabad. Navajivan Publishing.1992. 135
[43] ibid. 135

> Asia. She is no longer regarded as the champion throughout the world of fair dealing and the exponent of high principles, but as the upholder of Western race supremacy and the exploiter of those outside her borders. For Europe this is, in actual fact, a great moral defeat that has happened.[44]

He believed that this was the real beginning of a free and independent India, and that this achievement was made possible by Gandhi and his ideas. Even though Asia was still physically weak in relation to Europe, the tide had turned, and it would be only a matter of time before the English would be leaving India. Gandhi had said: "We in India may in a moment realize that one hundred thousand Englishmen need not frighten three hundred million human beings."[45]

AHIMSA*: THE LAW OF LOVE AND THE POWER OF NON-VIOLENCE*

Did Gandhi discover a Law of Love, which would dramatically change how people relate to each other? According to Gandhi, the object desired in the use of love is a change of heart of the person whom you are in conflict with. This must also involve the possibility of a change of heart on your own behalf as well. Within the process of *ahimsa* these changes would be permanent. These changes are brought about with the help and use of reason and conscience, and not by manipulation that by-passes these faculties, as described in works such as Huxley's *Brave New World.* Gandhi attempted to produce a system that could be used to bring about social change without the need to brutalise the participants. One of the main aims of *ahimsa* was: "to avoid the brutalisation of human nature."[46] Gandhi was well aware from his own experience that the appeal to reason had limited success in many conflicts. In particular, where prejudices were based on religious beliefs: "I have found that

[44] Fischer, 344.
[45] *All Men Are Brothers.* 136
[46] Ibid., Vol. LXIX., 323.

mere appeal to reason does not answer where prejudices are long and based on supposed religious authority…"[47]

Gandhi himself never wrote a thesis on the science of *ahimsa*. When he was asked to do so he said that it was beyond his powers:

> I am not built for academic writings. Action is my domain...Let anyone who can systematise *ahimsa* into a science do so, if indeed it lends itself to such treatment.[48]

Ahimsa as a principle can be taken to the extreme. Gandhi saw the danger in the extreme position taken by Jainism in relation to non-violence. He saw this as the negative aspect of a vital principle which has led to the distortion of *ahimsa*, where the emphasis is laid on the sacredness of sub-human life in preference to human life. Gandhi was very critical of those people who had made *ahimsa* a blind faith:

> They have put the greatest obstacle in the path of the spread of true *ahimsa* in our midst.[49]

This mistaken view of *ahimsa* is as dangerous as any blind faith. In Gandhi's opinion this view of *ahimsa:*

> Has drugged our conscience and rendered us insensible to a host of other and more insidious forms of *himsa*.[50]

Gandhi's pursuit of *ahimsa* did not prevent him from making and defending decisions that seemed to contradict the basic principles of *ahimsa*. In 1929 he defended his decision to have a calf that was in great suffering given an injection and put out of its pain. This caused a considerable controversy with other Hindus who believe the cow to be a sacred animal that is not to be killed under any circumstances. In his defence, Gandhi said that such mercy killing was the purest form of non-violence and

---

[47] Ibid., Vol. XXVI., 271.
[48] Iyer, 41.
[49] Gandhi, *Collected Works*, Vol. XXXVII. 312.
[50] Ibid.

that the same principles should hold true in relation to human beings as well. Gandhi said that in relation to himself or any friend of his where recovery is out of the question: "I would not see any *himsa* in putting an end to his suffering by death."[51] As his ideas and experience matured, Gandhi went even further than this:

> Should my child be attacked with rabies and there was no helpful remedy to relieve his agony, I should consider it my duty to take his life.[52]

No one should misunderstand what Gandhi meant by this. As Gandhi said himself:

> I have been practicing with scientific precision non-violence and its possibilities for an unbroken period of over 50 years. I have applied it in every walk of life domestic, institutional, economic and political. I know of no single case in which it has failed.[53]

SATYAGRAHA: *THE DIALECTICAL PROCESS OF HISTORY*

"What then is *satyagraha? Satyagraha* is the bringing of God into politics,"[54] although *satyagraha* is not only about bringing God into politics, because this by itself, has proven to be a very dangerous state of affairs. Gandhi's development of *satyagraha* lies somewhere between the concept of Jihad and the Marxist dialectical process of history. Bhikhu Parekh, in his analysis of Gandhi's political philosophy, has called *satyagraha* a "non-rationalist theory of rationality." He believes that:

> Gandhi's theory of *satyagraha* is at once both epistemological and political, a theory of both knowledge

---

[51] Ibid., Vol. XXXVII. 311.
[52] Gandhi, *All Men are Brothers*, 120.
[53] Ibid., 124.
[54] Simon Panter-Brick. *Gandhi Against Machiavellianism*. (London: Asia Publishing, 1966), 20.

> and action, and much misunderstood when seen as either alone.[55]

Gandhi accepted that rational discussion and persuasion were the best means of resolving conflicts. The basis of Gandhi's rational discussion was the ability of those involved in conflict to try and appreciate the other side's point of view. Rational discussion would not work if one or more of the parties to the conflict were not prepared to be sympathetic to the other's point of view. Hatred and bitterness will not be overcome by rational discussion: "To men steeped in prejudice, an appeal to reason is worse than useless."[56] The pre-conditions for rational discussion were, according to Gandhi, an open mind which presupposed an open heart. In practical terms the pre-conditions for rational discussion were very seldom in existence on the ground in real conflicts. The obvious limitations of rationality in violent situations, had according to Gandhi, led so many people to advocate violence as the only effective method of fighting for what they believed to be truth or justice. Violence, once it was used and justified, conceded that hatred and ill-will were more effective than love and truth in resolving fundamental conflicts.

Gandhi believed that the great religious traditions of mankind were the central storehouses of human wisdom and understanding. For Gandhi it was not just a question of which religion had the most truth; he believed that only a partial view of absolute truth can ever be identified. Each true religion will have different glimpses of truth and each glimpse will be valid in its own right: "But for me, truth is the sovereign principle, which includes numerous other principles."[57] Gandhi believed that each new generation has to solve the problem of truth for itself, using the intelligence and knowledge that exist at that particular time. This does not invalidate previous knowledge or traditional wisdom; in fact, a search for truth that is not built on the foundation of traditional wisdom will not produce very much. If we are aware that the wheel exists, it would not be

---

[55] Parekh. Ibid., 143
[56] Parekh 145
[57] Gandhi, *Autobiography*, 15.

very productive to try and re-invent it. Gandhi believed that if traditional moral wisdom tells us that killing is morally wrong, then we must build on that basis:

> The *rishis*, who discovered the law of non-violence in the midst of violence, were greater geniuses than Newton. They were themselves greater warriors than Wellington.[58]

Gandhi understood that the search for truth was an essential part of life. It would not end with any one individual or one generation. He was aware that: "the quest for truth was not going to end with him. It also did not begin with him."[59]
In the introduction to his autobiography Gandhi explained why he felt it necessary, even against strong advice, to write an autobiography. But the title that he chose, "The Story of My Experiments With Truth" reflects the importance that he gave to this undertaking. In his autobiography Gandhi uses his everyday experiences to outline and explain the basic principles of his philosophy. In the introduction to his autobiography he clearly outlines the principles which had evolved from his experience to-date. In relation to *satyagraha:*

> The doctrine came to mean the vindication of truth, not by infliction of suffering on the opponent, but on one's self. [60]

This autobiography was first published in 1927 and the introduction is dated the 26th of November 1925: "My purpose is to describe experiments in the science of *satyagraha.*"[61]

Gandhi did not attempt to produce from his beliefs an ideology by which society must live. In fact, Gandhi was very aware of what Herzen called: "the terrible power over human lives of ideological abstractions."[62] In this sense, Gandhi can be seen as the antithesis of Marx or Lenin. For Gandhi, the human

---

[58] *All Men Are Brothers*. 137
[59] Choudhuri, 45.
[60] Gandhi, *All Men are Brothers,* 114.
[61] Gandhi, *Autobiography,* 16.
[62] Isaiah Berlin, *Russian Thinkers,* ed. Henry Hardy and Aileen Kelly. (London: Penguin, 1978), 193.

condition does not lend itself to a symmetrical set of conclusions. Regardless of how lofty the motives are, the human spirit is such that it does not respond to standard formulae and neat solutions. In every area of discourse, from economics to ethics, Gandhi re-interprets the very framework of the debate. His philosophy of *satyagraha* rejects the biological concept of the struggle for existence and the survival of the fittest. It rejects Hobbes' conception of human life as "the struggle of all against all." Gandhi challenged the utilitarian formula "of the greatest good of the greatest number" and replaced it with "the greatest good of all" as the ideal that must be sought. According to Gandhi "the greatest good of all" is far superior as a doctrine, both as a means and as an end.

Gandhi proposes that the basis of human progress is the development of the awareness that human life is an organic whole, in which one person cannot injure a neighbour without injuring themselves. For Gandhi, s*atyagraha* solved the traditional moral dilemma between ends and means because, in fact, it was both a means and an end. Through its process the people who used it became stronger and more committed to the ideals of truth, and the opponents against whom it was used were also given a greater insight into the potential of truth.

THE CONQUEST OF VIOLENCE

Gandhi hoped that the development of the concept of *ahimsa* and the practical application of *satyagraha* into the political arena would be a significant development in the construction of an alternative to the use of violence. The Rowlatt s*atyagraha*, the Salt *satyagraha,* the *satyagraha* against war and the various other *satyagraha* campaigns were all part of the learning process for Gandhi himself. Simone Panter-Brick in his book "Gandhi against Machiavellianism"[63] highlights the diametrically opposed concepts between what he terms as Machiavellianism and Gandhism. The problematic relationship between the ends

---

[63] Panter-Brick. Ibid.,

sought and the means used has been part of philosophical debate down through the centuries:

> The belief that there is no connection between the means and the ends is a great mistake. Through that mistake, even men who have been considered religious have committed grievous crimes."[64]

Gandhi put forward very clear and strong ideas on this relationship. On numerous occasions he stated his belief that the understanding of the relationship between means and ends was one of the crucial elements in any philosophy: "Means and ends are convertible terms in my philosophy of life."[65] Gandhi's understanding of the relationship between the means used and the ends obtained became central concepts in his experiments with truth:

> They say 'means are, after all, means.' I would say 'means are, after all, everything.' As the means, so the end. There is no wall of separation between means and end.[66]

Gandhi's philosophy of peace is not easy to understand. There is no quick reference guide that can identify the principles involved. Many of Gandhi's actions and many of his written statements can be easily misunderstood or misinterpreted. The fact that he became, on his own admission, a recruiting sergeant for the British Army, if taken at face value, would seem to suggest that his philosophy of peace was not based on firm foundations. But this is exactly where Gandhi's strength lay; he did not feel himself bound by traditional interpretation of rules and taboos. His beliefs were shaped by the existential reality of human relations and social responsibility. He did not reject traditional moral wisdom, but he was not restricted by its shortcomings. Gandhi came on the stage of Indian history at a time of great tension and conflict. The stage was set within the

---

[64] Gandhi, *All Men are Brothers*, 106.
[65] Kripalani, 349.
[66] Ibid., 349.

context of the struggle for Indian independence. The struggle for independence aggravated other dangerous currents. Not least of these were the volatile question of Hindu-Muslim relationships, and the problem of Untouchability. The British colonial administration was able to capitalise on these potentially disastrous conflicts. For Gandhi, the Indian experience was seen as a world experience. If India, with all its cultural differences, with all its languages and all its religious traditions, could be held together and developed in peace and freedom, then there would be great hope for the whole world.

In 1915 Gandhi returned from South Africa to India where he worked for the rest of his life. His work in India was at times dominated by the struggle for Indian independence and the conflicts arising between the Hindus and Muslims. His awareness of the economic and social problems of the majority of rural dwellers in India helped develop what had been called his "critique of modern civilisation."[67] In this sense Gandhi has been seen as:

> One of the first non-Western thinkers of the modern age to develop a political theory grounded in the unique experiences and articulated in terms of the indigenous philosophical vocabulary of his country.[68]

Through his work in the constructive programme he hoped to bring about economic and social reform in Indian rural society. He worked always for the end of Untouchability. He was assassinated on January 30th 1948. During the last few years of his life Gandhi lived through some of the worst communal fighting in recent Indian history. At that very unhappy time for Gandhi he confessed that he felt that his lifelong teaching of non-violence seemed to have had little effect on so many people.

---

[67] Bhikhu Parekh, *Gandhi's Political Philosophy: A Critical Examination.* (Notre Dame: Universtiy of Notre Dame Press, 1989).
[68] Ibid., 3

8

ALBERT EINSTEIN: THE SCIENTIFIC FOUNDATION

It would seem that men always need some idiotic fiction in the name of which they can hate one another. Once it was religion. Now it is the State

One should not remain inactive in the face of such vital issues while those who are greedy and obsessed by power increasingly ravage the face of the planet

The nation-state is no longer capable of adequately protecting its citizens,
to increase the military strength of a nation no longer guarantees its security

I am convinced we are dealing with a kind of epidemic of the mind. I cannot otherwise comprehend how men who are thoroughly decent in their personal conduct can adopt such utterly antithetical views on general affairs

It is useless to proceed along this path, one cannot prepare for war and expect peace. There is no compromise possible between preparation for war, on the one hand and preparation of a world society based on law and order on the other

Albert Einstein

EINSTEIN'S ON PEACE

In relation to his contribution to peace, Albert Einstein can be seen as:

> The pacifist who encouraged men to arms and played a significant part in the birth of nuclear weapons.[1]

It is more than ironical that Einstein, who had spent so much of his time in promoting peace and trying to critically erode the rational justifications for war, should have made such a significant contribution to the development of nuclear weapons. In 1946, Einstein set out some of his mature beliefs in a letter to the Emergency Committee of Atomic Scientists:

> Our world faces a crisis as yet unperceived by those possessing the power to make great decisions for good and evil. The unleashed power of the atom has changed everything - except our mode of thinking - and thus we drift towards catastrophe.

The picture Einstein paints here is all too familiar. The twentieth century has seen major breakthroughs within the area of natural science. Science and technology have contributed to unprecedented developments. On the other hand, the understanding of man and his relationship to violence and aggression does not yet seem to have made any significant breakthrough. Einstein believed that in any evolutionary process, a species must adapt to changes or risk its survival, and that in the same way, the developments in nuclear weapons will force the human species to evolve beyond the institution of war and beyond the cultural habit of violence.

How significant is the contribution made by Einstein to the philosophy of peace? Einstein's unique contribution as a scientist to the field of science has been established beyond

---

[1] Ronald W. Clark, Einstein, The Life and Times. (London: Hodder @ Stoughton 1979) 20

question. Some of his contemporary critics in particular have said that once he moved outside of the field of science he became something: "between a crank and a buffoon."[2] Many of the statements made and opinions held by Einstein about the questions of war and peace were criticised by his contemporaries both inside and outside the peace movements. Einstein would seem to have underestimated the power and strength of the culture of war within the social system, but Einstein was not the only person to underestimate the tenacity of war in human society. While he may not have fully appreciated the role of violence and aggression in the human psyche, the ideas and the questions he attempted to answer are as valid as those of his most renowned critics. Notwithstanding the statements made, and the actions taken in passionate idealism, Einstein has made some invaluable contributions to the quest for peace in the twentieth century. The journey that Einstein undertook in his attempt critically to understand the causes of war and violence did not reach any indisputable conclusion, but this may reflect more on the nature of the problem rather than on the weakness of the approach.

There would seem to be two major trends in the criticisms laid against Einstein's ideas on peace and war. The first major criticism is related to Einstein's unrealistic expectations from conferences and international gatherings. The individuals who worked in the League of Nations and organised the disarmament conferences felt they played a useful purpose in attempting to put some restriction on the developments of various weapons systems, and believed that these conferences served a useful purpose in restricting the outbreaks of war. Einstein would not accept this approach. He felt that these conferences put a civilised veneer on the production of weapons and gave the arms manufacturers a respectability that they did not deserve. Einstein's position was clear enough, he had already developed a very critical attitude to the Disarmament Conference in Geneva, which he had called a tragedy.

---

[2] Ibid. 353.

The second set of criticisms about Einstein's ideas on war and violence came from individuals within the various peace movements. At one stage Roman Rolland stated, rather unfairly, that Einstein's: "constant about-faces, hesitations and contradictions are worse that the inexorable tenacity of a declared enemy."[3] It may well be that Einstein had not thought through the absolute implications of some of his early pacifist beliefs. The "Two per cent" speech made in New York in December 1930 is a good example. Einstein stated: "Even if only two per cent of those assigned to perform military service should announce their refusal to fight."[4] This, he believed, would make such a difference that governments would be unable to act against such a large number. The "Two per cent" motto became very popular among some anti-war movements, but they seemed to have overlooked the fact that, in the same speech, Einstein had also pleaded with those governments that enforce conscription, to provide alternative service for pacifists. It may be possible that Einstein did not understand the inherent contradiction in this position but, as one of his biographers said:

> There is another explanation of his evolving pacifist attitudes Perhaps in pacifism, as in space, there should be no absolute; a standpoint which makes more comprehensible his attitude of 1931.[5]

According to Lord Brockway, the then chairman of W.R.I. (War Resisters International), after a meeting with Einstein in 1931 states: "As he sees the problem, there are two ways of resisting war, the legal way and the revolutionary way."[6] The legal way involves the use of compromise on certain issues. In relation to conscientious objection, it would involve the acceptance of alternative service in a civilian area. The revolutionary way would involve uncompromising resistance to the principle of military conscription in any form. Lord Brockway concludes by saying that for Einstein: "both tendencies are valuable, and that

---

[3] Ibid.
[4] Ibid., 351.
[5] Ibid.
[6] Ibid.

certain circumstances justify the one and certain circumstances, the other."[7]

According to Einstein himself his suspicion and mistrust of any sort of authority was a very important factor in the evolution of both his scientific ideas and general philosophy of peace. He traced his rejection and scepticism of authority right back to his early childhood. His teacher's remarks on his departure from the Gymnasium reflect this early scepticism for authority: "Your presence in the class destroys the respect (for me) of the students."[8] When he had just turned fifteen years old, Einstein renounced his German citizenship. Such an action could be seen as somewhat typical of a high-school dropout, but it also shows a much deeper and more thought-out action than a normal teenage rebellion.

EINSTEIN'S PHILOSOPHY OF PEACE

Einstein's philosophy of peace can be traced along two distinct principles. Firstly, there must be considered his basic belief in people rather than institutions or organisations. Einstein believed above all else that people as individuals, rather than governments and other groups with vested interests, would seek peace rather than war. While this belief evolved and matured over time, Einstein's belief in this basic principle never faltered. In this regard Einstein believed that intellectuals in particular, in various countries, could develop a solidarity which would force their respective governments and organisations to seek civilised solutions to the various conflicts that would arise from time to time. Secondly, Einstein believed that where institutions were concerned, an institution like the League of Nations or the United Nations with strong legal authority, was the only possible way of guaranteeing international security. This security would be a vital component in bringing about peace in the chaos of international relations. Einstein believed that the League of Nations, or a similar organisation, must have a Court of

---

[7] Ibid.

[8] Paul A. Schilpp, *Albert Einstein: Philosopher-Scientist,* Vol. I. (New York: Harper Torchbooks, 1959), 15.

International Arbitration which would have some form of compulsory power to enforce legitimate decisions.
Around these two basic principles it is possible to get a clearer picture of some of the deeper developments in Einstein's philosophy of peace. Einstein stated quite clearly that his pacifism was not derived from any intellectual theory but was based on his deepest antipathy to every kind of cruelty and hatred:

> It would seem that men always need some idiotic fiction in the name of which they can hate one another. Once it was religion. Now it is the State.[9]

The various developments that can be traced in Einstein's philosophy of peace reflect quite clearly the profound political and personal experience of living in Europe, and in Germany in particular, through the First World War and the rise of Nazism. While it can be said that part of Einstein's basic political philosophy, his belief in democracy and socialism, did not undergo any significant changes during his lifetime; his belief in the practicality and utility of non-violence seems to have changed dramatically during the 1930s. At a crucial time in the early 1930s, particularly after 1932, Einstein seemed to have made a fundamental change in his attitude to pacifism and in his ideas about the utility of war. Many of the various peace movements and organisations who saw Einstein as their most influential supporter felt badly let down when Einstein began to support the rearmament of the Allies against the rise of militarism in Germany. Some in the contemporary peace organizations called this Einstein's 'Great Betrayal'. The general feeling of despondency in the peace movement can be summed up in this statement:

> Advocates of peace who are not prepared to stand for peace in time of war are useless. There are so many fictitious peace societies. They are prepared to speak of peace in time of peace, but are not dependable in time of

[9] Ottto Nathan and Heinz Norden, *Einstein on Peace*.(London: Methuen), 11.

war.[10]

Einstein's writings, and his activity in the various peace movements before the 1930s, reflected the ideas put forward by contemporary peace organisations such as the War Resisters International and the German League for Human Rights. Many of these organisations laid the responsibility for peace firmly on the individual. There was a general belief that individual action was the key to the abolition of war; put quite simply, war will cease when men as individuals refuse to fight.

THE PROBLEM OF NAZISM

In the early years of the rise of Nazism in Germany, Einstein felt that he could no longer advocate the policy of war resistance which he had so passionately promoted in previous years. Einstein was not the only person to re-examine the principles of pacifism in the light of the rise of Nazism, but his change of mind caused much bitterness in the peace movement. Einstein made a number of statements explaining his changed position:

> Until quite recently we in Europe could assume that personal war resistance constituted an effective attack on militarism. Today, we face an altogether different situation. In the heart of Europe lies a power, Germany, that is obviously pushing towards war with all available means.[11]

and even more clearly:

> There are two kinds of pacifism: sound and unsound. Sound pacifism tries to prevent wars through a world order based on power, not through a purely passive attitude towards international problems. Unsound, irresponsible pacifism contributed in large measure to the defeat of France as well as to the difficult situation in

---

[10] Ibid., 140.
[11] Ibid., 229.

which England finds herself today.[12]

There can be no question that Einstein ruffled a lot of feathers when he was seen to change his mind so dramatically on such an important social issue. At the time a number of explanations were given by his contemporaries in the various peace movements and scientific organisations. There is a general tendency to believe that any particular individual who is outstanding in one area of science or the arts should be automatically outstanding in all other areas. Of course, it is not necessary or correct to assume that someone like Einstein, who has made major and fundamental advances in the physical sciences, will also be blessed with creative wisdom in the area of human social structures, of politics, of religion and morality. In fact, the opposite might well be the case. Einstein's devotion to science may well have restricted the time left to him to develop comparable knowledge of the less developed and more complicated subject of the science of human understanding. Specialised knowledge and understanding in one specific area does not necessarily transfer into other areas.

Many of Einstein's contemporaries felt that he was way out of his depth when he became involved in political and social issues. One example was his attitude to the League of Nations, his inability or unwillingness to admit that whatever the fine intentions of the League, it had to operate in the world of fallible men and dangerous if not evil passions. With the passing of time, it is now possible to get a more objective analysis of Einstein's beliefs in relation to war and violence, to outline Einstein's philosophy of peace based on his writings, and to show Einstein's contribution to the evolving peace philosophy of the twentieth century. A number of examples of Einstein's relationship to the contemporary questions of war and peace, violence and non-violence, can help paint a more balanced picture of the evolution of his beliefs on these questions.

---

[12] Ibid., 319.

THE MANIFESTO TO EUROPEANS

The *Manifesto to Europeans* that Einstein was closely associated with, and which was to add to his trouble with the German authorities at a later stage, was written as a direct result of the *Manifesto to the Civilised World* which was published in October 1914. *The Manifesto to the Civilised World* was signed by ninety three of Germany's leading scientists and intellectuals including Max Plank and Paul Ehrlich. The invasion by Germany of neutral Belgium had caused problems in other countries especially with those who had some sympathy with the German position. The *Manifesto to the Civilised World* attempted, among other things, to justify the German invasion of Belgium, and to give a more balanced view of the German position to the rest of the world. The general trend of the manifesto was that Russian hordes had been unleashed against European civilisation and:

> Were it not for German militarism, German culture would have been wiped off the face of the earth.[13]

The *Manifesto* also served another purpose, it implied that anyone who opposed German militarism also opposed German culture and, by implication, European civilisation. The *Manifesto* concluded:

> We cannot wrest from our enemies' hand the venomous weapon of the lie. We can only cry out to the whole world that they bear false witness against us. To you who know us...a nation that holds the legacy of Goethe, Beethoven and Kant no less sacred than heart and home.[14]

What really annoyed Einstein about this manifesto was the way that these scientists were allowing themselves to be used:

---

[13] Nathan and Norden, 3.

[14] Hermann Sudermann, *The Manifesto to the Civilised World* Georg F. Nicolai, (Die Bioloqie Des Krieget, trans. Orell Fussli Zurica, 1916).

> How could scientists do in the name of the state what had once been done in the name of religion?

Within a few days of the publication of this manifesto, Georg F. Nicolai, a professor at the University of Berlin and a noted pacifist, drew up a response which he called the *Manifesto to Europeans*.
Given the atmosphere in Germany at this time it is nor surprising that this manifesto received so little support. In the end only three people including Einstein were prepared to sign it, and with so little support, *the Manifesto to Europeans* was not published until some years later. Nicolai credits Einstein as a co-author of the *Manifesto to Europeans. In Einstein On Peace* Otto Nathan says that *The Manifesto to Europeans* foreshadows many of the ideals to which Einstein was to give lifelong devotion."[15] The *Manifesto to Europeans* was very carefully worded. In its structure it was strongly pro-European and went out of its way not to be seen as anti-German. The manifesto stated that:

> The struggle raging today can scarcely yield a "victor"; all nations that participate in it will, in all likelihood, pay an exceedingly high price. Hence it appears not only wise but imperative for men of education in all countries to exert their influence for the kind of peace treaty that will not carry the seeds of future wars, whatever the outcome of the present conflict may be"[16]

In November 1914 a new pacifist group, *The New Fatherland League* was formed, of which Einstein was a founding member. The purpose of the League was to; "promote achievement of a just peace without annexations."[17] This was quite a radical proposition given the belligerent atmosphere in Germany during the early months of the war. The League attracted a number of influential German people, members of the aristocracy, retired diplomats and bankers. In April 1915 some members of the

[15] Nathan and Norden, 7.
[16] Ibid., 5.
[17] Nathan and Norden, 9.

League attended a conference organised by the Dutch Anti-War Council which was an attempt to organise an international association to promote a peaceful resolution of the conflict. The League came under continuous pressure from the German authorities and eventually it was proscribed in early 1916.

THE COMMITTEE OF INTERNATIONAL CO-OPERATION

Some of the strengths and weaknesses in the development of Einstein's philosophy of peace can be identified in his relationship with the League of Nations and its various committees. In 1922 Einstein was invited to become a member of the International Committee on Intellectual Co-operation of the League. From the very beginning, his membership of this committee was problematic. Some of the French members did not want any Germans on the committee, Einstein himself did not want to be seen as the German representative. Within two months of him accepting the invitation to become a member, and before the first official meeting of the committee, he had resigned. At this stage Einstein was asked to reconsider his resignation. Madame Curie wrote to him on a personal basis and asked him to think again. The Committee members felt that the resignation would do grave damage to the impartial image that the committee was hoping to create. Eventually Einstein withdrew his resignation.

Shortly after this, Einstein left on a long voyage overseas which included a visit to Japan. In March 1923, on his way home, he stopped in Zurich and again resigned from the committee on which he still had not attended a meeting. This time his resignation was made public and in this letter he was very critical of the League:

> I have recently become convinced that the League of Nations had neither the force nor the goodwill necessary for the accomplishment of its task. As a convinced pacifist it does not seem to me to be a good thing to have any relations whatsoever with it. I ask you to strike my

name from the list of committee members.[18]

This action by Einstein left bitter feelings among some other members of the committee. He later admitted that the action was caused by a passing mood of despondency. One of the causes of this despondency was the invasion and occupation of the Ruhr by the French. France was one of the leading members of the League of Nations, and by implication, one of the chief supporters of the Committee of Intellectual Co-operation. Einstein also felt that it was not appropriate for him to be seen as the German representative on the committee. Einstein was again persuaded to rejoin the committee and attended his first meeting in July 1924. The committee never lived up to the hopes and expectations of Einstein or many of its other members. By January 1926 he was identifying the weaknesses in the whole idea of having an International Committee which should help to contribute to better international relations:

> It must be admitted that scientists and artists, at least in the countries with which I am familiar, are guided by narrow nationalism to a much greater extant than are public men.[19]

The Committee of Intellectual Co-operation had a flawed weakness right at the centre of its structure. The principle it was constructed around was that scientists in particular, and men and women of learning in general, would not be so easily manipulated by national passions at times of international crises. Experience from the First World War did not give much confidence in this belief. Bertrand Russell in his *Justice In War-Time* published in 1916, had been very critical of the supposed impartiality of Men of Learning when international conflicts arose: "The guardians of the temple of truth have betrayed it to the idolaters."[20]

In 1932 Einstein was the subject of much criticism for his feelings toward, and public statements about, the *World Disarmament Conference* which was taking place or, as seen by

---

[18] Clark, 342.

[19] Ibid., 334.

[20] Bertrand Russell, *Justice in War-Time* (Illinois: The Open Court, 1917), 1.

many, dragging on in Geneva. Einstein attended one session where various delegates were debating the importance of aircraft carriers and the mobility of the planes they carried and how this might effect the balance of air or naval power. It can never be known for certain just what he expected to find. Einstein found a peace conference in Geneva which, like so many other peace conferences since, was more about war than about peace. When told by a friend that they had come to Geneva to watch the: "comedy of peace," Einstein said that: "this is not a comedy, it is a tragedy."[21] At a press conference on the same day as his visit to the conference Einstein stated that the conference itself was:

> The greatest tragedy of modern times, the delegates were unintelligent and insincere and nothing but puppets moved by strings in the hands of politicians at home - politicians and ammunition manufacturers.[22]

The criticism of the various delegates and the conference in general was not very diplomatic, but Einstein was no diplomat, and it is possible that he felt afterwards that he had been too critical of some of the individuals who were doing their best under the circumstances. The central point of Einstein's statement was more important than the criticism of particular individuals or of the conference set-up. In this statement he said:

> One does not make wars less likely to occur by formulating rules of warfare. War cannot be humanised. It can only be abolished. People must be prepared to refuse all military service.[23]

EINSTEIN ON EDUCATION

Throughout most of his life, Einstein expressed very strong feelings about the role and contribution of education to the development of a more just and less violent world. His

---

[21] Clark, 355.
[22] Ibid.
[23] Ibid., 354.

experience with German education both before and after the First World War sowed the seeds of these very strong feelings. But Einstein also realised that it was not just the German education system that was at fault:

> The trouble with Europe is that her people have been educated on a wrong psychology. Our schoolbooks glorify war and conceal its horrors. They indoctrinate children with hatred.[24]

One of Einstein's major areas of interest in his work with the League of Nations and its various committees, was in the potential of education in general for promoting the possibilities of peace and reducing the bitterness and mistrust that contribute so much to the causes of war. Einstein felt that education held the key for removing the misunderstandings and hatreds which help to make war both possible and, more importantly, popular and attractive among young people generally:

> To my mind the main task he said is how generally to improve the education of the young. The League can do no greater work than help make better the elementary school system throughout the world.[25]

In practical terms this would mean having some influence on the school history books of both France and Germany. This could be done by reducing the interpretation of events which provoked and nourished the traditional feelings of hostility and hatred between these two countries. The idea of producing a school history book that can be accepted in any two countries which have a history of conflict between them has proved much harder than was originally imagined by Einstein or by the committee of the League of Nations. Some progress has been made in recent times. Sixty years and many wars later this idea is still at an experimental stage. In recent years, teacher organisations and historians have produced an historical text book, under the

---

[24]Otto Nathan & Heinz Norden, *Einstein On Peace* (London: Methuen, 1963), 126.
[25] Clark, 346.

Education for Mutual Understanding (EMU) project, that will be suitable for schools in the Irish Republic and in Northern Ireland. At the same time, teachers and historians in both Germany and Poland have produced a preliminary text book that may be acceptable for both countries.
Einstein's work with the League of Nations reflected one of his basic beliefs in the role of education in the promotion of peace. He believed that the basic contribution of educated individuals would be for the promotion of peace as against war. Men and women of education, of science, of intelligence would not be so easily swayed by the jingoism of war. Many other writers in this area believed the very opposite, and identified what they termed "the treason of the intellectuals." J. A. Hobson in *The Psychology of Jingoism* (1901) identified the peculiar susceptibility of the educated for war fever and that education, as constructed, offered no protection against raw aggression and the justification of the use of force. In fact, Hobson's view seems to suggest that the educated elite were very attracted to violence and aggression.

"WHY WAR?" ALBERT EINSTEIN AND SIGMUND FREUD

The Committee of Intellectual Co-operation decided that it would commission a number of letters or statements from some of the leading intellectuals on areas of general international importance. These statements were to promote the common interests of the League of Nations and were to be published as widely as possible. The first volume of these letters was entitled *A League of Minds* and published letters from a number of leading writers and artists including Paul Valery, Gilbert Murry, and M. Henri Focillon. Einstein was asked to co-operate with the publication of the second volume. The contents and subject matter would be left generally to Einstein's discretion. The original idea was for Einstein to set out two letters; one was to be addressed jointly to German and French organisations and would deal with the content of history books. The central question was how to teach history in such a way so as to reduce the amount of recrimination and bitterness between countries that have traditionally been in conflict. In the end this approach did not materialise and a different tack was taken by Einstein.

The second volume was eventually published in the form of an open letter from Einstein to Sigmund Freud with Freud's response, and published in 1933 under the title *Why War?* There had been some dispute over what title the publication should be given. The original idea was for the title to be: *Law and Violence* which gives some indication of the type of direction in which it was hoped the debate would develop. In the end the title that was agreed was simply: *Why War?* Einstein's gesture in turning to Freud to look for an answer to this question has significant symbolism in relation to Einstein's faith in science to address these questions. Einstein's letter to Freud was dated July 30th 1932 and it posed one simple central question: "Is there any way of delivering mankind from the menace of war?"[26] This, as Einstein stated, is one of the: "most insistent of all the problems civilisation has to face."[27] Einstein had his own ideas as an answer to such a major question. At the international level at least, Einstein felt that the answers lay in the development of the League of Nations and of the World Court of International Justice, which would have some form of compulsory powers of arbitration in international disputes. In his letter to Freud, Einstein identified certain interest groups that prevented any real progressive movement towards the conditions of peace. In particular:

> The craving for power which characterises the governing class in every nation. The determined group regard warfare, the manufacture and sale of arms, simply as an occasion to advance their personal interest and enlarge their personal authority.[28]

Einstein also identified the role of schools and the media in influencing the population in general:

> The ruling class at present, has the schools and the press,

---

[26] Nathan and Norden, 188.
[27] Ibid.
[28] Ibid., 189.

usually the Church as well, under its thumb.[29]

But the particular question that Einstein wanted Freud to answer related to the debate about Man's instinct. Has Homo Sapiens an instinct for hatred and destruction and is psychoanalysis a better approach to addressing these issues than science or religion? Einstein almost answered his own questions, when he stated that he believed: "man has within him a lust for hatred and destruction."[30]
The central question of *Why War?* was divided by Einstein into a number of secondary questions which Einstein felt were all interlinked into one another. see Table: 7.1

Table 8:1
EINSTEIN'S QUESTIONS ON AGGRESSION AND WAR.

1. Is it possible to understand and do something with all Man's Aggressive instincts?

2. Is it possible to bring an end to the collective psychosis of war? (Einstein wanted to examine the craving for power of certain individuals and groups.)

3. Why are such groups so successful in rousing men to such wild enthusiasm, even to sacrifice their lives?

4. What were the strong psychological factors at work which are paralysing the efforts of the League of Nations?

5. Why was an International Legislative and Judicial body like the League of Nations, not able to function?.

Einstein recognised his own limitations on such a vast subject. He believed that many of the questions arising out of any inquiry into the causes of war would need to look into: "the dark places of human will and feeling."[31] He believed that the political and

---

[29] Ibid., 190.
[30] Ibid.
[31] Ibid., 188.

social structures, important as they were, only reflected the aggressive instinct of man. Einstein was aware of problems being faced by the League of Nations. Why were the League of Nations and the principles upon which it was based, so unable to produce the necessary results? This was one of the central questions he addressed to Freud; in Many ways Einstein's contribution to: *Why War?* represents some of his most reflective thinking on the problems of war and aggression.

FREUD'S RESPONSE

On the questions that Einstein put to Freud in relation to war and aggression, Freud stated that: “I was dumbfounded on the thought of my (of our, I almost wrote) incompetence.”[32]

In his reply Freud initially stated that he had no direct answers to the fundamental questions raised by Einstein. Freud believed that his contribution to these questions could not be as direct as Einstein wanted. In one sense these questions were very unfair to Freud because, in answering them, Freud would have, in effect, to outline not only a very detailed theory of civilisation but also a detailed theory of the instinctual nature of the individual. Given Freud's detailed study of these forces, a pamphlet or letter was not the place to answer these questions in any detail. Nevertheless Freud's answer, which included less than four thousand words, was quite significant, and Einstein stated his thanks by saying:

> You have made a most gratifying gift to the League of Nations and myself with your truly classic reply.[33]

This exchange of ideas of two of the greatest minds of the twentieth century was published in German in an edition of less than two thousand copies, and a similar number was published in an English translation.

Freud attempted to take up some of Einstein's more direct questions but he also raised and attempted to answer a few of his

---

[32] Ibid., 191.

[33] Ibid., 202.

own. Freud took up the debate on the importance of an international authority like the League of Nations:

> To me the kernel of the matter is: the suppression of brute force by the transfer of power to a larger combination, founded on the community of sentiments linking up its members. All the rest is mere tautology and glosses.[34]

Freud took up the debate on the relationship between "might", and "right" which he felt that Einstein had not fully appreciated. But for the term "might," Freud wrote:

> I would substitute a tougher and more telling word: 'violence.' In right and violence we have today an obvious antinomy[35]

One of the dangers, according to Freud, of the measures of institutional reform which Einstein seemed to be so attracted to, was that they can be treated as panaceas. Institutional reforms by themselves will not bring about any fundamental changes in human nature and, according to Freud, could bring about the dangerous belief that the fundamental problems of human society are due to problems within society rather than within human nature. Freud believed that in general, the control of individual aggression can be helped or hindered by different forms of social institutions. Freud accepted that Man would seem to have a lust for hatred and destruction and that there is very little likelihood of suppressing Man's aggressive tendencies. As early as 1915 in his paper *On Transience* Freud had set out his ideas on war in very clear language:

> War- shattered our pride in the achievements of our civilisation,...it revealed our instincts in all their nakedness and let loose the evil spirits within us which we thought had been tamed for ever by centuries of continuous

---

[34] Ibid., 194.
[35] Ibid., 192.

education by the noblest minds.[36]

Freud identified what he believed were a number of different, if not distinct, ways of controlling aggression. He believed that aggression could be regulated in the more traditional ways by intensifying communal feelings through the attachment to a leader. But Freud was aware that this form of "regulation" would involve an increase in intolerance for anyone outside a particular "in" group. Freud did believe that some aggression can be controlled by removing what he determined as the occasions of aggression. In particular, he identified the institution of nationhood and the institutions of property as two of the key occasions of aggression. But he produced no grand design or blueprint on how this could be done. In fact he outlined the dangers in such social engineering:

> For so often in the denunciation of this or that historical form of society, what was being attacked was something essential to society itself.[37]

For Freud, the basic ingredients of human nature cannot be abolished by future political decree or some grand Utopian plan. There will always be the conflict between the individual and society and as importantly, within the individual himself. In: *Civilisation and its Discontents* published in 1930, Freud examined the types of questions for which Einstein hoped there would be short or specific answers. One of Freud's comments on the Russian revolution is revealing:

> That the experiment was undertaken prematurely, that a sweeping alteration of the social order has little prospect of success until new discoveries have increased our control over the forces of Nature and so made easier the satisfaction of our needs. Only then perhaps may it become possible for a new social order not only to put an end to the material need of

---

[36] Sigmund Freud in Daniel Pick, *War Machine* (London: Yale University Press, 1993), 194.
[37] Nathan and Norden, 199.

> the masses but also to give a hearing to the cultural demands of the individual. Even then we shall still have to struggle for an incalculable time with the difficulties which the untamable character of human nature presents to every kind of social community.[38]

Freud, like so many of his predecessors on the questions of aggression, proposed the replacement of instinct by intellect as one of the ideal methods of reducing and controlling aggression:

> If a culture has not got beyond a point at which the satisfaction of one portion of its participants depends upon the suppression of another, and perhaps larger, portion - and this is the case in all present day cultures - then that culture will not last.[39]

Freud identified four different if not distinct ways of controlling aggression. Two were related to the institutions and social structures of society and two were related to different aspects of human nature.

EINSTEIN'S CORE PRINCIPLES

Einstein developed his beliefs on war and peace around a number of very clear concepts which he passionately promoted to the very end of his life. He had said from an early stage that:

> His pacifism was not derived from any intellectual theory but was based on his deepest antipathy to every kind of cruelty and hatred.[40]

This statement is one of the key concepts in the foundation for Einstein's lifelong commitment to the search for peace. In relation to the tidal wave of militarism and jingoistic nationalism that swept over Europe in the early part of the twentieth century

---

[38] Sigmund Freud, *The Complete Psychological Works*. Vol. XXI. *Civilisation and its Discontents,* ed. J. Strachey. (London: Hogarth, 1930), 181.
[39] Ibid., Vol. XXI., 12.
[40] Nathen and Norden, ix.

Einstein held a very strong view. One of the problems that Einstein identified and came back to on numerous occasions was the ease in which whole populations can be manipulated by certain vested interests with their use of jingoism. In one of his darker moments in 1929 he stated that:

> The political apathy of people in time of peace indicates that they will readily allow themselves to be led to slaughter later.[41]

Even allowing for some darker moments, Einstein always remained optimistic that people generally, given the right basic education, would be able to overcome the attempts at manipulation by the various vested interests. He believed that people of education had a significant contribution to make:

> One should not remain inactive in the face of such vital issues while those who are greedy and obsessed by power increasingly ravage the face of the planet.[42]

Einstein did not produce any neat or all-embracing formulas in the area of war and peace. It may well be that the nature of the debate in this area of human understanding does not lend itself to any neat formulas. While the views expressed by Einstein after the Second World War showed some maturity on earlier expressions, his basic beliefs had not altered to any considerable extent. It is possible to identify in a subjective manner some of the key concepts that guided Einstein's search for the structures of peace? The best answer to this is to let Einstein speak in his own words. But at least two distinct approaches can be identified, in the first place, there are Einstein's ideas concerning national and international relations, and secondly, there are his ideas on the contribution of the individual.

At the international level, the following principles are a reflection of some of his ideas which have stood the test of time.

Principle of national security:

---

[41] Ibid.

[42] Ibid., 104.

The nation-state is no longer capable of adequately protecting its citizens,

to increase the military strength of a nation no longer guarantees its security.[43]

Principle of sovereignty:

> The developments of science and technology have determined that the peoples of the world are no longer able to live under competing national sovereignties with war as the ultimate arbitrator.[44]

Principle of balance of power and deterrence:

> The release of atomic energy has created a new world in which old ways of thinking that include old diplomatic conventions
> and balance of power politics have become utterly meaningless.[45]

Principle of disarmament:

> It is useless to proceed along this path, one cannot prepare for war and expect peace. There is no compromise possible between preparation for war, on the one hand and preparation of a world society based on law and order on the other.[46]

At the individual level it is also possible to identify a number of important principles in relation to war and violence which Einstein recognised as significant, and to which he made reference on a number of occasions, from his early work right up to his last.

Principle of instinct:

---

[43] Ibid., 407
[44] Ibid., 412
[45] Ibid., 407
[46] Ibid., 411, 441

> None of us realised how much more powerful is instinct compared to intelligence. We would do well to bear this in mind or the tragic errors of the past may be repeated.[47]

Principle of war and violence:

> I am convinced we are dealing with a kind of epidemic of the mind. I cannot otherwise comprehend how men who are thoroughly decent in their personal conduct can adopt such utterly antithetical views on general affairs.[48]

Principle of killing:

To me the killing of any human being is murder. It is also murder when it takes place on a large scale as an instrument of policy.[49]

These principles, as outlined, give some guide to Einstein's ideas as they matured over time with his own personal experiences of the problems and the possibilities of the conditions of peace. None of these principles can be tested and proved on the same level as the theory of relativity or any other scientific theory but these are the very clear principles which Einstein himself believed would guide the way to a more peaceful world. In the years since Einstein formulated these principles nothing has happened in the field of war and violence that would contradict these basic principles.

---

[47] Ibid., 26
[48] Ibid., 18
[49] Ibid., 93

9

RATIONAL THOUGHT AND THE COLLAPSE OF WAR

The Delusion of War and Violence:
There is no delusion greater than the delusion that we have no delusion.
And no one should underestimate the Human capacity for self delusion.

Anon.

Who creates such fears among the American people that they should be obliged to accept permanent military bondage?

Albert Einstein

The hope…that by the single-minded pursuit of wealth, without bothering our heads about spiritual and moral questions, we could establish peace on earth, is an unrealistic, unscientific and irrational hope.

E.F. Schumacher

No amount of violence could have achieved, in a hundred years, what peaceful political action achieved in Europe since 1988.

Anon.

THE COLLAPSE OF WAR

Since the end of the Second World War one of the most dominant theories on the underlying causes of war and violent conflict has developed around the traditional and long established "sin theory"[1] of war. The belief that wars are made by criminals or the criminally insane was strengthened by the Nuremberg and Tokyo war crime trials. The problem with this approach is that the Cold War warriors and their intellectual supporters built themselves an almost impregnable moral foundation to justify their support for the planning of ever more destructive conventional and nuclear war. The distortion of historical understanding in the service of contemporary political culture is not new; it was one of the factors that so annoyed Bertrand Russell during the early part of the First World War. Adolf Hitler and the dangers that arise from demented ideologies have been used to justify almost every war that has taken place since the end of the Second World War.

In 1961 A. J. P. Taylor was one of the first British historians to question the monopoly of self-righteousness that passed for historical analysis on the origins of the Second World War.[2] His impertinence in even raising the question of British and Allied war aims was criticised from all sides. One of the results of the almost total failure of so many historians to open up a genuine debate on the causes of war, has been the encouragement and space given to the revisionist historians of the new right. Because of Ireland's military neutrality in the Second World War the "sin theory" of war was not as readily accepted in Ireland. The problem was that Irish neutrality did not fit into the Hollywood version of the war that was passing for historical analysis. A number of British and Irish-trained British historians took on the task of attempting to discredit all aspects

---

[1] D. Cameron Watt, *How War Came*. (London: Longmans, 1957; reprint, London: Heinemann 1989).

[2] A. J. P. Taylor, *The Origins of the Second World War*. (London: Penguin, 1961).

of Irish neutrality. One such book: *Unneutral Ireland*[3] reflected much of the "think tank" thinking of various strategic institutes on the annoying problem of neutrality.

The sudden collapse of the iron curtain in 1989 caught the Cold War warriors with their trousers down. The ideological theorists of the Cold War should have been exposed in all their sterility and perversion but, like the phoenix, they attempted to rise out of the ashes of history. Within a very short space of time, new enemies, new dangers and new fears had been manufactured by ideologues:

> Islamic fundamentalism is at least as dangerous as Communism was. Please do not underestimate this risk. Fundamentalism and democracy cannot be reconciled, NATO can help counter the threat as the alliance redefines its role after winning the Cold War. NATO is much more than a military alliance. It has committed itself to defending the basic principles of civilisation that bind North America and Western Europe.[4]

It is quite understandable that the NATO bureaucracy should have a strong instinct for self-preservation. But the real problem arises when this distorted picture is accepted as factual interpretation by the majority of political analysts and their academic counterparts. Very little critical analysis was heard when NATO suddenly turned itself into a "Partnership for Peace." The age-old fallacy that you can create peace by preparing for war is still deeply ingrained in the mind-set of the one remaining superpower and its minions. In 1915 the Irish writer George Russell (A. E.) summed up his feelings on this type of debate:

> They tell us that they war on war. Why do they treat our wit with scorn? The Dragon from the Dragon seed, the

[3]Trevor C. Salmon, *Unneutral Ireland*. (Oxford: Clarendon, 1989).
[4] Willy Class, Secretary General, NATO, quoted in *Irish Times*. (3rd February 1995).

breed runs true since life was born.[5]

RATIONAL THOUGHT

The conviction that rational thought could lay the foundation of peaceful co-existence at an international level was one of the most important contributions from the Age of Enlightenment to the debate on war and peace. The process of rational thought attempted to reaffirm some of the principles set out in Aristotle's "Ethics" without reference to the theology of God. The liberal thesis still holds to the belief that the development of understanding will produce workable solutions to the problems that generate violent conflict. The traditional religious interpretations and justifications of war and violence in human society were substantially undermined but not completely abandoned. Religious violence, which, in one sense should be seen as a contradiction in terms, was in fact a central factor in the history of violence in European culture for hundreds of years. Violence fuelled by religious hatred and bigotry was a primary factor in some of the most voracious conflicts in the sixteenth and seventeenth centuries. The treaty of Westphalia in 1648 brought an end to some of the most destructive of the various wars of religion. After the destructiveness of the Thirty Years War a new maturity seemed to emerge. It was hoped that the suspicion, the fear and the hatred aroused by economic and political competition would never be as strong as similar emotions aroused by religious intolerance.

Towards the end of the First World War two important figures emerged upon the stage of European and world history, each with a very distinct vision of how peace and a new world order might be constructed. One was Woodrow Wilson and other Vladimir Lenin. Many of the conflicts of the twentieth century were fought around the opposing principles set out in their conflicting world-views:

---

[5] G.W. Russell, (A. E.), quoted in Henry Summerfield, *That Myriad Minded Man: A Bioghraphy of G. W. Russell - A. E.* (London: Collins Smyth, 1975), 173.

> The President and his advisers were determined to redraw the map of Europe so that the peoples released from imperial rule could have countries of their own.[6]

When Wilson set out across the Atlantic in the liner *George Washington,* he took with him tons of maps, books and all sorts of ethnographic studies and census reports. In January 1914, Wilson had outlined possible peace aims in his famous "Fourteen Points." Many of the principles outlined by Wilson were seen by the statesmen of the warring powers to be very lofty and not to be taken too seriously; the ideal of "open covenants openly arrived at" was not going to change the ways things were done. The first five principles outlined general assumptions of peacemaking:

> Behind these five general aims lay an implicit theory of what had caused the war: secret treaties, naval jealousies, tariffs, competition in armaments, and colonialism. Remove these causes of war and peace would result.[7]

There is some truth in the saying that: "All wars end in peace" but peace treaties and peace conferences themselves can be very mixed blessings. The treaties of Westphalia (1648), Utrecht (1713), Vienna (1815) and Versailles (1919) established peace periods that were to last for various lengths of time. In so far as the treaties and conferences failed, or were unable to address the central issues of the conflicts, they were not in a position to create a stable international peace. Versailles attempted to create new international norms that would help to develop means of resolving conflicts as they arose. But conceit and arrogance dressed up as national pride and self-respect won the day at Versailles. Many peace treaties revolve around conditions the conditions; for the cessation of violence rather than the construction of Peace. Pope Innocent X left little doubt of his view of the treaty of Westphalia, which, he stated:

> Is null, void, invalid, unjust, damnable, reprobate, inane, empty of meaning and effect for all time.

---

[6] Strobe Talbott, "When Empires Crumble," *Time.* (22nd June 1992.)

[7] Thomson. *Europe Since Napoleoan.*

In the years after Versailles, Wilson was blamed for raising the hopes of too many peoples with his lofty idealism; which was seen by many as a heavy liability in relation to the practical settlement of national and international disputes. Thomson's view was that:

> Wilson stood, in general, for the culmination of all the liberal, democratic, nationalist ideals which since 1789 had fermented in Europe. The war became, in his eyes, a war to make the world safe for democracy and small nations.[8]

Lenin, the quintessential revolutionary, had no real intention of freeing any of the national groups that made up the Russian Empire. His successors were determined that whatever the cost, no popular nationalist movements would be tolerated.
As the century came to a close it could be said that Wilson's legacy has made a spectacular re-emergence on the stage of European, if not world, history. The liberal principles, whose very concepts caused the statesmen at Versailles so much trouble, were eventually swept under the carpet. The price of refusing to face up to these principles condemned the world to even greater conflicts into the future.

THE HYPOTHESIS PROVEN

This book sets out to identify and trace in outline the set of ideas and the knowledge that have made the collapse of the war system inevitable. In order to do that it was necessary to identify and trace the ideas and knowledge that has evolved in the study of peace during the twentieth century. Such an approach required not only identifying the theories put forward, but more importantly, recognizing the perceptions and assumptions behind those theories, and analysing the framework of reference within which these theories were constructed. It was hoped to show that the four individuals and their ideas reflected the central aspects of these developments. It was

---

[8] Ibid., 571.

necessary to trace the historical evolution of the ideas and concepts that make up the philosophy of peace and to identify the cultural components of the culture of war and violence. Because the culture of violence is so ingrained in the mind-set of Western Civilisation it may take nothing less than a paradigm-shift in outlook to acknowledge the culture of peace. But paradigm shifts can and do happen, in fact paradigm shifts are the key to the advancement of science.

One of the central aims of this book was to identify the body of thought that can be recognised and associated with philosophical foundation on which peace in all its meanings will be constructed. Any number of approaches could be taken for this task. Anatol Rapoport[9], in his outline of the philosophy of war, identified a number of individuals who had a profound influence on their respective disciplines. Some examples given were Francis Bacon's "Novum Organum" on the philosophy of science, Machiavelli's "The Prince" on the philosophy of politics, and Adam Smith's "Wealth of Nations" on the philosophy of economics. It was hoped that in a similar way the ideas of the four individuals analysed would reflect distinct but intrinsic aspects of the philosophy of peace, and the profound changes that have occurred in the balance of the debate for war and peace, and for violence and non-violence.

It was not intended to construct a gospel of peace according to Tolstoy, Russell, Gandhi or Einstein. It was hoped to have identified some of the underlying patterns of thought that relate these individuals to each other, and to a broader reality of war and violence, peace and non-violence. It is hoped that the propositions identified for each of these individuals reflect the fundamental principles of their peace philosophies. The ideas, theories and analyses found in their public writings must be balanced against their active participation in the social and political problems of their day. None of the four individuals were under any illusion about the complexities of the problems of war and violence and the enormity of the task that lay ahead

[9] Anatol Rapoport. (Ed) *On Wa*. By Carl Von Clausewitz. London. Penguin. 1968

in the attempt to break, once and for all, our addiction to violence. Each of the individuals became actively engaged in various attempts to reject war and violence. Some of the contradictions that can be identified in their beliefs have arisen out of their refusal to reject war and violence *absolutely*. But this in no way takes away from the vital nature of the contribution they have made in the debate and of course their active participation in attempts to modify the conditions that produce war.

It has been a deliberate decision not to make direct comparisons of the ideas put forward by Tolstoy, Russell, Gandhi or Einstein. At one level, their ideas stand alone for clarity and comprehension, and it is part of the hypothesis of this book that each has constructed a different aspect of the philosophy of peace. It is hoped to have shown that the ideas and beliefs of each of the four individuals analysed have helped to undermine the foundations of the some of the central mythologies of war and violence. Their ideas and beliefs were not specifically original, because they built on centuries of tradition which challenged the logical and moral basis of violence. The uniqueness of their contributions relates to their refusal to accept traditional justifications for organised violence. The book attempted to abstract and clarify the core peace concepts as expressed by the individuals as their ideas matured and developed with experience. Very different approaches could be, and have been, taken to the beliefs and principles as expressed by these individuals. Tolstoy and Russell left vast amounts of written material on almost very topic under the sun. Gandhi's writings and the application of his beliefs to the political and social problems of India are a rich source of material for any analysis of social transformation. Einstein stands in a unique position in relation to his contribution to the scientific developments of the twentieth century and his experience of European militarism. The ideas of the four individuals have been analysed by numerous critics. The approach taken in this work has a number of problems associated with it. The ground to be covered was so extensive that in-depth analysis could not be pursued in many of the more interesting areas. In some aspects this weakness was also a strength; it was a deliberate decision to move away from in-depth research and move towards an overall interpretation and analysis of the knowledge already produced. This is partly a reaction to a western system of education that makes the study of wisdom a very marginal discipline, and an university system saturated with research almost to the exclusion of analysis.

TOLSTOY: AND THE MYTHOLOGIES OF WAR

Tolstoy challenged the age-old gospel that force is the most effective and efficient means of resolving conflict and, by implication that non-violence does not work. He believed that this mythology of violence was a central aspect of the traditional ideologies of power, of the state, of the Church, the aristocracy, the revolutionary groups and their modern counterparts. Tolstoy believed that historical evidence proved his ideas to be far more authentic than traditional interpretations. In the final analysis force had failed to resolve any of the fundamental questions surrounding the bitter religious conflicts of the sixteenth and seventeenth centuries. He believed that Napoleon was not the master of violence but its victim. He argued that the reality of violence was deliberately fashioned and distorted by the vested interests of the various ruling elites and the revolutionary groups and their institutions down through the ages. His prime example of such utter distortion of the truth was the attitude of the Christian Churches to violence, because he felt that their distortion of the gospel of peace was far more reprehensible. For Tolstoy, Christianity is pacifism, and pacifism is Christianity. Pacifism arises out of, and is fundamental to the Christian World View.

Tolstoy attempted to construct a moral framework on which a philosophy of peace could be formulated. Many of his critics have said that he failed to face up to the reality of violence both in personal relationships and the social structures of society. Against this Tolstoy, could be compared to the great men of history - was their view of reality more authentic than Tolstoy's? He contemptuously dismissed the historical figure of Napoleon:

> Napoleon, throughout the whole (Russian) campaign was like a child seated in a carriage clasping the sides, and imagining it is he that makes the horses go.[10]

Tolstoy attempted to point out what he believed was the truth about war, although not many people in positions of authority wanted to hear what he had to say. Tolstoy believed, above all else, that the antidote to hate and violence in human society and in individuals was love and forgiveness. Those who thought that this was a weak message were, according to Tolstoy, hypnotised by the magnetism of power and violence. Governments, or the revolutionary groups that aspire to be in government, could never accept what Tolstoy was saying. If they believed Tolstoy, that would lead to their own undoing.

Tolstoy can be seen, in one sense, as a voice crying in the wilderness. Both his ex-communication from the Russian Orthodox Church and the attempts to silence him by the Russian government reflect the danger that was seen in his ideas. He objected in the strongest possible terms to the ridiculous idea that governments generally expect people to believe that they made war for the sake of peace.

RUSSELL: AND THE MYTHOLOGIES OF JUSTIFICATION

In his early writings Russell attacked the logic of violence on every front. The political, social, economic and moral bases of violence were, according to Russell, untenable from any rational perspective. While some violence could be justified, and some wars could be rationalised, the central theme of most of Russell's writings identified the justifications and rationalisations which were used as distortions and were untenable. The fact that Russell reluctantly supported the Second World War does not in itself invalidate his original ideas. He could, as he was aware himself, be a victim of irrational fears and illogical justifications.

---

[10] Sampson, *Causes of War,* 10.

Russell believed that the concept of violence and the concept of non-violence were the bases of two fundamentally opposing theories of reality. Within the concept of violence, the absurdities of logic were far greater than in the concept of non-violence. The belief that crimes committed against civilian populations in the names of freedom or justice or the state are somehow less evil than the same crimes committed for some other reason is, according to Russell, totally illogical. It leads on to other equally problematic beliefs, for example, that weapons of mass extermination are not really weapons of mass extermination when they are used for security, defence or some other perceived higher principle.

Russell has been charged with inconsistency in his pacifist stance, but he never committed himself to a totally pacifist position. He stood firmly against the First World War when it was a very unpopular stand to take. He was prepared to go to jail rather than stay silent. Many of those who criticise him have done far less for such principles. Russell has done more than any other modern philosopher to highlight the inconsistencies in the logic of war and violence.

GANDHI: AND THE MYTHOLOGIES OF VIOLENCE

Gandhi's legacy on the reality of war and violence has not, as yet, made a significant breakthrough. The type of revolutionary changes that Gandhi looked for will not come about instantaneously because his message is not to the elites of this world, but to people at grass-roots level every where. The essence of *satyagraha* and *ahimsa* are so fundamental that they will produce a metamorphosis in the nature of power in society. Such a metamorphosis will threaten so many vested interests that it will be sabotaged at every level. The Gandhian methods themselves may well be used for non-Gandhian purposes. Gandhi believed that there were two basic, and mutually exclusive, methods of bringing about social change; through the method of violence or through the method of non-violence. Such a simple division can be very misleading, but Gandhi believed that this division was fundamental. Violence and non-violence are not only poles apart, they are the tips of two very separate cultural icebergs. The changes brought about through the use of violence will be fundamentally different to the changes brought about through the use of non-violence. Gandhi's challenge to the mythologies of violence centered around the doctrine that the means cannot justify the ends; for the simple and obvious reason that the means used determines the nature of the ends sought. This is where Gandhi differs so radically from the Machiavellian view of means and ends.

EINSTEIN: AND THE MYTHOLOGIES OF SECURITY

In one sense Einstein was the most problematic of the four individuals. His total commitment to conscientious objection in the early part of his life, and then his strong rejection of it during the 1930s, was a major source of antagonism between Einstein and various members of the peace movements. Even his own explanation for this change of conviction was not very convincing. While accepting this and other problems, it was hoped to obtain a more balanced view of his over-all contribution to the concepts of peace. Einstein lived through some of the great upheavals of the twentieth century. It is not surprising that his view on specific approaches to war and peace would change with the rise of the demented ideology of Nazism.

Einstein held to his belief that the international system based on balance of power concepts was a menace to peaceful international relations. He was voracious in his criticism of the principles that underlay this system of international relations. Einstein rejected, as fatally flawed, the principle *si vis pacem, para bellum*, "if you want peace prepare for war." Einstein believed from a purely logical point of view that if you want peace you must prepare for peace. The people who really annoyed Einstein were those who tried to justify war preparation by turning logic on its head. If you want peace; prepare for peace, educate for peace, construct international systems that will promote peace. That is the simple logic that Einstein felt was basis for any culture of peace.

Since the end of the Second World War, concepts of security have been dominated by what could be called techno-scientific mind-sets. The idea that it was possible to measure security in millions of tons of T.N.T. or thousands of nuclear and other weapons of mass extermination, has been accepted as a central aspect of international wisdom. The inconvenient fact that the single most important characteristic of international relations since 1945 has been insecurity rather than security tends to be overlooked. The national security state as it has evolved in the nuclear age has placed its citizens in a position of unprecedented danger. The apologists for this state of affairs say that there is no alternative to the very system that they helped to create. Einstein said we must ask the question: "Who creates such fears among the American people that they should be obliged to accept permanent military bondage?"[11] The ideas that the introduction of more and more sophisticated weapons of mass destruction might impose limits on war has failed repeatedly over time, from the interdict on the crossbow in the eleventh century to the attempts to control the Dreadnoughts in the early part of the twentieth century. Einstein believed that what he saw as passing for arms control was a sham; the very people who operate the arms control process have little real interest in reducing the amount of money being spent on arms. In the final analysis, Einstein looked to the ordinary peoples of the world as the only hope to overcome the addiction to violence. He felt that this could be done through the proper education of the young, and the establishment of democratic politics in countries throughout the world. This would be a gradual process with no instantaneous results.

PEACE AND DEVELOPMENT ISSUES

The struggle against poverty, repression and exploitation must be seen as a central aspect of any peace debate. President Eisenhower, in his famous farewell address, highlighted the issue:

---

[11] Nathan and Norden, 343.

> Every gun that is made, every warship launched, every rocket fired, signifies a theft from those who hunger and are not fed, from those who are cold and are not clothed.

Pope Paul VI declared that: "Development is the new name for peace." The relationships between peace and development issues were highlighted by a number of studies and reports. In 1977 the General Assembly of the United Nations convened the first special session on disarmament which was to highlight the nature of the relationship between disarmament and development issues. In 1980 the Brant report: *North-South: A Programme for Survival*[12] analysed the possible impact on development of a certain reduction in the level of military spending, which would then be diverted to development issues. The report attempted to identify the economic and social consequences of continuous large-scale spending on military hardware, research and development. The Brant report maintained that if only a fraction of the money, manpower and resources was diverted to socially useful developments, the effects would be of enormous benefit. In 1981 the Thorssen report, which had been commissioned after the first special session on disarmament of the General Assembly, established a definite negative relationship between military spending and development. Various cycles of "poverty, repression and militarisation" were identified.

From the Gandhian point of view the relationship between peace and development issues had a number of serious complications. Gandhi himself, on numerous occasions had questioned the development process. It was quite possible that the development process was actually creating many of the conflicts and fueling the cycle of poverty and repression. E. F. Schumacher took a critical look at this issue in *Small is Beautiful*[13]:

> The dominant modern belief is that the soundest

[12] The Independent Commission, *North South: A Programme for Survival.* (London: Pan 1980).
[13] E. F. Schumacher, *Small is Beautiful: A Study of Economics as if People Mattered.* (London: Abacus, 1973).

> foundation of peace would be universal prosperity. One may look in vain for historical evidence that the rich have regularly been more peaceful than the poor,...The road to peace, it is argued, is to follow the road to riches.[14]

Schumacher goes on to argue that the relationship between peace and development can only be positive if the right development paths are chosen:

> The hope...that by the single-minded pursuit of wealth, without bothering our heads about spiritual and moral questions, we could establish peace on earth, is an unrealistic, unscientific and irrational hope.[15]

A number of attempts have been made to try and establish a "New International Economic Order". At the United Nations Conference on Trade and Development in 1964, countries from the weaker economies established the Group of 77, which had grown to a membership of 128 by the early 1990s. The adoption of declarations on a more just international system would not, by itself, create any real shift in the balance of power. The Bretton Woods systems of the World Bank and the International Monetary Fund and their more recent manifestations were not going to give up their controlling interests without major political change. By the time of the "Earth Summit" in Rio in 1992, the relationship between peace and development issues and major environmental problems had started to move towards the centre-stage of political awareness.

---

[14] Ibid., 21.
[15] Ibid., 30-31.

PEACEFUL CHANGE IN EUROPEAN SOCIETY

Since the time of the French revolution, a belief in the utility of violence has been established almost beyond question in European culture and society. It had become almost an accepted fact that political change in Europe was always accompanied by bloody social upheavals. The incredible implications of the developments of "The Velvet Revolution" of 1989 have only just begun to move some way towards undermining the cultural enthrallment to political violence:

> No amount of violence could have achieved, in a hundred years, what peaceful political action achieved in Europe since 1988.

"The Velvet Revolution" liberated the peoples of East Germany, Poland, Hungary, Czechoslovakia, Bulgaria and, to a lesser extent, Romania. At the same time the peoples within the Soviet Empire from Estonia to Uzbek reasserted their national and regional autonomy.

Until quite recently, the long history of peaceful political change has been ignored and dismissed in most European countries. Within Irish historical traditions the extraordinary achievements of Daniel O'Connell in his use of the techniques of non-violence have been ignored for political reasons and in some cases denied. The Catholic association, founded by O'Connell in 1823 introduced novel methods of organisation, which produced revolutionary results. The subscription of 1d a month opened the association to membership of the mass of the people. This was to have an important psychological effect on the poorest of the peasants who were suddenly given a vested interest in the politics of Emancipation. Campaigns of Civil Disobedience and passive resistance were successfully introduced into Irish politics by O'Connell and his associates. O'Connell was only one of a long tradition of Irish political leaders who rejected the use of violence as a political instrument. Michael Davitt, one of the founders of the Land League, spoke on numerous occasions against the use of violence. He passionately believed that the aims of the Land League would not be served by violence. The League has,

> A higher aim, a nobler object, than taking vengeance on individuals, and anyone engaged in it who advocated any such thing was guilty of great folly.[16]

Given Davitt's personal history of imprisonment and abuse by the British authorities, his attitude towards the use of violence is all the more remarkable. He claimed that violence and revenge were ignoble and self destroying: "let the victims of the Land League movement be injustice, ignorance, social degradation, and pauperism."[17]

THE EUROPEAN CULTURE OF VIOLENCE

The culture of violence and the tradition of physical force have been very powerful factors in European society and civilisation for over a thousand years. The Christian Churches, one of the central historical pillars of European society, became, and remained one of the great Warrior Religions of mankind. The attempts by the Christian Churches to come to terms with the use of physical force have not been very successful. The just war theory has become less and less functional, particularly in relation to the "dirty little wars" that have come to characterise the second half of the twentieth and the early part of the twenty-first centuries. The historical experience and tradition of the European Enlightenment created some significant new perspectives on the question of violence. But the violent revolutions that stemmed from the ideals of the enlightenment created a new culture of violence that almost extinguished those new perspectives.

The "romantic illusion of violence" is still so ingrained in the ideologies of most European cultures that it is almost hidden and beyond question. The violent conflict on the island of Ireland in

---

[16] T. W. Moody, *Davit and Irish Revolution.* (Oxford: Clarendon, 1982), 322.
[17] Ibid., 444.

recent times reflects an even deeper crises in European culture. The Irish experience has brought people face to face with the romantic illusion of violence and it has become harder and harder to justify the romance of that illusion. In France and Britain, and many other European countries that illusion is so ingrained in the mind-set of their respective cultures that it is almost beyond question. The continent of Europe is still saturated with weapons of mass extermination, including nuclear, chemical and biological systems. Many European Governments are still heavily involved in the appalling production and distribution of land-mines. The veneer of respectability given to this reign of terror reflects the persistence of the illusion of violence in European culture. The irony and the hypocrisy of those governments preaching non-violence to terrorist groups is not lost on these ogranisations.

How persistent, dangerous and deep-routed is the culture of violence in European civilisation, can be seen by the tragic re-emergence of Genocide on the European stage of history. In 1914 the Carnegie Endowment for International Peace sent a commission of eminent people to examine the nature of the violent conflicts in the Balkan region. In 1993 a new commission was established by the Carnegie Endowment to try again to do what the original commission had set out to do. One of the more important emphasis of the commission was to lay aside the idea that these conflicts were somehow endemic to the Balkan region and its people. There was a belief that the real ingredients of the conflict in the Balkans was "a clash of civilisations" based on "ancestral hatreds," and so, little or nothing could be done about them. While these historical conditions do exist to a greater or lesser extent, it must be seen as a dangerous misconception to blame the war on these factors alone. The war in the former Yugoslavia, like every other war of the twentieth century, was not created by spontaneous combustion. It was created with deliberate calculation by certain individuals who believed that war could be fought on the Clausewitzian principles of rational instrumentality. One contemporary view of this particular conflict is that it has been deliberately started by intellectuals:

> This is probably the only war in history which was planned and led by writers, and they have pursued it for three-and-a-half-years fanatically.[18]

But individuals like ideologies need the oxygen of culture in which to survive and prosper.

AN AGENDA FOR PEACE

In 1992 Boutros Boutros-Ghali, the then Secretary-General of the United Nations, produced his report: *An Agenda for Peace.*[19] The basis of this report was the hope that the end of the Cold War would create a new environment in which the United Nations could work in a positive way for the principles of peace and international security as laid out in its original charter. He stated that:

> The Nations and peoples of the United Nations are fortunate in a way that those of the League of Nations were not. We have been given a second chance to create the world of our Charter that they were denied....there is a need to ensure that the lessons of the past four decades are learned and that the errors, or variations of them, are not repeated. For there may not be a third opportunity for our planet, which now, for different reasons, remains endangered.[20]

Given the bitter ideological disputes of the Cold War period it would seem almost a miracle that the United Nations has survived at all in a meaningful form. Much criticism has been laid at the door of the United Nations over its failure to act in a positive manner when large-scale violence is either threatened or breaks out.

---

[18] Marko Vesovic,-Yugoslavian author quoted in Irish Times. 28th September 1995.

[19] Boutros Boutros-Ghali, *An Agenda for Peace*. (New York: United Nations, 1992).

[20] Ibid., 45.

Since the end of the Second World War an appalling catalogue of genocidal conflicts has been recorded. Sean MacBride, in an address to Amnesty International in 1979 condemned:

> The present world phase of unprecedented violence and cruelty, and near total breakdown in public and private morality.[21]

He went on to identify a long list of genocidal conflicts that had taken place since the adoption of the Convention on Genocide by the United Nations in 1948:

> In historical terms, war has always led towards genocide. There is no shortage of historical accounts of exterminations amounting to genocidal levels.[22]

But the nature of the symbiotic relationship between war and genocide has only just begun to be studied and understood. The more recent genocidal conflicts in Rwanda and in former Yugoslavia and in numerous other areas can be seen as a major failure of the United Nations system. But the failure of the United Nations is only a reflection of the failure of the individual countries that go to make up the permanent membership of the Security Council, which has the specific mandate for upholding international peace. There can be no question that the United Nations system needs reforms but the basic principles, as outlined in the original charter, are a beacon of hope for future generations. Lance Morrow, writing about peaceful developments in South Africa and the Middle East, sums up some of the central problems and the possibilities of peace:

> Low in the central brain lies the limbic system (hypothalamus, hippocampus, amygdala) where the aggression seems to start. But there is a higher brain as

---

[21] Sean MacBride quoted in Leo Kuper, *Genocide.* (London: Penguin, 1981), 186.

[22] Israel W. Charny, ed. *Genocide: A Critical Bibliographic Review*. (London: Mansell, 1988).

> well. If war originates as an impulse of the lower brain, then peace is an accomplishment of the higher, and the ascent from the brain's basement, where the crocodile lives, to the upper chambers may be the most important climb that Humans attempt.[23]

One of the central themes of the analysis of the ideas highlighted in this book is the belief that in relation to the philosophy of peace there are few if any moral absolutes. The philosophy of peace, by its very nature, deals with questions that defy simple solutions and involve many moral ambiguities. It may be felt by some, that peace studies, and indeed, a philosophy of peace, should by their very nature contribute a set of moral absolutes around which a particular world-view can be built. The modern concept of "Fuzzy Logic" would seem, by many, to be inadmissible to any serious philosophy. But "Fuzzy Logic" or its philosophical equivalent has been a central part of most philosophical frameworks. The individuals whose ideas have been outlined have attempted to put some clarity into the ambiguities that surround the questions of war and peace. Traditional attempts at promoting one set of philosophical values by demonising another set have contributed little to the progressive synthesis. It should not be that in times of war the philosopher should be silent.

One of the central arguments of the tradition that rationalises the use of violence relates to the question of power outlined so clearly in the Melian dialogue in the history of the Peloponesian wars. The central aspects of this debate have still not been fully resolved. There is still to be found the general belief that there is no real alternative to violence, and that peace does not produce the necessary results. Within these parameters can be found some of the more absurd arguments in relation to peace and war. Again and again it is possible to identify an almost infantile approach to peace and its possibilities. It is assumed almost as a fact, that peace has some magical properties, and that once peace has been reached, as in the cessation of hostilities, for whatever reason, the problems that created the conflict in the

---

[23] Lance Morrow, "To Conquer the Past." *Time*. (3rd January, 1994), 16.

first place will disappear. Nothing could be further from the truth. Yet, such a belief exists against all historical experience.

10

THE FOUNDATIONS OF A NEW ENLIGHTENMENT

The greatest tragedy of this period of social transitions was not the strident clamor of the bad people, but the appalling silence of the good people

Martin Luther King, JR.

This is the Way of Peace:

Overcome Evil with Good,

And Falsehood with Truth,

And Hatred with Love.

The Peace Pilgrim (1908-1981)

THE COST OF THE IDEOLOGY OF VIOLENCE

Much information is available concerning the actual economic cost of the ideology of violence. The figures show quite clearly that every year thousands of billions of euro are spent collectively on the war system. The actual amount of money spent since the McCloy-Zorin proposals (1961) for General and Complete Disarmament (GCD), if it could be accurately estimated, would be staggering. But this is a very false picture. The thousands of trillions of euros wasted in the last half century is literally only the tip of this appalling iceberg. The real cost of the Ideology of Violence for our civilizations and our planet are immeasurably higher. In one sense this is the real crime of the war system. It is also a mistake to believe that we can measure the damage done by war and violence by counting the number of individuals killed and injured. Because the real damage is, as Bertrand Russell pointed out, far more widespread and deeply entrenched in all aspects of culture and society. War and the fear of violence had a double effect in retarding social progress. According to Russell the greatest evil of war is the spiritual damage done to society, and this from a man who was in no way religious. Russell's approach of logical analysis was outraged at the acceptance of what he termed the whole mythologies of falsehoods that are inflicted on society in order to support, justify and rationalise the ideology of the war system.

The greatest paradox that has been created by, and resulted from, the pursuit of the ideology of violence has been the creation of insecurity rather than security. This insecurity is truly on an unparalleled level. The war system created the incredible situation where the citizens of Europe, the United States and the Soviet Union were threatened with almost instant nuclear omnicide and the unimaginable consequences of such action. No demented suicidal ideologist could have created a more dangerous system than this. The war system whose very reason for existence was supposed to have been to improve the security of the actors involved, created the very opposite of security. This situation did not arise accidentally, nor as a bolt out of the blue. From the very start of the nuclear arms race many of the scientists involved warned of the explicit dangers. The Russell- Einstein Manifesto[1] published under the auspices of the Pugwash group of scientists was just one such warning. The real question is how can such logical absurdities be passed off as rational analysis? We warn our children that if they play with fire they are sure to get burned. It is a simple lesson.

DIRECT AND STRUCTURAL VIOLENCE

War and the violence associated with modern warfare have the potential for levels of violence of unimaginable devastation. But on a constant basis war itself is no longer the most deadly form of violence. Far more people are killed and have their lives impaired as a result of the insidious nature of structural violence. The ideology of violence which underlines the culture of violence takes many different forms and shapes. While the recognised differences between direct and structural violence are very significant, structural violence is only made possible by the ideological foundations of direct violence and not the other way round. In relation to violence, both direct and cultural, some pessimists would argue that we have already passed the point of no return; that our industrial civilisation would collapse without persistent and widespread violence both direct and structural. One of the paradoxes at the heart of the culture of violence is built into the relationship between power and violence. The paradox concerns how power is constructed in society. The ruling elite of whatever culture will always attempt to monopolise the legitimacy of violence. So that it will always be in the interest of the ruling elite to differentiate between 'legitimate' and 'illegitimate violence'. If there is any chance of breaking the paradox of violence we need to move beyond the endless debate on the legitimacy of violence.

---

[1] Bertrand Russell and Albert Einstein. *The Russell Einstein Manifesto*. London 1955

ENGINEERING THE STRUCTURES OF PEACE

Quincy Wright in his classical work: *A Study of War*[2] published originally in 1942, identified the problems of constructing a viable peace in the following scenario. An engineer or an architect who wants to construct a bridge, must produce a blueprint of the structure of the bridge with the details of the design before the work begins. What sort of bridge would we get without an intelligent plan or blueprint? But an engineer building a bridge has some great advantages over those who are trying to build a culture of peace. Any engineer must know and accept that there are certain laws of physics that must be taken into account or the structure will be unstable and collapse. The fundamental laws associated with gravity and the laws of mass and weight etc. must be incorporated into the construction. Architects and engineers can interpret these laws to produce functional or aesthetic variations depending on the material used. But anyone who tries to build a bridge while ignoring the fundamental laws of gravity will construct a dangerous and unstable bridge.

Robert Schuman one of the founding fathers of the European Union was a real architect of peace. Schuman himself had come from a part of Europe which had been fought over continuously by France and Germany - the Alsace-Lorraine region. He experienced first hand the ravages of war. He believed that if there was ever going to be peace in Europe, then the age old antagonism between France and Germany would have to be addressed. Many people believed that this was just not possible. Schuman and other contemporaries like Jean Monnet had the creative imagination to build institutions that would make redundant many of the most significant age old national animosities of Europe. The key for Schuman was in the open nature of the agreement:

[2] Quincy Wright. *A Study of War*. University of Chicago Press. Chicago. 1983

> Europe will not be made at once or according to a single plan. It will be built through concrete achievements which first create a de facto solidarity.[3]

At the hearth of the Schuman plan (1950) drafted by Jean Monnet was the proposal of placing the massive coal and steel resources under joint control. National arguments over the control of these and other resources had contributed to much of the instability in Europe over the previous decades. This step-by-step gradual approach was the key concept in the European architecture of peace. It led to the position that Schuman had believed that war would become "not merely unthinkable, but materially impossible."[4]
In the same way the construction of peace, for example, in international affairs will have certain fundamental laws that must be considered for the stability of the system. But Wright in his: *Study of War* believed that planning for peace was much more problematic than planning for building a bridge or other structure. He believed that the objective of peace cannot be identified as a given variable. The objective of peace will change with experience so that the fundamental conditions for the construction of peace cannot be predicted in advance. Under these conditions engineering plans for peace cannot be as scientific as conditions pertaining to the natural world. Even allowing for such differences, the fundamental principles for constructing peace have been identified and studied in many cultures in many ages. There is no mystery or magical formula associated with these ideas; they are at this stage of our knowledge almost self evident. see Table 10.1

Table 10.1
SOME OF THE SOCIAL AND POLITICAL FOUNDATIONS FOR THE STRUCTURES OF PEACE

1. World Community: Beyond Nation States and Empires.

---

[3] Robert Schuman. An Architect of Peace. Irish Times. Dublin 27.03.2007. Supplement p 3
[4] Ibid.

A Federation of peoples, or world Government however defined.

2. International Relations: Beyond the Law of the Jungle.
    A World Court with the moral and legal authority to arbitrate on conflicts.

3. Security: Beyond the Insanity of Mutually Assured Destruction. (MAD)
    General and Complete Disarmament: Similar to the Zorin-McCloy proposals.

4. Economics: Beyond the Capitalist Model.
    An Economic Order with sustainability and fairness as the key dynamic.

5. Environment: Beyond the Ideology of Destruction.
    An Environmental Order in which sustainability is the norm.

These five and other related principles are both of local and global importance. We know for example that there are just under two hundred nation states represented in the United Nations. But as Elsie Boulding pointed out in her: *Cultures of Peace*[5] there are over ten thousand societies that make up the whole of human culture. In many cases the nation state is more of a hindrance then a help in fulfilling the potential of these societies. The model of the European Union of unity in diversity would seem to be a much more positive approach.

However, the very foundations for the structures of peace are the individual humans that make up our cultures. *The Seville Statement on Violence* [6] is quite clear that individually we are not genetically programmed towards violence. That we need not be enslaved to the reptilian part of our brain. That we, as individuals, can break our addiction to violence.

---

[5] Elise Boulding. *Cultures of Peace*. Syracuse University Press. New York 2000

[6] UNESCO. The Seville Statement On Violence. UNESCO. Paris. 1986

Again the principles of peace, however defined, that apply to individuals are known and have been clearly stated down through the ages. There are no absolutes in this area, but the principles can be clearly identified.
see Table 10.2

Table 10.2
THE HUMAN FOUNDATIONS FOR THE STRUCTURES OF PEACE:
SOME PRINCIPLES

1. A Recognition of the Five Commandments:
   i. Do not kill. ii. Do not lie. iii. Do not steal.
   iv. Do not practice immorality.
   v. Respect parents and love children.

2. The Acknowledge of the Golden Rule:
   Whatever you want people to do to you, do also to them.

3. The Critical Role of Tolerance.
   The practice of religions and cultural tolerance in relation to differences.

4. The Role of Education and Wisdom.
   Education that balances morality and ethics with science and economics.

This is where the building of peace goes beyond the engineering parameters. Any structure of peace will of course have to have a moral foundation, at the level of the individual will lie the concept of tolerance

The Crash of Civilisation

Questions arising out of the idea of the: 'Clash of Civilisations' have become popular since the publication of the book by that title: *The Clash of Civilisations*[7]. But the real danger from the

[7] Samuel, P Huntington. *Clash of Civilizations?* Norton. London. 1997

pursuit of the ideology of violence must be the possibility of the crash of civilisation rather than the class of civilisations. Towards the end of his life Sigmund Freud, wrote very pessimistically about the future of civilization. In particular he was pessimistic about the future of European society. He painted the following picture. European culture with its two thousand years of Christianity, its hundreds of years of enlightenment, its scientific tradition, its education, its literature, its art, its philosophy was still a very violent and savage place. For him the First World War had shown just how thin the veneer of civilization really was – it was barely skin deep. He was shocked at how easy the men of learning in particular, were in justifying and rationalising war and violence. In *Civilization and Its Discontents*[8] he ended his analysis by saying that it would probably take another five hundred years of the gradual process of civilization to have any effect on our violent instincts and in reducing the levels of violence in European culture. His analysis might have been even more pessimistic if he had lived to see the savagery and brutality of the Second World War. Given the levels of violence in Europe during the first half of the twentieth century it would seem almost miraculous that a European Community has evolved against all the odds. But the European Community was not founded on any magical formulas. The principles which underlay the foundations of the Community were not newly invented in the nineteen fifties. They have been recognised by many philosophers and critical thinkers throughout history.

It has always been problematic to argue, from a non-violent perspective, against the utilitarian effectiveness of violence in social conflict or the efficiency of military force in political conflict. Because it is always easier to sow the seeds of doubt and fear than to sow the seeds of trust and tolerance. But we know that there are limits to the use of and to the effectiveness of violence. General Maxwell's famous statement when he signed the last of the execution orders in Dublin after the Irish Rebellion of 1916 is a good example: 'that is the last you will hear of an Irish Republic.' The point being that from a military

---

[8] Sigmund Freud. Civilization and Its Discontents. Penguin. London 2004

perspective General Maxwell had done a perfectly good job. Many people think that the world changed significantly after the attacks on United States of America in 2001. While the spectacular nature and the level of sophistication in the planning of these attacks had some novel features, the attacks themselves where just more of the same on a long continuum of the ideology of violence.

In his classical work: *Power and the Pursuit of Peace*[9] Professor F. H. Hinsley develops a number of controversial points. He argues that in general we are living in an age of unprecedented peace. Even in western culture it is not very long ago that the torture of individuals by the state was a normal practice. The hanging of men and women for stealing turnips was the accepted punishment. In some ways we are living in an age of unprecedented peace as Hinsley points out that in the personal relationships:

> Of man to man, of man to woman, of master to man, of adult to child, - witnessed a greater rise of tolerance and regulation, a greater decline in violence and chaos, than had been registered in all previous history[10]

The argument he makes is that most of the violence that we are aware of today comes through the news media and the media has for whatever reasons developed an unparalleled efficiency in bringing violence to men's attention. Regardless of how valid this analysis may be Hinsley rightly points out that:

> A civilisation which has broken through immense barriers in almost every other direction, and which has surpassed all its predecessors on innumerable fronts, should still hold views and pursue programmes in international politics that it held and pursued when it was young- this is the outstanding failure of recent

[9] Hinsely, F.H. Power and the Pursuit of Peace. London,. Cambridge UP. 1985
[10] Ibid. 277

> times. Only one thing is more surprising: we do not yet recognise this failure.[11]

The book was broadly based around three propositions in relation to the collapse of the war system. Firstly, in relation to what can be described as the ideology of war, the book starts from the position that the ideology of war is a central part of the structural framework of the culture of violence. This is relevant because if we are going to dismantle our culture of violence we must first dismantle the war system. So therefore the collapse of the war system is a vital step in the creation of the culture of peace.

The second proposition is the following. All the information and knowledge that is required for us as individuals to live in peace and all the information that is required for us to construct peaceful societies is well known and freely available. So the problem of peace is not so much the knowledge of peace but is our failure to either recognise that knowledge or to act on that knowledge.

Thirdly, the knowledge of peace involves almost every area of human social interaction. So the project of understanding peace is probably more complex than the project of mapping the human DNA sequence. There is no one area of knowledge from which peace will arise. But the knowledge of peace and the wisdom associated with that knowledge is to be found in most of the main cultures of the world.

There is one definition of madness which sums up much of the ideology of violence 'To Keep doing the same thing and expect different results'. Many people, today, sincerely believe that in historical terms the war system has served Homo Sapiens well. But that paradigm is as relevant today as a Flat Earth paradigm. There are of course still enormous vested interests in the war system. But the war paradigm is false and dangerous. In particular in relation thermo-nuclear war the pursuit of the war paradigm is criminal and suicidal. The symbiotic relationship

[11] Ibid.3

between the war system and our cultures of violence has the characteristics of a virus that is potentially disastrous. But the antidote for this virus of violence can be clearly seen and is now freely available.

BIBLIOGRAPHY

Adams, David. The Seville Statement on Violence. Jr. of Peace Research No 2. 1989.

Ansbro, John. Martin Luther King, The Making of a Mind. New York: Orbis. 1982.

Arendt, Hannah. On revolution, London: Penguin, 1965.

________.On Violence. London: Harvest. 1970

________.The Origins of Totalitarianism. London: Harvest.1976.

________.Eichmann in Jerusalem. New York. Penguin. 1994.

Arnold, Sir Edwin. The Song Celestial. London: 1885.

Ashley, Richard K. et al Last Words about War. Journal of Conflict Resolution. 1984.

Ayer, A.J., Russell And Moore: The Analytical Heritage. London: Macmillan. 1971.

________. Russell. London: The Woburn Press, 1974.

Azar, Edward E. International Conflict Resolution. Brighton: Wheatsheaf, 1986.

Barash, David P. (ed) Approaches to Peace. Oxford: OUP. 2000

Barrie and Jenkins. The Russell Lectures. 1972.

Beer, Francis. Peace Against War. San Francisco: Freeman. 1981.

Beg, Moazziz Ali. The Ideological Integration of East and West.

New Delhi: Global Vision 2005

Bentham, Jeremy. A Plan for a Universal and Perpetual Peace. London:
Grotious Society. 1927.

Berkeley, George. The Principles of Human Knowledge. (1710) Ed. by G.J. Warnock.
Glasgow: Fontana. 1962.

Berlin, Isaiah. The Hedgehog and the Fox. London: Weidenfeld,1953.

________. Fathers and Children. Romanes Lecture 1970. Oxford: OUP. 1972.

________. Introduction to Ivan Sergeyevich Turgenev. Fathers and Sons.
Trans. by Rosemary Edmonds. London: Penguin, 1965.

________. Russian Thinkers. Edited by Henry Hardy and Aileen Kelly. London:
Penguin. 1978.

Bernstein, Jeremy. Einstein. London: Fontana.1973.

Bhaktivedanta Swami Prabhupada, A. C. Bhagavad-Gita As It Is. Los Angeles: Bhaktivedanta Book Trust. 1981.

Bobbitt, Philip. The Shield of Achilles. London: Allen Lane 2002.

Borras, Professor F. M. Maxim Gorky on Tolstoy. Leeds: Leeds UP. 1968.

Boulding, Elise Cultures of Peace: The Hidden Side of History. Syracuse UP. 2000.

Boulding, Kenneth E. Peace and the War Industry. New Jersey: Transaction. 1973.

Bouthol, Gaston. War. New York: Walker, 1970.

Boutros-Ghali, Boutros. An Agenda for Peace. New York: United Nations. 1992.

Bradford, Ernle. The Sword and the Scimitar. London: Gollancz. 1974.

Braudel, Fernand. A History of Civilisations. Trans.by Richard Mayne. London:
Penguin. 1993.

Brock, Peter. 20th Century Pacifism - The Roots of War. New York: Van Nostrand-
Reinhold. 1977.

Brock, Peter. A Brief History of Pacifism from Jesus to Tolstoy. Toronto: Syracuse University Press 1992.

Calvocoressi, Peter. A Time For Peace. London: Hutchinson. 1987.

Cameron Watt, D. How War Came. London: Heinemann. 1989.

Camus, Albert. Neither Victims Nor Executioners. Philadelphia: New Society, 1986.

Cardenal, Rodolfo. "The Role of the University in Establishing a Just Society." Irish
School of Ecumenics paper quoted in Irish Times, 15th July 1994.

Carr, Brian, ed. Bertrand Russell An Introduction. London: Allen and Unwin, 1975.

Charleton, Peter. Lies in a Mirror. Dublin: Blackhall. 2006.

Charny, Israel W. Genocide: A Critical Bibliographic Review. London: Mansell,
1988.

Chelcicky, Peter. "Net of Faith", quoted in Peter Brock A Brief History of Pacifism
from Jesus to Tolstoy, . Toronto: Syracuse University Press, 1992.

Chomsky, Noam. Problems of Knowledge and Freedom. London: Fontana, 1972.

________. Deterring Democracy. London: Vintage, 1992.
________. Rogue States. London: Pluto Press. 2000

________. Hegemony or Survival. London: Penguin Books 2003

Chopra. Deepak. Peace is the Way. London: Rider. 2005.

Choudhuri, Manmohan. Exploring Gandhi. New Delhi: The Gandhi Peace
Foundation, 1989.

Christian, Reginald F. Tolstoy A Critical Introduction. Cambridge: Cambridge
University Press, 1969.

________. Ed. and trans. Tolstoy's Diaries. London: The Athlone Press: 1985; reprint,
London: Flamingo 1994.

Clark, Ian. Waging War: A Philosophical Introduction. Oxford: Clarendon, 1990.

Clark, Ronald W. Einstein, The Life and Times. London: Hodder & Stoughton, 1979.

________. The Life of Bertrand Russell. London: Penguin, 1978.

Class, Willy. Secretary General NATO, quoted in Irish Times. 3rd February 1995.

Claude, Inis L. The Heritage of Quincy Wright. Journal of Conflict Resolution.
No. 4, 1970.

Clausewitz, Carl von. On War. Edited by Anatol Rapoport. London: Penguin. 1968.

Collingwood, R.G. The Idea of History. Oxford: Oxford University Press. 1993.

Cook, Paul. Darwinism: War and History. Cambridge: CU. 1994.

Copleston, Frederick, S. J. A History of Philosophy. Vol. I. New York:
Image Books, 1961.

Cox, Caroline and R. Scruton. Peace Studies: A Critical Survey. London: the Institute
for European Defence and Strategic Studies. Occasional Paper No. 7, 1984.

Cremin, Peadar, ed. Education for Peace. Dublin: Education Studies Association of
Ireland, 1993.

Cruise O' Brien, Conor. Reflections on Political Violence. London: Hutchinson, 1978.

DeBenedetti, Charles. The Peace Reform in American History. Bloomington: Indiana
University Press, 1980.

Dewey, John. "The Influence of Darwin of Philosophy" in Darwin, edited by P. Appleman.New York: Norton, 1970.

Dhawan, Gopinath. The Political Philosophy of Mahatma Gandhi. 4th ed. Delhi: Gandhi Peace Foundation, 1990.

Dillon, Martin. The Shankill Butchers. London: Arrow Books, 1990.

Dostoyevsky, Fyodor Mikhail. The Devils. London: Penguin, 1953.

Duncan, Ronald, ed. Selected Writings of Mahatma Gandhi. London: Faber and Faber Ltd., 1951; reprint, London: Fontana 1972.

Dunn, Ted. A Search for Alternatives to War and Violence. London: Clark, 1967.

________. Foundations of Peace and Freedom. Swansea: Christopher Davies, 1975.

________. A Step By Step Approach to World Peace. Chichester: Gooday, 1988.

Edwards, Stewart, ed. Selected Writings of Pierre-Joseph Proudhon. Translated by Elizabeth Fraser. London: Macmillan 1969.

Egan, David, and Melinda A. Egan, Leo Tolstoy, an Annotated Bibliography of English- Language Sources to 1978. London: Scarecrow, 1979.

Einstein, Albert. The World As I See It. By Alan Harris. London: Watts, 1949.

________. Ideas And Opinions. By Sonja Bargmann. New Jersey: Wings. 1954.

________. Out Of My Later Years. New York: Philosophical Library, 1
New Jersey: Wings Books, 1993.

Einstein, Albert and Sigmund Freud. Why War. London: 1934.

Elshtain, Jean B. ed. Just War Theory. Oxford: Blackwell, 1992.

Fahey, Joseph J. War and the Christian Conscience. New York: Orbis 2005.

Fanon, Frantz. The Wretched of the Earth. Translated by Constance Farrington.
London: Pelican, 1983.

Farley, Christopher and David Hodgson, compiled by, The Life Of Bertrand Russell
in Pictures and his Own Words. Nottingham: Spokesman, 1972.

Fergusion, Niall. The War of the World. London: Allen Lane. 2006

Fink, Clinton F. and Christopher Wright. Quincy Wright on War and Peace: Journal
of Conflict Resolution. Vol. XIV, No.4, Dec. 1970.

Fischer, Louis. The Life of Mahatma Gandhi. London: Grafton Books. 1988.

Freud, Sigmund. The Complete Psychological Works. Vol. XXI. Civilisation and its
Discontents. Edited by J. Strachey. London: Hogarth, 1930.

Fry, Douglas P. The Human Potential for Peace. Oxford, OUP. 2006

Freyer, Grattan. W.B.Yeats And the Anti-Democratic Tradition. Dublin: Gill and
Macmillan, 1981.

Fukuyama, Francis. The End of History and the Last Man. Penguin (1992)

Fuller, J. C. K. The Decisive Battles of the Western World. Edited by John Terrine.
London: Granada, 1971.

Fussell, Paul. The Great War and Modern Memory. Oxford: Oxford University Press,
1975.

Gallie, W. B. Philosophies of Peace and War. Cambridge: Cambridge
University Press, 1979.

________. Understanding War. London: Routledge, 1991.

Galtung, Johan. Towards a Definition of Peace Research. Paris: UNESCO, 1979.

________. "Social Cosmology and the Concept of Peace." Journal Of Peace Research.
Vol. XVIII, No. 2, 1981.

________. (et al.) Searching for Peace. Pluto Press. London. 2002

________. Peace By Peaceful Means. Sage. London. 1996

Gandhi, M. K. All Men are Brothers. Compiled and edited by Krishna Kripalani.
Ahmedabad: Navajivan Trust, 1960.

________. An Autobiography or the Story of My Experiments with Truth. Translated by Mahadev Desai. reprinted as one volume, London: Penguin, 1982

Gardiner, Patrick. Theories of History.The Free Press. London: Allen & Unwin, 1969.

Gelditsch, Nils P. John Galtung: A Bibliography: Oslo: PRIO, 1980.

Genoves, Santiago. Is Peace Inevitable? London: George Allen and Unwin, 1972.

Gifford, Henry, ed. Leo Tolstoy A Critical Anthology. London: Penguin, 1971.

Girard, René. Violence and the Sacred. Tran.P. Grergory. London: Continuum. 2005.

Glover, Edward. War, Sadism and Pacifism. 1933.

Goldsmith, Maurice. Einstein: The First Hundred Years. Oxford: OUP. 1980.

Gray, John. Al Qaeda and What It Means to be Modern. London: Faber. 2002.

Green, Paula. The Buddhist Roots of Active Non-violence. Reconciliation International, Volume No. IV, 1990.

Green, Martin. Tolstoy and Gandhi: Men of Peace. New York: 1983.

Griffin, Nicholas, ed. The Selected Letters of Bertrand Russell. Volume I: The Private Years, 1884-1914. London: Allen Lane, 1992.

Grotius, Hugo. The Rights of War and Peace. (1623). Translated by A. G. Campbell.
London: Universal Classics Library, 1901.

Grossman, David. On Killing. New York. Back Bay Books. 1996

Gunn, John. Violence in Human Society. London: David and Charles, 1973.

Hailsham, Lord. The Dilemma of Democracy. London: Collins, 1978.

Haring, Bernard. The Healing Power of Peace. Slough: St. Paul, 1986.

Harle, Vilho. Towards a Comparative Study of Peace Ideas. Journal of Peace
Research. Vol. XXVI. No. 4, 1989.

Hegel, G. W. F. The Philosophy of Right. (1821). Translated by T. M. Knox. Oxford:
Clarendon, 1942.

Hellwig, Monika K. A Case for Peace in Reason and Faith. Minnesota: Liturgical
Press,1992.

Hemleben, Sylvester J. Plans for World Peace Through Six Centuries. 1945.

Hendrickx, Herman. A Time for Peace: Reflections on the Meaning of Peace and
Violence in the Bible. London: Claretian, 1986.

Highfield, Roger The Private Lives of Albert Einstein. London: Faber 1993.

Hinde, Robert & Rotblat, Joseph. War No More. London. Pluto. 2003

Hinsley, F.H. Power and the Pursuit of Peace. Cambridge: CUP. 1963.

Hollins, Elizabeth Jay, ed. Peace is Possible. New York: Grossman, 1966.

Holsti, Kalevi J. Peace and War: Armed Conflicts and International Order 1648-1989.
Cambridge: Cambridge University Press, 1991.

Holton, Gerald. Albert Einstein: Historical and Cultural Perspectives. Princeton
University Press, 1982.

Homer. The Iliad. Translated by Martin Hammond. London: Penguin, 1987.

Hope, Marjorie and James Young. The Struggle for Humanity. London: Orbis, 1977.

Hope Mason, John. The Indispensable Rousseau. New York: Quartet, 1979.

Horowitz, Irving L. War and Peace in Contemporary Social and Philosophical
Theory. London: Condor, 1973.

Howard, Michael. War and the Liberal Conscience. Oxford: OUP. 1981.

________. War in European History. Oxford: Oxford University Press, 1987

________. The Invention of Peace: The Reinvention of War. Profile. London 2000

Howell, Signe, and Roy Willas. Societies at Peace. London: Routledge, 1989.

Hume, David. A Treatise of Human Nature. Edited by Pall S. Ardal. London:
Fontana, 1972.

Huxley, Aldous. The Perennial Philosophy. London: Grafton, 1989.

________. Pacifism and Philosophy. London: Peace Pledge Union, 1994.

Huxley, Julian. Essays of a Humanist. London: Chatto and Windus, 1964.

Independent Commission. North South: A Programme for Survival. London: Pan.
1980.

Iyer, Raghavan, ed. The Essential Writings Of Mahatma Gandhi. Ahmedabad:
Navajivan Trust, 1990; reprint, Delhi: Oxford University Press, 1994.

Jack, Homer A., ed. Religion for Peace: Proceedings of the Kyoto Conference. New
Delhi: 1973.

Jager, Ronald. The Development of Bertrand Russell's Philosophy. London: George
Allen and Unwin, 1972.

Jensen, Derrick. Endgame: Volume I The Problem of Civilization. Seven Stories.
New York 2006

Jeong, Ho Won. Peace and Conflict Studies. London: Ashgate. 2000.

John XXIII. Pacem in Terris. New York: America Press, 1963.

Jones, Malcolm, ed. New Essays On Tolstoy. Cambridge: CUP. 1978.

Josephson, Harold. "Albert Einstein: The Search for World Order." In Peace Heroes.
Charles DeBenedetti. Bloomington: Indiana University Press, 1988.

Joyce, Avery James. The War Machine. 1980.

Kainz, Howard P. Philosophical Perspectives on Peace: An Anthology of Classical
and Modern Sources. London: Macmillan Press, 1987.
Keen, David. Endless War. London: Pluto. 2006

Kende, Istvan. The History of Peace: Concepts and Organisations from the Late
Middle Ages to the 1870s. Journal of Peace Research. No. 3, 1989.

Kennedy, Paul. The Rise and Fall of the Great Powers. London: Fontana Press, 1988.

King, Martin Luther, JR. I Have A Dream.. Haper Collins. New York New York 1992

________________. A Call To Conscience. London. Little Brown. 2001

________________. In My Own Words. London. Hodder & Stoughton. 2002

Kitchen, Martin. Fascism. London: Macmillan, 1976.

Knowles, A. V. ed. Tolstoy: The Critical Heritage. London: Routledge, 1978.

Knutsen, Torbjorn. Re-reading Rousseau in the Post-Cold War World.
Journal of PeaceResearch, Vol. XXXI, No.3, 1994.

Kripalani, J. B. Gandhi His Life and Thought. New Delhi: Publications Division,
Ministry of Information and Broadcasting, Government of India. reprint, 1991.

Kumar, Krishan. Utopianism. Milton Keynes: Open University Press, 1991.

Kung, Hans. Global Responsibility: In Search of a New World Ethic. London:
SCM Press, 1991.

Kuper, Leo. The Pity of It All. London: Duckworth, 1977.

________. Genocide. London: Penguin, 1981.

Kutash, Irwin L. Violence: Perspectives on Murder and Aggression. London:
Jossey-Bass. 1978.

Lavik, Nils J. Contributions from Psychiatry on the Peace War Issue.
Bulletin of Peace Proposals, Vol. XX, No.2, June 1989.

Lenin, V. I. Socialism and War - Collected Works. Vol. XXI. 1915.London: Progress
Publishers, 1960-80.

Lentz, Theodore F. Towards a Science of Peace. London: Halcyon Press, 1955.

Lévy, Bernard-Henri. War, Evil and the End of History. London. Duckworth. 2004

Lief, Alfred. The Fight Against War. New York: 1933.

Lindqvist, Sven. A History of Bombing. Granta Books London 2001

Lopez, George A. Peace Studies Past and Future. The Annals of the American
Academy of Political and Social Science, Vol. 504. London: Sage, July 1989.

Lorenz, Konrad. On Aggression. London: Methuen, 1966.

Luterbacher, Urs. Last Words about War. Journal of Conflict Resolution.
Vol. XXVIII.No. 1, 1984.

MacFarlane, L. J. Violence and the State. Oxford: Nelson, 1974.

Macquarrie, John. The Concept of Peace. London: SCM Press, 1973.

MacQueen, Graeme. Peace Studies and Metanarrative. Gandhi Marg. Vol. XVI. 1995.

Malthus, Thomas. Essay on the Principles of Population 1798; Edited by Geoffrey
Gilbert. Oxford: Oxford University Press, 1993.

Marshall, Peter. Demanding the Impossible. London: Fontana, 1973.

Martin, David. Does Christianity Cause War? Oxford: Clarendon Press 1997

Martin, James. The Meaning of the 21st Century. London. Eden Project.2006

Marx, Karl, and Friedrich Engels. The Selected Works. Moscow: Progress, 1973.

Matlaw, Ralph E. ed. Tolstoy: A Collection of Critical Essays. New Jersey: Prentice-Hall, 1967.

Maude, Aylmer. The Life of Tolstoy. Oxford: OUP. reprint, 1987.

May, John D'Arcy. Transcendence and Violence. New York: Continuum. 2003.

McCarthy, Fr. Emmanuel Charles, University of Notre Dame. The Christian Philosophy of Peace. Lecture on R.T.E. radio, 16th March 1996.

McLellan, David. The Thoughts of Karl Marx. London: Macmillan, 1995.

McSorley, Richard. New Testament Basis of Peace. New York: Hearld Press (1985)

Melko, Matthew and Richard D. Weiger. Peace in the Ancient World. Jefferson. North Carolina: McFarland, 1981.

Melman, Seymore. The Peace Race. London: Gollancz, 1962.

Mills, John O. Justice Peace and Dominicans 1216-2001. Dominicans. Dublin 2001

Modelski, George and Patrick M. Morgan. Understanding Global War. Journal of Conflict Resolution, 1985.

Monbiot, George. The Age of Consent: A Manifesto for a New World Order. London: Flamingo. 2003

Montagu, Ashley. Learning Non-Aggression. New York: OUP. 1978.

Moody, T. W. Davitt and Irish Revolution. Oxford: Clarendon, 1982.

Moore, Barrington, Jnr. Social Origins of Dictatorship and Democracy. London:
Penguin, 1966.

Moorehead, Caroline. Troublesome People: Enemies of War 1916-1986.
London: Hamish Hamilton, 1987.

________. Bertrand Russell: A Life. London: Sinclair-Stevenson, 1992.

More, Thomas. Utopia. Translated by Paul Turner. London: Penguin, 1965.

Morgan, T. Clifton. "The Concept of War." Peace and Change. Vol. XV. No. 4,
October 1990.

Morris, William. News from Nowhere. Edited by Krishan Kumar. Cambridge:
Cambridge University Press, 1995.

Morrow, Lance. "To Conquer the Past." Time. 3rd January 1994.

Mumford, Lewis. The Conduct of Life. London: Harcourt, 1951.

________. The City in History. London: Pelican, 1961.

Murphy, Daniel. Tolstoy And Education. Dublin: Irish Academic Press, 1992.

Myrdal, Alva. The Game of Disarmament. New York: Spokesman, 1978.

Nandy, Ashis. "Gandhi after Gandhi." The Gandhi Way. No. 49, 1996.

Nathan, Otto and Heinz Norden, ed. Einstein on Peace. London: Methuen, 1963.

Nef, John U. War and Human Progress: An Essay on the Rise of Industrial Civilisation. New York: Norton, 1968.

Newman, Cardinal John Henry. The Idea of a University. Edited by Frank M. Turner. New Haven: Yale University Press, 1996.

Nisbet, Robert. The Social Philosophers: Community and Conflict in Western Thought. London: Heinemann, 1974.

North, Robert C. Wright on War. Journal of Conflict Resolution. No. 4. 1970

O'Connell, James. Approaches to the Study of Peace. Conference Paper: Education for Peace, University of Limerick, 1991.

Pais, Abraham. Einstein Lived Here. Oxford: Oxford University Press, 1994.

Pandiri, Ananda M., Robert C. Cox, and P. Krishna Mohan. Mahatma Gandhi: An American Perspective. Connecticut: Connecticut College Press, 1981.

Panter-Brick, Simon. Gandhi Against Machiavellianism. London: Asia Pub. 1966.

Parekh, Bhikhu. Gandhi's Political Philosophy: A Critical Examination. Notre Dame: Notre Dame University Press, 1989.

Pauling, Linus, Ervin Laszlo, and Jong Youl Yoo, ed. World Encyclopaedia of Peace.

Oxford: Pergamon, 1986.

Paz, Octavio. One Earth, Four or Five Worlds. Translated by Helen R. Lane.
Manchester:Carcanet, 1985.

Philips, M. M. Erasmus and his Times. Cambridge: CUP. 1967.

Pick, Daniel. War Machine. London: Yale University Press, 1993.

Pinch, Alan, and Michael Armstrong, ed. Tolstoy on Education. Translated by Alan
Pinch. London: Athlone Press, 1982.

Priestland, Gerald. The Future of Violence. London: Hamish Hamilton, 1974.

Proudhon, Pierre-Joseph. What is Property? Vol. I. Translated by B. R. Tucker.
Boston: 1888; reprint, London: Constable, 1970.

Randle Robert F. The Origins of Peace. New York: The Free Press, 1973.

Rawls, John. A Theory of Justice. Oxford: Oxford University Press, 1971.

Redfearn, David. Tolstoy: Principles for a New World Order. London:
Shepheard-Walwyn. 1992.

Redhead, Brian. Plato to Nato. London: BBC Books, 1984.

Reiss, Hans, ed. Kant Political Writings. Translated by H. B. Nisbet. 2nd edition.
Cambridge: Cambridge University Press, 1991.

Rempel, Richard A. et al. Prophecy and Dissent 1914-1916. Vol. XIII. The Collected Papers of Bertrand Russell. London: Unwin Hyman, 1988.

Richardson, Lewis Fry. Arms and Insecurity: A Mathematical Study of the Causes and Origins of War. Ed. N. Rashevsky. London: Stevens, 1960.

________. The Statistics of Deadly Quarrels. Edited by Quincy Wright. London: Stevens, 1960.

Richardson, Stephen A. Lewis. F. Richardson: A Personal Biography. Journal of Conflict Resolution, Vol. I, No. 3, 1957.

Robbins, Keith. The Abolition of War: The 'Peace Movement' in Britain 1914-1919. Cardiff: University of Wales Press, 1976.

Roll, Eric. A History of Economic Thought. New Jersey: Prentice-Hall 1953.

Roper, Hugh Trevor. Review of War and Human Progress: An Essay on the Rise of Industrial Civilisation, by John U. Nef. In Sunday Times, 1951.

Rorty, Amelie, Oksenberg. From Passions to Sentiments: The Structure of Hume's Treatise. Berkeley: University of California, April 1993.

Rousseau, Jean-Jacques. Judgement sur la Paix Perpetuelle. (1756). Translated by C. E. Vaughan. New York: 1915.

Russell, Bertrand. Principles of Social Reconstruction. London: Allen & Unwin 1916.

________. Justice in War-Time. Illinois: The Open Court, 1917.

________. Which Way to Peace?. London: M. Joseph. 1936.

________. Logic And Knowledge. Ed. R. C. Marsh. London: Allen &Unwin. 1956.

________. The Problems of Philosophy. London: Williams and Norgate, 1912;
Oxford: Oxford University Press, 1967.

________. War Crimes in Vietnam. London: George Allen and Unwin. 1967.

________. An Outline Of Philosophy. London: George Allen and Unwin, 1979.

________. My Philosophical Development. London. George Allen and Unwin, 1985.

________. Roads To Freedom. London: George Allen and Unwin. 1985.

________. History Of Western Philosophy. London: Routledge, 1991.

________.The Autobiography of Bertrand Russell 1872-1914. (Vol. I), London:
George Allen and Unwin. 1967.

________. The Autobiography of Bertrand Russell 1914-1944. (Vol. II), London:
George Allen and Unwin. 1968.

________. The Autobiography of Bertrand Russell 1944-1967. (Vol. III), London:

George Allen and Unwin. 1969.

Ryan, Alan. Bertrand Russell: A Political Life. London: Penguin. 1988.

Said, Edward W. Power, Politics and Culture. London: Bloombury. 2005.

Salmon, Trevor C. Unneutral Ireland. Oxford: Clarendon, 1989.

Sampson, Ronald V. Tolstoy: The Discovery of Peace. London: Heinemann, 1973.

________. Tolstoy on the Causes of War. London: Peace Pledge Union, 1987.

Schell, Jonathan. The Unconquerable World. London: Allen Lane. 2003.

Schilpp, Paul Arthur, ed. The Philosophy of Bertrand Russell. Illinois: Open Court,
1944; revised edition, 1971.

________.Albert Einstein: Philosopher-Scientist. Vol. I. New York: Harper
Torchbooks, 1959.

Schumacher, E. F. Small is Beautiful: A Study of Economics as if People Mattered.
London. Abacus. 1973.

Sebald, W. G. On the Natural History of Destruction. Penguin. London. 2003

Seckel, Al. Bertrand Russell on God and Religion. New York. Prometheus, 1986.

________. Bertrand Russell on Ethics, Sex and Marriage. New York. Prometheus,
1987.

Semmel, Bernard, ed. Marxism and the Science of War. London: OUP. 1981.

Sharp, Gene. The Politics Of Non-violent Action. Boston. Porter Sargent, 1973.

Simmons, Ernest J. Introduction to Tolstoy's Writings. Chicago: University of Chicago Press,1969.

Singer, Joel David. "From 'A Study of War' to Peace Research: Some Criteria and
Strategies." Journal Of Conflict Resolution, Vol. XIV, No. 4. 1970.

________. Explaining War. London: Sage, 1979.

________. The Correlates of War - II. New York: Free Press. 1980.

________. Accounting for International War: the State of the Discipline. Journal
of Peace Research. Vol. XVIII. No. 1, 1981.

Singer, Joel David and Melvin Small. The Wages of War 1816-1915. New York:
Wiley, 1972.

S.I.P.R.I. Policies for Common Security. London: Taylor and Francis, 1985.

Smoker, Paul, Ruth Davies. A Reader in Peace Studies. Oxford: Pergamon, 1990.

Sorel, Georges. Reflections on Violence. Translated by T. E. Hulme. London. George

Unwin and Allen. 1917.

________. The Illusions of Progress. Translated by John Stanley and Charlotte Stanley. Berkeley and Los Angeles: University of California Press. 1969.

Sorokin, Pitirin. Social and Cultural Dynamics. New York: American Books, 1937.

Soros, George. The Age of Fallibility. Weidenfeld& Nicolson. London. 2006

Spence, G. W. Tolstoy the Ascetic. Edinburgh. Oliver and Boyd, 1967.

Stain, Arthur A. The Nation at War. Baltimore: John Hopkins University Press, 1980.

________. Last Words about War. Journal of Conflict Resolution, 1984.

Starke, J.G. An Introduction to the Science of Peace (Irenology). Leyden.1968.

Stephenson, Carolyn M. ed. Alternative Methods for International Security. Washington D. C.: University Press of America. 1982.

Storr, Anthony. Human Aggression. London: Penguin. 1968.

Sudermann, Hermann. The Manifesto to the Civilised World. Georg F. Nicolai Die Bioloqie Des Krieget. Translated by Orell Fussli Zurica. 1916.

Summerfield, Henry. That Myriad Minded Man: A Biography of G.W. Russell - A.E.

London.Collins Smyth. 1975.

Suter, Keith D. Reshaping the Global Agenda - the UN at 40. Sydney: United Nations Association, 1986.

________.Alternative to War: The Peaceful Settlement of International Disputes. Victoria: Women's International League for Peace & Freedom.

Swift, Jonathan. Gulliver's Travels. London: Penguin, 1994.

Talbott, Strobe. When Empires Crumble. Time. 22nd June, 1992.

Taylor, A. J. P. The Origins of the Second World War. London: Penguin, 1961.

Thompson, Henry O. Praxis: Peace Preachment and Practice. International Journal of World Peace. Vol. VII. No. 1 1990.

Thomson, David. Europe Since Napoleon. London. Penguin, 1966.

Thoreau, Henry David. Walden and Civil Disobedience. London: Penguin, 1983.

Tolstoy, Leo. The Death of Ivan Illich and Other Stories. Translated by Rosemary Edmonds. London: Penguin, 1960.

________. Resurrection. Translated by Rosemary Edmonds. London: Penguin, 1966.

________. War and Peace. Translated by Louise Maude and Aylmer Maude. Edited by George Gibian. New York: Norton, 1966.

________. War and Peace. Translated by Rosemary Edmonds. London:
Penguin, 1982.

________. The Slavery of Our Times. Translated by Aylmer Maude. London:
Briant, 1972.

________. Master and Man. . Trans. P. Foote. London: Penguin 1977.

________. The Inevitable Revolution. Trans. R. Sampson. London: Housmans, 1981.

________. The Kreutzer Sonata Trans. David Mc Duff. London: Penguin, 1985.

________. Writings on Civil Disobedience and Non-violence. Santa Cruz:
New Society, 1987.

________. What Then Must We Do? Trans. A. Maude. London: Green Books, 1991.

Toffler, Alvin. Third Wave. Sunday Times, 17th June 1984

Toynbee, Arnold J. A Study of History. Abridged by D. C. Somervell. 2 vols.
Oxford: OUP. 1974.

Turgenev, Ivan Sergeyevich. Fathers and Sons. Trans. Rosemary Edmonds.
London. Penguin, 1965.

Tzu, Sun. The Art of War. Trans. Samuel B. Griffith. London: OUP. 1971.

UNESCO. Violence and Its Causes. Paris: UNESCO, 1981.

Van Den Dungen. Peter. Peace Research and the Search for Peace.
International Journal of World Peace. Vol. XI. No.3, Jul. 1985.

Vanderhaar, Gerard. Non-violence in Christian Tradition. London: Pax Christi, 1983.

Vayrynen, Raimo, ed. The Quest for Peace. International Social Science Council,
London: Sage, 1987.

Vellacott, Jo. Bertrand Russell and the Pacifists in the First World War. Brighton:
Harvester Press, 1980.

Vesovic, Marko. Yugoslavian author quoted in Irish Times. 28th September 1995.

Vidal, Gore. Perpetual War for Perpetual Peace. Nation Books New York 2002

Vogt, Wolfgang, ed. Frieden als Zivilisierung Sprojket. Baden Baden, 1995.

Voltaire. "De la Paix Perpetuelle." (1769). In Istvan Kende. The History of Peace:
Concepts and Organisations. Journal of Peace Research. No. 3, 1989.

Waldheim, Kurt. Building the Future Order. London: Macmillan. 1980.

Walzer, Michael. Just and Unjust War. New York: Basic Books. 1992.

Weston, Burns H. ed. Towards Nuclear Disarmament and Global Security. Boulder,
Colorado: Westview 1984.

Wessells, Michael G. The Role of Peace Education in a Culture of Peace. Peace
Environment and Education. No. 18, 1994.

Whyte, John. Interpreting Northern Ireland. Oxford: Clarendon. 1991.

Wilson, A. N. Tolstoy. London: Penguin Books. 1989.

Wilson, Andrew. The Disarmers Handbook. London: Penguin, 1983.

Wilson, Edward O. Sociology: The New Synthesis. Cambridge. Mass. 1975.

Wollheim, Richard. Freud. London: Fontana, 1973.

Wright, Quincy. A Study of War. Chicago: University of Chicago Press. 1965.

Wright, Quincy, W. F. Cottrell, and C. H. Boasson. Research For Peace. Amsterdam:
North-Holland, 1954.

Wright, Quincy, William M. Evan and Morton Deutsch. Preventing World War III.
New York. Simon and Schuster, 1962.

Yergin, Daniel. Shattered Peace. London: Penguin, 1980.

Young, Nigel. Studying Peace: Problems and Possibilities. London: Housmans, 1985.

Zampaglione, Gerrardo. The Idea of Peace in Antiquity. Translated by Richard Dunn.
Notre Dame, Indiana: Notre Dame Press, 1973.

Other Sources.

Ambler, Rex. A Guide to the Study of Gandhi: An Annotated Bibliography London:
Housemans, 1986.

Carroll, Berenice A., Clinton F. Fink and Jane E. Mohraz. The War/Peace
Bibliography Series. Santa Barbara: Clio Press, 1983.

Conference Papers on the Teaching of Peace and Conflict Studies at British
Universities, University of Bradford, (1989).

Gandhi: The Collected Works of Mahatma Gandhi. (Ninety volumes). New Delhi:
Publications Division of the Government of India, Navajivan, 1958-1984.

Garland Library of War and Peace, the, edited by Blanche Wiesen Cook, Charles
Chatfield and Sandy Cooper. New York: Garland, 1971.

International Reace Research Association Newsletter. Quarterly Journal of I.P.R.A.

Journal of Conflict Resolution, Vol. XIV, No. 4, December 1970, - a special edition
devoted to the writings of Quincy Wright.

Peaceful Peoples: An Annotated Bibliography. Edited by Bruce D. Bonta. London:
Scarecrow, 1993.

Peace Research Abstracts Journal. Ontario: Sage Periodicals.

Russell: The Collected Papers of Bertrand Russell, produced by the Bertrand Russell

Editorial Project. At McMaster University, Hamilton, Ontario. 13 Volumes.

Russell: The Journal of the Bertrand Russell Archives. Hamilton, Ontario: McMaster University Press. A bi-annual journal since 1971.

Tolstoy: The Complete Works of Tolstoy. (Ninety volumes) Compiled by V. G. Chertkov. Moscow, 1956.

UNESCO. Executive Board Document (27 C/ 126) 1993. Action programme to promote a culture of peace.

UNESCO: Declaration on the Role of Religion in the Promotion of a Culture of Peace. Barcelona Centre UNESCO de Catalunya, 1994.

United Nations: The Charter of The United Nations, 26th June 1945.

United Nations: The Constitution of The United Nations Educational, Scientific and Cultural Organisation. 1948.

World Conference on Religion and Peace. Religion for Peace Newsletters. Geneva, Switzerland.